CONTENTS

D0009134

*The Contents includes the full citation for the study that is featured in each reading selection of this text.

3 LEARNING AND CONDITIONING 64

4 INTELLIGENCE, COGNITION, AND MEMORY 94

5 HUMAN DEVELOPMENT 126

6 EMOTION AND MOTIVATION 158

7 PERSONALITY 186

8 PSYCHOPATHOLOGY 219

PREFACE

Science moves through history in many ways and at many speeds. There are slow times, all too frequently, when it seems to stagnate, making little or no progress. Then there are those exciting, dynamic periods when new discoveries spark waves of dialog, attention, research, and progress. These discoveries quite literally change what we know about how the world works. Within this frame, the history of psychology is no different from the other sciences. There have been psychological research endeavors that have had remarkable and lasting effects on the various disciplines that comprise the science we call psychology. The findings generated from these studies have changed our knowledge of human behavior, and they have set the stage for countless subsequent projects and research programs. Even when the results of some of these pivotal studies have later been drawn into controversy and question, their effect and influence in a historical context are never diminished. They continue to be cited in new articles; they continue to be the topic of academic discussion; they continue to form the foundation for textbook chapters; and they continue to hold a special place in the minds of psychologists.

The concept for this book grew out of my many years of teaching psychology. All psychology textbooks are based on many key studies that have shaped the science of psychology over its relatively brief history. Textbooks, however, seldom give the original studies themselves the attention they richly deserve. Usually the research processes are summarized and diluted to the point that little of the life and excitement of the discoveries remain. And sometimes the way the methods and findings are reported can even mislead the reader about the study's true impact and influence. This is in no way a criticism of the textbook writers who work under length constraints and must make many difficult choices as to what gets included and in how much detail. The situation is, however, unfortunate, since the foundation of all of psychology is research, and it is through a century of ingenious and elegant studies that our knowledge and understanding of human behavior have been expanded and refined to the level of sophistication that exists today.

So, this book is an attempt to fill the rather large gap between the psychology textbooks and the research that made them possible. It is a journey through the "headline history" of psychology. My hope is that the way the 40 chosen studies are presented will, in essence, bring them back to life so that you, the reader, can experience them for yourself. This book is intended for anyone who wishes a greater understanding of the true roots of psychology.

CHOOSING THE STUDIES

The studies included in this book were carefully chosen from those found in psychology texts and journals and from those suggested by leading authorities in the many fields of psychology summarized in the table of contents. The number (40) wasn't planned, but as the studies were selected this number seemed to be about right both from a historical point of view and in terms of length. The studies chosen are arguably the most famous, the most important, or the most influential in the history of psychology. I use the word "arguably" since many who read this book may wish to dispute some of the choices. One thing is sure: There is no single list of 40 studies that would satisfy everyone. However, the studies included here are the ones that continue to be cited most frequently, stirred up the most controversy when they were published, sparked the most subsequent related research, opened new fields of psychological exploration, and changed most dramatically our knowledge of human behavior. These studies are organized according to the subfield into which they best fit. The subfields are: Biology and Human Behavior; Consciousness; Learning and Conditioning; Intelligence, Cognition, and Memory; Human Development; Emotion and Motivation; Personality; Psychopathology; Psychotherapy; and Social Psychology.

PRESENTING THE STUDIES

The basic format used throughout the book allows for a clear understanding of each study presented. Each chapter contains:

1. An exact, readily available reference for where the original study can be found.
2. A brief introduction summarizing the background in the field leading up to the study and the reasons the researcher carried out the project.
3. The theoretical propositions or hypotheses on which the research rests.
4. A detailed account of the experimental design and methods used to carry out the research, including, where appropriate, who the subjects were and how they were recruited; descriptions of any apparatus and materials used; and the actual procedures followed in carrying out the research.
5. A summary of the results of the study in clear, understandable, non-technical, non-statistical, no-jargon language.
6. An interpretation of the meaning of the findings based on the author's own discussion in the original article.
7. The significance of the study to the field of psychology, or, how did this study change psychology?
8. A brief discussion of supportive or contradictory follow-up research findings and subsequent questioning or criticism from others in the field.
9. A few references for additional and updated reading relating to the study.

The primary goal of this book is to make these discoveries meaningful and accessible to the reader. Often, scientists speak in languages that are not easily understood (even by other scientists!). Therefore, I hope that the presentations as outlined above will allow the reader to experience the drama of these remarkable and important discoveries in accessible, relevant, and interesting ways. Additionally, where possible and appropriate, the studies presented here have been simplified and edited for ease of reading and understanding. However, this has been done in such a way that the meaning and elegance of the work is preserved and the impact of the research is distilled and clarified.

THE ETHICS OF RESEARCH INVOLVING HUMAN
OR ANIMAL SUBJECTS

Without subjects, there is virtually no scientific research possible. In physics the subjects are subatomic particles; in botany they are plants; in chemistry they are the elements of the periodic table; and in psychology the subjects are people. At times certain research procedures or behaviors under study do not permit the use of human subjects, so animal subjects are substituted. However, the goal of animal research is to better understand humans, not the animals themselves. In the following pages, you will be reading about research involving both human and animal subjects. Some of the studies may cause you to question the ethics of the researchers in regard to the procedures used with the subjects. Usually, when painful or stressful procedures are part of a study being discussed, the question of ethics will be noted in the chapter. However, since this is such a volatile issue (especially currently with the animal rights movement), a brief discussion of the ethical guidelines followed by present-day psychologists should be discussed here in preparation for some of the studies described in this book.

Research with Human Subjects

The American Psychological Association (APA) has issued strict and clear guidelines that researchers must follow when carrying out experiments involving human participants. A portion of the introduction to those guidelines reads as follows:

> Psychologists respect the dignity and worth of the individual and strive for the preservation and protection of fundamental human rights. They are committed to increasing knowledge of human behavior and of people's understanding of themselves and others and to the utilization of such knowledge for the promotion of human welfare. While pursuing these objectives, they must make every effort to protect the welfare . . . of the research participants that may be the object of study. [from American Psychological Association (1981) Ethical principles of psychologists. *American Psychologist, 36*, 633–38]

In order to adhere to those principles, researchers follow certain basic rules for all studies involving human subjects:

1. *Informed consent.* A researcher must explain to potential subjects what the experiment is about and what procedures will be used so that the individual is able to make an informed decision whether to participate. If the person then agrees to participate, this is called "informed consent." There are times, as you will see in this book, when the true purposes of an experiment cannot be revealed because this would alter the behavior of the subjects and contaminate the results. In such cases, when deception is used, a subject still must be given adequate information for informed consent and the portions of the experiment that are hidden must be justifiable based on the importance of the potential findings.

2. *Freedom to withdraw at any time.* All human subjects in all research projects must know that they may withdraw freely from the experiment at any time. This may seem an unnecessary rule, since it would seem obvious that any subject who is too uncomfortable with the procedures can simply

leave. However, this is not always so straightforward. For example, undergraduate students are often given course credit for participating as subjects in psychological experiments. They may feel that withdrawing will influence the credit they receive and they will not, therefore, feel free to do so. In other cases when subjects are paid to participate, if they are made to feel that their completion of the experiment is a requirement for payment, this could produce an unethical inducement to avoid withdrawing when they wish to do so. To avoid this problem, subjects should be given credit or paid at the beginning of the procedure "just for showing up."

3. *Debriefing and protection from harm.* Experimenters have the responsibility to protect their subjects from all physical and psychological harm that might be produced by the research procedures. Most psychological research involves methods that are completely harmless, both during and after the study. However, even seemingly harmless procedures can sometimes produce negative effects such as frustration, embarrassment, or concern. One common safeguard against those effects is the ethical requirement of the debriefing. After subjects have completed an experiment, especially one involving any form of deception, they should be debriefed. During debriefing, the true purpose and goals of the experiment are explained to them and they are given the opportunity to ask any questions about their experiences. If there is any possibility of lingering aftereffects from the experiment, the researchers should provide subjects with their phone numbers for further discussion if necessary.

4. *Confidentiality.* All results from subjects in experiments should be kept in complete confidence unless specific agreements have been made with the subjects. This does not mean that results cannot be reported and published, but this is done in such a way that individual data cannot be identified. Often, no identifying information is even acquired from subjects, and all data are combined to arrive at *average* differences among groups.

Of course, in research involving children, the same ethical guidelines apply with the children's parents.

As you read through the studies included in this book, you may find a few studies that appear to have violated some of these ethical principles. In general, these studies were carried out long before formal ethical guidelines existed, and probably they could not be replicated today. The lack of guidelines, however, does not excuse past researchers for abuses. Judgment of those investigators must now be made by each of us individually and we must learn, as psychologists have, from past mistakes, however few they have been.

Research Involving Animal Subjects

One of the hottest topics of discussion in and outside of the scientific community is the question of the ethics of animal research. Animal rights groups are growing in number and are becoming increasingly vocal and militant. There is clearly more controversy today over animal subjects than human subjects, probably because of the correct perception that animals cannot be protected, as humans can, with informed consent, freedom to withdraw, or debriefing. Additionally, the most radical animal rights activists take the view that all living things are ordered in value by their ability to sense pain. In this conceptualization animals are equal in value to humans and, therefore, any use of animals by humans is seen as unethical. This use includes eating a chicken, wearing leather, and owning pets (which according to radical animal rights activists is a form of slavery). It should be made clear that many people believe that research with animals, even though it is only a very small percentage of the ways humans use animals, is inhumane and unethical, and should be prohibited.

Nearly all scientists and most American citizens, however, believe that the limited and humane use of animals in scientific research is necessary and beneficial. Many lifesaving drugs and medical techniques have been developed through the use of animal experimental subjects. Animals have also often been subjects in psychological research to study such issues as depression, brain development, overcrowding, and learning processes. The primary reason animals are used in research is that to carry out similar research on humans would be clearly unethical. For example, suppose you wanted to study the effect on brain development and intelligence of raising infants in an enriched environment with many activities and toys vs. an impoverished environment with little to do. To assign human infants to these different conditions would simply not be possible. However, rats could be used as subjects without exposing them to harm and discoveries potentially important to humans might be produced (see the reading on research such as this by Rosenzweig and Bennett).

The American Psychological Association, in addition to its guidelines on human subjects, has strict rules and laws governing research with animal subjects designed to ensure humane treatment. These laws require that research animals receive proper housing, feeding, cleanliness, and health care. All unnecessary pain to the animal is prohibited. A portion of the APA's "Care and Use of Animals" reads as follows:

> Psychologists make every effort to minimize discomfort, illness, and pain of animals. A procedure subjecting animals to pain, stress, or privation is used only when an alternative procedure is unavailable and the goal is justified by its prospective scientific, educational, or applied value. [from American Psychological Association (1981) Ethical principles of psychologists. *American Psychologist*, 36, 633–38]

In this book there are several studies involving animal subjects. Besides the ethical considerations of such research there are also the usual difficulties of generalizing from animal findings to humans. These issues are discussed within each chapter that includes animal research. Some of this research may seem cruel and unethical to you. The bottom line of all this is that each individual, whether a researcher, a student, or an enthusiast of psychology, must make his or her own decisions about animal research in general and the justifiability of using animal subjects in any specific instance. If you allow that animal research is acceptable under some circumstances, then for each study involving animals in this book, you must decide if the value of the study's findings support the methods used.

One final note related to this issue involves a development in animal research that is a response to public concerns about potential mistreatment. Cambridge, Massachusetts, one of the major research centers of the world with such institutions as Harvard University and M.I.T., recently created a new official position called Commissioner of Laboratory Animals. This is the first such government position ever formed, and Dr. Stuart Wiles has been named as the first person to fill the post. Cambridge contains 22 research laboratories that house approximately 60,000 animals of all types. The new commissioner's job is to ensure humane and proper treatment of all animal subjects, from how the experimental treatments are administered to the quality of the animals' living quarters. If he discovers a lab that is in violation of Cambridge's strict laws concerning the humane care of lab animals, he is authorized to impose fines of $300 per day (*People Magazine*, May 27, 1991, p. 71).

I would like to express my sincere gratitude to Charlyce Jones Owen, Editor-in-Chief at Prentice Hall's College Division, for her commitment to and support of this project from the beginning. I would also like to thank Katy Bsales for her organized and thorough work as production editor. Finally, I would like to thank the reviewers of this edition: Edward L. Pencer, St. Francis Xavier University; Eliot Shimoff, University of Maryland Baltimore County; James Huntermark, Missouri Western State College; Jeremy Wolfe, Massachusetts Institute of Technology; and Valda Robinson, Hillsborough (FL) Community College.

The studies you are about to experience in this book have benefited all of humankind in many ways and to varying degrees. The history of psychological research is a relatively short one, but it is filled with the richness and excitement of discovering human nature.

Roger R. Hock

ONE

BIOLOGY AND HUMAN BEHAVIOR

Nearly all general psychology texts begin with the chapters relating to the biology of human behavior, and this book does so as well. This is not simply due to convention or convenience, but rather it is because biological or physiological processes form the basis of *all* behavior. Each of the other subfields of psychology included in this book rests upon this biological foundation. The branch of psychological research that studies these processes is called *physiological psychology*, which focuses on the interaction of your brain and nervous system, the processes of receiving stimulation and information from the environment around you through your senses, and the ways in which your brain organizes all this information to create your perceptions of the world.

   The studies chosen to represent this basic component of psychological reseach include a wide range of research and are clearly among the most influential and most often cited. The first study discusses a famous research program on right-brain/left-brain specialization that shaped much of our present knowledge of how the brain functions. Next is a study that surprised the scientific community by demonstrating how a stimulating "childhood" might produce a more highly developed brain. The third study takes us to a faraway culture to reveal how our perceptions of the world around us are shaped by a lifetime of specific sensory input. And fourth is the invention of

1

the famous "visual cliff" method of studying infants' abilities to perceive depth. All these studies, the latter two in particular, also address an issue that underlies and connects nearly all areas of psychology and provides for an ongoing and fascinating debate: the *nature-nurture* controversy.

ONE BRAIN OR TWO?

Gazzaniga, M.S. (1967) The split brain in man. *Scientific American*, 217, 24–29.

You are probably aware that the two halves of your brain are not the same and that they perform different functions. For one thing, the left side of your brain is responsible for movement in the right side of your body, and vice versa. Even beyond this, though, the two brain hemispheres appear to have even greater specialized abilities.

It has come to be rather common knowledge that, for most of us, the left brain controls the ability to use language while the right is involved more in spatial relationships, such as those needed for artistic activities. It is well known that stroke or accident victims who suffer damage to the left side of the brain will usually lose their ability to speak (often this skill returns with practice and training). Many people believe that each half, or "hemisphere," of your brain may actually be a completely separate mental system with its own individual abilities for learning, remembering, perceiving the world, and even feeling emotions.

These ideas have become extremely popular, as evidenced by best-selling books such as *Drawing on the Right Side of Your Brain*. But the concepts underlying this popular awareness are the result of many years of rigorous scientific research on the effects of splitting the brain in two: on *hemispheric specialization*.

Research in this area was pioneered by R.W. Sperry, beginning about 15 years prior to the article examined in this chapter. In his early work with animal subjects, Sperry made many remarkable discoveries. For example, consider a cat that has had surgery to cut the connection between the two halves of its brain and to alter its optic nerves so that its left eye only transmitted information to the left hemisphere and the right eye only to the right hemisphere. Following surgery, the cat appeared to behave normally and exhibited virtually no ill effects. Then the cat's right eye was covered and the cat learned a new behavior, such as walking through a short maze to find food. After the cat became skilled at maneuvering through the maze, the eye cover was shifted to its left eye. Now when the cat was placed in the maze, its left brain had no idea where to turn and the animal had to relearn the entire maze from the beginning.

Sperry conducted many related studies over the next 30 years and received the Nobel Prize for his work on the specialized abilities of the two halves of the brain. When these research endeavors turned to human subjects in the early 1960s, he was joined in his work by Michael Gazzaniga. Although Sperry is considered the founder of split-brain research, Gazzaniga's article has been chosen here because it is a clear, concise summary of their early collaborative work with human subjects and is cited consistently in nearly all general psychology texts. Its selection is in no way intended to overlook or overshadow either Sperry's leadership in this field or his great contributions.

In order to understand split-brain research, a little awareness of physiology is required. The two hemispheres of your brain are in constant communication with one another via the *corpus callosum*, a structure made up of about 200 million nerve fibers. If your corpus callosum is cut, this major line of communication is disrupted and the two halves of your brain are left to function independently. So, if we want to study each half of your brain separately, all we need to do is surgically sever your corpus callosum.

But can scientists divide the brains of humans? This sounds like psychology à la Dr. Frankenstein! Obviously, research ethics would never allow such drastic methods simply for the purpose of studying the specialized abilities of the brain's two hemispheres. However, in the late 1950s, the field of medicine provided psychologists with a golden opportunity. In some people with very rare and very extreme cases of uncontrollable epilepsy, it was found that their seizures could be virtually eliminated by surgically severing the corpus callosum. This operation was (and is) extremely successful, as a last resort, for those patients who cannot be helped by any other means. When this article was written in 1966, there had been 10 such operations, and four of the patients had consented to participate in examination and testing by Sperry and Gazzaniga to determine how their perceptual and intellectual skills were affected as a result of this surgical treatment.

THEORETICAL PROPOSITIONS

The researchers wanted to explore the extent to which the two halves of the human brain are able to function independently, and whether they have separate and unique abilities. If the information traveling between the two halves of your brain is interrupted, would the right side of your body suddenly be unable to coordinate with the left? If language is controlled by the left side of the brain, how would your ability to speak and understand words be affected by this surgery? Would thinking and reasoning processes exist in both halves separately? If the brain is really two separate brains, would a person be capable of functioning normally when these two brains are no longer able to communicate? Since we receive sensory input from both the right and the left, how would the senses of vision, hearing, and touch be affected? Sperry and Gazzaniga would attempt to answer these and many other questions in their studies of split-brain individuals.

METHOD

There were three different types of tests developed to explore a wide range of mental (cognitive) capabilities of the patients. One was designed to examine visual abilities. A technique was devised so that a picture of an object, a word, or parts of words could be transmitted only to the visual area (called a "field") in either the right- or left-brain hemisphere, and not to both. It should be noted that, normally, both of your eyes send information to both sides of your brain. However, with exact placement of items or words in front of you, and with your eyes fixed on a specific point, images can be fed to only the right *or* the left visual field of your brain.

Another testing situation was designed for tactile (touch) stimulation. Here an object, a block letter, or even a word in block letters could be felt, but not seen. Very simply, this apparatus consisted of a screen with a space under it for the subject to reach through and touch the items without being able to see them. The visual and the tactile devices could be used simultaneously so that, for example, a picture of a pen could be projected to one side of the brain and the same object could be searched for by either hand among various objects behind the screen (see Figure 1).

Finally, testing auditory abilities was somewhat more tricky. When sound enters either of your ears, sensations are sent to both sides of your brain. Therefore, it is not possible to limit auditory input to only one side of the brain even in split-brain patients. However, it is possible to limit the *response* to such input to one brain hemisphere. Here is how this was done. Imagine that several well-known objects (a spoon, a pen, a marble) are placed into a cloth bag, and you are then asked to find certain items by touch. You would probably have no trouble doing so. If you place your left hand in the bag, it is being controlled by the right side of your brain, and vice versa. Do you think either side of your brain could do this task alone? As you will see in a moment, both halves of the

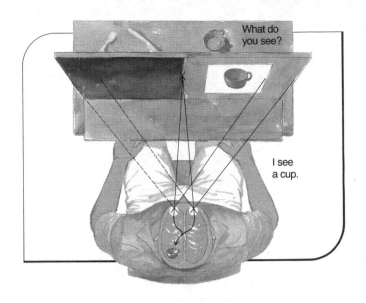

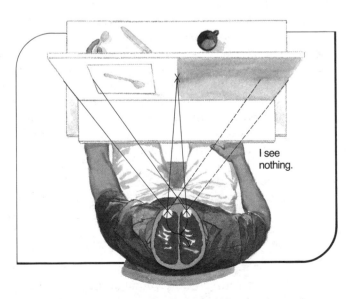

FIGURE 1 A typical visual testing device for split-brain subjects. (Carol Wald/© 1987 Discover Magazine)

brain are not equally capable of performing this task. What if you are not asked for specific objects, but are simply requested to reach into the bag and identify objects by touch? Again, this would not be difficult for you, but it would be quite difficult for a split-brain patient.

Gazzaniga combined all of these testing techniques to reveal some fascinating findings about how the brain functions.

RESULTS

First of all, it should be noted that following this radical brain surgery, the patients were the same people they were before the operation; that is, their intelligence level, personality, typical emotional reactions, and so on were unchanged. Moreover, they were very happy and relieved that they were now free of seizures. It was reported that one patient, while still groggy from surgery, joked that he had "a splitting headache." When testing began, however, these subjects demonstrated many unusual abilities.

Visual Abilities

One of the first tests involved simply a board with a horizontal row of lights. When a patient sat in front of this board and stared at a point in the middle of the lights, the bulbs would flash across both the right and left visual fields. However, when the patients were asked to explain what they saw, they said that only the lights on the right side of the board had flashed. Then the researchers flashed only the lights on the left side of the visual field, and the patients claimed to have seen nothing. A logical conclusion from these findings was that the right side of the brain is blind. Then an amazing thing happened. The lights were flashed again, only this time the patients were asked to point to the lights that had flashed. Although they had *said* they only saw the lights on the right, they pointed to all the lights in both visual fields. Using this method of pointing, it was found that both halves of the brain had seen the lights and were equally skilled in visual perception. The important point here is that when the patients failed to *say* that they had seen all the lights, it was not because they didn't see them, but because the center for *speech* is located in the brain's left hemisphere. In other words, in order for you to say you saw something, the object has to have been seen by the left side of your brain.

Tactile Abilities

You can try this test yourself. Put your hands behind your back. Then have someone place familiar objects (a spoon, a pen, a book, a watch) in either your right or your left hand and see if you can identify the object. You would not find this task to be very difficult, would you? This is basically what Sperry and Gazzaniga did with the split-brain patients. When an object was placed in the right hand in such a way that the patient could not see or hear it, messages about the object would travel to the left hemisphere and the patient was able to name the object and describe it and its uses. Then, when the same objects were placed in the left hand (connected to the right hemisphere), the patients could not name them or describe them in any way. But did the patients know what the object was? In order for the researchers to find out, the subjects were asked to match the object in their left hand (without seeing it, remember) to a group of various objects presented to them. This they could do as easily as you or I. Again, this places verbal ability in the left hemisphere of the brain. Keep in mind that the reason *you* are able to name unseen objects in your left hand is that the information from the right side of your brain is transmitted via the corpus callosum to the left side, where your center for language says "that's a spoon"!

Visual Plus Tactile Tests

Combining these two types of tests provided support for the findings above and also offered additional interesting results. If subjects were shown a picture of an object to the right hemisphere only, they were unable to name it or describe it. In fact, there might be no verbal response at all or even a denial that anything had been presented. But if the patients were allowed to reach under the screen with their left hand and touch a selection of objects, they were always able to find the one that had been presented visually.

The right hemisphere was found to be able to *think* about and analyze objects as well. Gazzaniga reported that when the right hemisphere was shown a picture of an item such as a cigarette, the subjects could touch 10 objects behind the screen that did not include a cigarette, and select an object that was most closely related to the item pictured — in this case an ashtray. He went on to explain:

> Oddly enough, however, even after their correct response, and while they were holding the ashtray in their left hand, they were unable to name or describe the object or the picture of the cigarette. Evidently, the left hemisphere was completely divorced, in perception and knowledge, from the right (p. 26).

Other tests were conducted to shed additional light on the language-processing abilities of the right hemisphere. One very famous, ingenious, and revealing use of the visual apparatus came when the word HEART was projected to the patients so that "HE" was sent to the right visual field and "ART" was sent to the left. Now, keeping in mind (your *connected* mind) the functions of the two hemispheres, what do you think the patients verbally reported seeing? If you said "ART," you were correct. However, and here is the revealing part, when the subjects were presented with two cards with the words "HE" and "ART" printed on them and asked to point with the *left hand* to the word they had seen, they all pointed to "HE"! This demonstrated that the right hemisphere is able to comprehend language, although it does so in a different way from the left: in a non-verbal way.

The auditory tests conducted with the patients produced similar results. When patients were asked to reach with their left hand into a grab bag hidden from view and pull out certain specific objects (a watch, a marble, a comb, a coin) they had no trouble doing this. This clearly demonstrated that the right hemisphere was comprehending language. It was even possible to describe a related aspect of an item with the same accurate results. An example given by Gazzaniga was when the patients were asked to find in a grab bag full of plastic fruit "the fruit monkeys like best," they retrieved a banana. Or when told "Sunkist sells a lot of them," they pulled out an orange. However, if these same pieces of fruit were placed out of view in the patients' left hand, they were unable to say what they were. In other words, when a verbal response was required, the right hemisphere was unable to speak.

One last example of this amazing difference between the two hemispheres involved plastic block letters on the table behind the screen. When patients were asked to spell various words by feel with the left hand they had an easy time doing so. Even if three or four letters that spelled specific words were placed behind the screen, they were able, left-handed, to arrange them correctly into words.However, immediately after completing this task, the subjects could not name the word they had just spelled.

So, clearly, the left hemisphere of the brain is superior to the right for speech (in some left-handed people, this is reversed). But in what skills, if any, does the right hemisphere excel? Sperry and Gazzaniga found in this early work that visual tasks involving spatial relationships and shapes were performed with greater proficiency by the left hand (even though these patients were all right-handed). As can be seen in Figure 2, copying three-dimensional drawings (using the pencil behind the screen) was much more successful with the left hand.

Finally, the researchers wanted to explore emotional reactions of split-brain patients. While performing visual experiments, Sperry and Gazzaniga suddenly flashed a picture of a nude woman to either the left or right hemisphere. In one instance, when this picture was shown to the left hemisphere of a female patient:

> She laughed and verbally identified the picture of a nude. When it was later presented to the right hemisphere, she said . . . she saw nothing, but

almost immediately a sly smile spread over her face and she began to chuckle. Asked what she was laughing at, she said: "I don't know . . . nothing . . . oh—that funny machine." Although the right hemisphere could not describe what it had seen, the sight nevertheless elicited an emotional response like the one evoked in the left hemisphere (p. 29).

DISCUSSION

The overall conclusion drawn from the research reported in this article was that there are two different brains within each person's cranium, each with complex abilities. Gazzaniga notes the possibility that if our

FIGURE 2 Drawings made by split-brain patients. From "The Split Brain in Man," by Michael S. Gazzaniga. Reprinted by permission of the author.

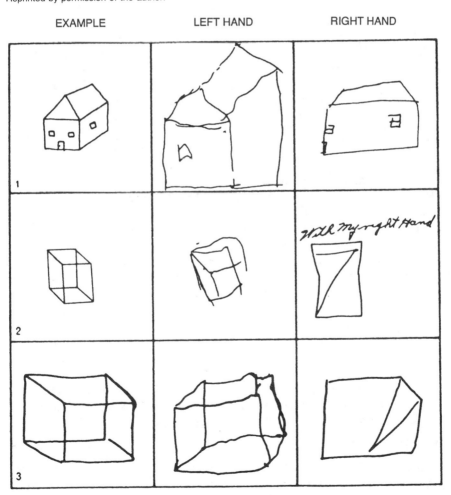

EXAMPLE   LEFT HAND   RIGHT HAND

brain is really two brains, then perhaps we have the potential to process twice as much information if the two halves are divided. Indeed, there is some research evidence to suggest that split-brain patients have the ability to perform two cognitive tasks as fast as a normal person can carry out one.

SIGNIFICANCE OF FINDINGS

These findings and the subsequent research carried out by Sperry and Gazzaniga and others are extremely significant and far-reaching in many areas. There is now evidence that the two halves of your brain have many specialized skills and functions. Your left brain is better at speaking, writing, mathematical calculation, and reading, and is the primary center for language. Your right hemisphere, however, possesses superior capabilities for recognizing faces, solving problems involving spatial relationships, symbolic reasoning, and artistic activities.

Our increased knowledge of the specialized functioning of the two hemispheres of the brain allows us to better treat victims of stroke or head injury. By knowing the location of the damage, we can predict what deficits are likely to exist as the patient recovers. Through this knowledge, appropriate relearning and rehabilitation strategies can be employed to help patients recover as fully and quickly as possible.

Gazzaniga and Sperry, through their years of continuous work in this area, have concluded that each hemisphere of your brain really is a mind of its own. In a later study, split-brain patients were tested on much more complex problems than have been discussed here. One question asked was, "What profession would you choose?" A male patient verbally (left hemisphere) responded that he would choose to be a draftsman, but his left hand (right hemisphere) spelled by touch in block letters "automobile race" (Gazzaniga and LeDoux, 1978). In fact, Gazzaniga has taken this theory a step further. He now maintains that even in people whose brains are normal and intact, there may not be complete communication between the two hemispheres (Gazzaniga, 1985). For example, if certain bits of information, such as those forming an emotion, are not stored in a language format, the left hemisphere may not have access to it. The result of this is that you may feel sad and not be able to say why. Since this is an uncomfortable cognitive situation, the left hemisphere may try to find a verbal reason to explain the sadness (after all, language is its main job). However, since your left hemisphere does not have all the necessary data, its explanation may actually be wrong!

CRITICISMS

It is clear that the findings from the split-brain studies carried out over the years by Sperry, Gazzaniga, and others have been quite accurate and rarely in dispute. The main body of criticism about this research has focused instead on the way the idea of right- and left-brain specialization has filtered down to popular culture and the media.

There is now a widely believed myth that some people are more "right-brained" or more "left-brained," or that one side of your brain needs to be developed in order for you to improve certain skills. Jarre Levy, a psychobiologist at the University of Chicago, has been in the forefront of scientists who are trying to dispel the notion that we have two separately functioning brains. She claims that it is precisely *because* each hemisphere has separate functions that they must integrate their abilities instead of separating them, as is commonly believed. Through such integration, your brain is able to perform in ways that are greater than *and different* from the abilities of either side alone.

When you read a story, for example, your right hemisphere is specializing in emotional content (humor, pathos), picturing visual descriptions, keeping track of the story structure as a whole, and appreciating artistic writing style (such as the use of metaphors). While all this is happening, your left hemisphere is understanding the written words, deriving meaning from the complex relationships among words and sentences, and translating words into their phonetic sounds so that they can be understood as language. The reason you are able to read, understand, and appreciate a story is that your brain functions as a single, integrated structure (Levy, 1985).

In fact, Levy explains that there is no human activity that uses only one side of the brain. "The popular myths are interpretations and wishes, not the observations of scientists. Normal people have not half a brain, nor two brains, but one gloriously differentiated brain, with each hemisphere contributing its specialized abilities" (Levy, 1985, p. 44).

GAZZANIGA, M.S. (1985) *The social brain*. New York: Basic Books.
GAZZANIGA, M.S., and LEDOUX, J.E. (1978) *The integrated mind*. New York: Plenum.
LEVY, J. (1985) Right brain, left brain: Fact and fiction. *Psychology Today*, May, 42–44.

MORE EXPERIENCE = BIGGER BRAIN?
Rosenzweig, Mark R., Bennett, Edward L., and Diamond, Marian
   C. (1972) Brain changes in response to experience. *Scientific American*, 226, 22–29.

If you were to enter the baby's room in a typical American middle-class home today, you would probably see a crib full of stuffed animals, and various colorful toys dangling directly over and within reach of the infant. Some of these may even light up, move, play music, or do all three. What do you suppose is the reasoning behind supplying infants with so much to see and do? Well, aside from the fact that babies seem to enjoy and respond positively to these things, it is most parents' belief, acknowledged or not, that children need a stimulating environment for optimal intellectual development and proper development of the brain.

The question of whether certain experiences produce physical changes in the brain has been a topic of conjecture and research among philosophers and scientists for centuries. In 1785, Malacarne, an Italian anatomist, studied pairs of dogs from the same litter and pairs of birds from the same batches of eggs. For each pair, he would train one subject extensively over a long period of time while the other would be equally well cared for, but not trained. He discovered later, in autopsies of the animals, that the brains of the trained animals appeared more complex, with a greater number of folds and fissures. However, this line of research, was, for unknown reasons, discontinued. In the late 19th century, there were attempts to relate the circumference of the human head with the amount of learning a person had experienced. While some early findings claimed such a relationship, later research determined that this was not a valid measure of brain development.

Finally, by the 1960s new technologies had been developed that gave scientists the ability to measure brain changes with great precision using high magnification techniques and assessment of levels of various brain enzymes and neurotransmitter chemicals. Mark Rosenzweig and his colleagues Edward Bennett and Marian Diamond, at the University of California in Berkeley, incorporated those technologies in an ambitious series of 16 experiments over a period of 10 years to try to address the issue of the effect of experience on the brain. Their findings were reported in the article discussed in this chapter. For reasons that will become obvious, they did not use humans in their studies, but rather, as in many classic psychological experiments, their subjects were rats.

THEORETICAL PROPOSITIONS

Since psychologists are ultimately interested in humans, not rats, the use of non-human subjects must be justified. In these studies, then, part of the theoretical foundation concerned why rats had been chosen as subjects. The authors explained that for several reasons, it is more convenient to use rodents than to use higher mammals such as carnivores or primates. The part of the brain that is the main focus of this research is smooth in the rat, not folded and complex as it is in higher animals. Therefore, it can be examined and measured more easily to yield the desired results. In addition, rats are small and inexpensive, which is an important consideration in the world of research laboratories (usually underfunded and lacking in space). Rats bear large litters, and this allows for members from the same litters to be assigned to different experimental conditions. Finally, the authors point out, various strains of inbred rats have been produced, and this allows researchers to include the effects of genetics in their studies if desired.

Implicit in Rosenzweig's research was the belief that animals raised in highly stimulating environments will demonstrate differences in brain growth and chemistry when compared with animals reared in plain or dull circumstances. In each of the experiments reported in this article, 12 sets of three male rats, each set from the same litter, were studied.

METHOD

Three male rats were chosen from each litter. They were then randomly assigned to one of three conditions. One rat remained in the laboratory cage with the rest of the colony; another was assigned to what Rosenzweig termed the "enriched" environment cage; and the third was assigned to the "impoverished" cage. Remember that there were 12 rats in each of these conditions for each of the 16 experiments.

The three different environments were described as follows. The standard laboratory colony cage contained several rats in an adequate space with food and water always available. The impoverished environment was a slightly smaller cage isolated in a separate room in which the rat was placed alone with adequate food and water. The enriched environment was virtually a rat's Disneyland (no offense intended to Mickey!). Six to eight rats lived in a "large cage furnished with a variety of objects with which they could play. A new set of playthings, drawn out of a pool of 25 objects, was placed in the cage every day" (p. 22). The three environments are illustrated in Figure 1.

The rats were allowed to live in these different environments for various periods of time, ranging from four to 10 weeks. Following this differential treatment period, the experimental rodents were humanely sacrificed so that autopsies could be carried out on their brains to determine if any differences had developed. In order to be sure that no experimenter bias would occur, the examinations were done in random order by code number so that the person doing the autopsy would not know in which condition the rat was raised. The researchers' primary focus was on the differences in the brains of the enriched rats vs. the impoverished rats.

The rats' brains were dissected and the various sections were measured, weighed, and analyzed to determine amount of cell growth

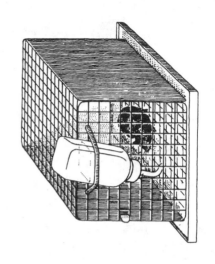

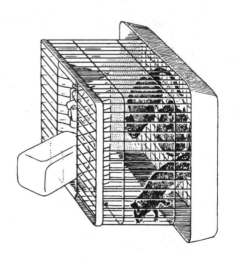

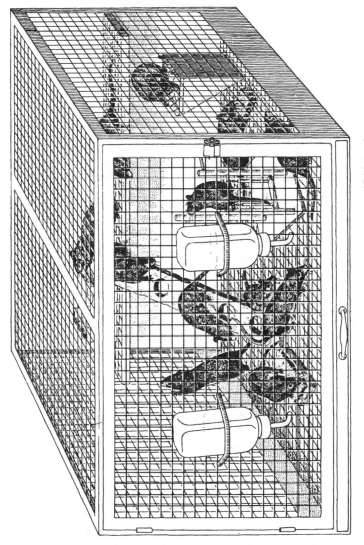

FIGURE 1 The three cage environments. From M. R. Rosenzweig, E. L. Bennett, and M. C. Diamond, "Brain changes in response to experience." Copyright © 1972 by Scientific American, Inc. All rights reserved.

and levels of neurotransmitter activity. In this latter measurement there was one brain enzyme of particular interest called "acetylcholinesterase." This chemical is important because it allows for faster and more efficient transmission of impulses among brain cells.

So, did Rosenzweig and his associates find differences in the brains of rats raised in enriched vs. impoverished environments? Here are their results.

RESULTS

Results indicated that the brains of the enriched rats were different from the impoverished rats in many ways. The cerebral cortex of the enriched rats was significantly heavier and thicker. The cortex is the part of the brain that responds to experience and is responsible for movement, memory, learning, and all sensory input (vision, hearing, touch, taste, smell). Also, greater activity of the nervous system enzyme, acetylcholinesterase, mentioned previously, was found in the brain tissue of the rats with the enriched experience.

In your brain as well as in the brains of rats there are millions of cells called "glial cells." They are not involved directly in the transmission of nerve impulses (this is carried out by neurons), but serve several crucial auxiliary functions. Glial cells are involved in the formation of the myelin sheath or covering that insulates nerves and promotes the fast movement of signals along neural pathways. These glial cells also serve to nourish and cleanse neurons in the brain. The analyses in these studies found a significantly greater number of glial cells in the enriched rats' brains compared with the rats raised in the dull environment.

While there were no significant differences found between the two groups of rats in the number of brain cells (called neurons), the enriched environment produced *larger* neurons. Related to this was the finding that the ratio of RNA to DNA, the two most important brain chemicals for cell growth, was greater for the enriched rats. Without going into detail, this meant that there had been a higher level of chemical activity in the enriched rats' brains.

Rosenzweig and his colleagues stated that "although the brain differences induced by environment are not large, we are confident that they are genuine. When the experiments are replicated, the same pattern of differences is found repeatedly. . . . The most consistent effect of experience on the brain that we found was the ratio of the weight of the cortex to the weight of the rest of the brain: the sub-cortex. It appears that the cortex increases in weight quite readily in response to experience whereas the rest of the brain changes little" (p. 25). This measurement of the ratio of the cortex to the rest of the brain was the most accurate measurement of brain changes. This was because the overall weight of the brain varies with the overall weight of each individual animal. By considering this ratio, such individual differences are canceled out. Figure 2 illustrates this finding for all of the 16 studies. As you can see, in only one experiment was the difference not statistically significant.

Finally, there was a finding reported relating to the synapses of the brains of the two groups of rats. The synapse is the point at which two neurons meet. Most brain activity occurs at the synapse, where a nerve impulse is either passed from one neuron to the next so that it continues on, or it is inhibited and stopped. Under great magnification using the electron microscope, it was found that the synapses themselves of the enriched rats' brains were 50 percent larger than those of the impoverished rats.

DISCUSSION AND CRITICISMS

After nearly 10 years of research, Rosenzweig, Bennett, and Diamond were willing to state with confidence, "There can now be no doubt that many aspects of brain anatomy and brain chemistry are changed by experience" (p. 27). However, they are also quick to acknowledge that

FIGURE 2   Ratio of cortex to test of brain enriched compared with impoverished environment.*

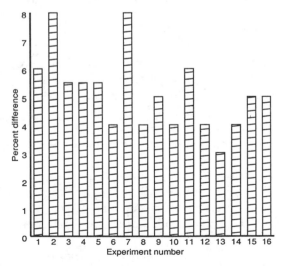

*Results in experiments 2 through 26 were statistifcally significant.
(adapted from p. 26)

when they first reported their findings many other scientists were skeptical, since such effects had not been so clearly demonstrated in past research. There were criticisms contending that perhaps it was not the enriched environment that produced the brain changes, but other differences in the treatment of the rats such as mere handling or stress.

The criticism of differential handling was a valid one in that the enriched rats were handled twice each day when they were removed from the cage as the toys were being changed, while the impoverished rats were not handled. It was possible, therefore, that the handling might have caused the results and not the enriched environment. To respond to this potential confounding factor, the researchers handled one group of rats every day and did not handle another group of their litter mates (all were raised in the same environment). No differences in the brains of these two groups were found. Additionally, in their later studies, both the enriched and impoverished rats were handled equally and, still, the same pattern of results was found.

As for the criticisms relating to stress, the argument was that the isolation experienced by the impoverished rats was stressful and this was the reason for their less developed brains. Rosenzweig, et al., cited other research that had exposed rats to a daily routine of stress (cage rotation or mild electric shock) and had found no evidence of changes in brain development due to stress alone.

One of the problems of any research carried out in a laboratory is that it is necessarily artificial. Rosenzweig and his colleagues were curious about how various levels of stimulation might affect the brain development of animals in their natural environments. They pointed out that laboratory rats and mice often have been raised in artificial environments for as many as 100 generations and bear little resemblance genetically to rats in the wild. To explore this intriguing possibility, they began studying wild deer mice. After the mice were trapped, they were randomly placed in either natural outdoor conditions or the enriched laboratory cages. After four weeks the outdoor mice showed greater brain development than did those in the enriched laboratory environment. "This indicates that even the enriched laboratory environment is indeed impoverished in comparison with a natural environment" (p. 27).

Finally, the most important criticism of any research involving animal subjects is the question of its relationship, if any, to humans. There is no doubt that this line of research could never be performed on humans, but it is nevertheless the responsibility of the researchers to address this issue, and these scientists did so.

The authors explained that it is difficult to generalize from the findings of one set of rats to another set of rats, and consequently much more difficult to try to apply rat findings to monkeys or humans. And, although they report similar findings with several species of rodents, they admit that more research would be necessary before any assumptions could be made responsibly about the effects of experience on the human brain. They proposed, however, that the value of this kind of research on animals is that "it allows us to test concepts and techniques, some of which may later prove useful in research with human subjects."

Several potential benefits of this research were suggested by the authors in their article. One possible application was in the study of memory. Changes in the brain due to experience might lead to a better understanding of how memories are stored in the brain. This could, in turn, lead to new techniques for improving memory and preventing memory loss due to aging. Another area in which this research might prove helpful was in explaining the relationship between malnutrition and intelligence. The concept proposed by the authors in this regard was that malnutrition may make a person unresponsive to the stimulation available in the environment and consequently may limit brain development. And, the authors noted, some concurrent research suggested that the effects of malnutrition on brain growth may be either reduced by environmental enrichment or enhanced by deprivation.

Related Research

This work by Rosenzweig, Bennett, and Diamond served as a catalyst for continued research in this area. Over the past 20 or so years since the publication of their article, these scientists and many others have continued to confirm, refine, and expand on their findings.

For example, it has been found that learning itself is enhanced by enriched environmental experiences and that even the brains of adult animals raised in impoverished conditions can improve when placed in an enriched environment (see Bennett, 1976, for a complete review). Moreover, it has been found more recently that enriched experiences may increase the secretion of certain neurotransmitter chemicals that enhance learning (Woody, 1986).

Finally, there has been some evidence to indicate that experience does indeed alter brain development in humans. Through careful autopsies of humans who have died naturally, it appears that when a person develops a greater number of skills and abilities, the brain actually becomes more complex and heavier. Other findings come from examinations during autopsies of the brains of people who were unable to have certain experiences. For example, in a blind person's brain, the portion of the cortex used for vision is significantly less developed, less convoluted, and thinner than in the brain of a person with normal sight.

Marian Diamond, one of the authors of the original article, has applied the results of work in this area to the process of human intellectual development throughout life. She says: "For people's lives, I think we can take a more optimistic view of the aging brain. . . . The main factor is stimulation. The nerve cells are designed for stimulation. And I think curiosity is a key factor. If one maintains curiosity for a lifetime, that will surely stimulate neural tissue and the cortex may in turn respond. . . . I looked for people who were extremely active after 88 years of age. I found that the people who use their brains don't lose them. It was that simple" (Hopson, 1984, p.70).

BENNETT, E.L. (1976) Cerebral effects of differential experience and training. In M.R. Rosenzweig and E.L. Bennett (eds.), *Neural mechanisms of learning and memory*. Cambridge, Mass.: MIT Press.
HOPSON, J. (1984) A love affair with the brain: A PT conversation with Marian Diamond. *Psychology Today*, 11, 62–75.
WOODY, C. (1986) Understanding the cellular basis of learning and memory. *Annual Review of Psychology*, 37, 433–93.

WHAT YOU SEE IS WHAT YOU'VE LEARNED
Turnbull, C.M. (1961) Some observations regarding the experiences and behavior of the BaMbuti Pygmies. *American Journal of Psychology*, 74, 304–8.

This study is a somewhat unusual one to appear in this book. Turnbull did not have any specific theoretical propositions, there was no clear scientific method used, and the author is not a psychologist. Nevertheless, this short article has been frequently and widely cited to demonstrate some important psychological concepts relating to your ability to perceive the world around you. Before reaching the point where Turnbull's observations can be placed in the proper context, a considerable amount of conceptual explanation is necessary. Keep in mind that we *will* get to the study itself, even though we may seem to be taking the long way around. Let's begin by filling in the theory behind Turnbull's discoveries, which the brevity of his article did not allow him to do.

THEORETICAL PROPOSITIONS

Two large and important fields of study within psychology are those of sensation and perception. These are fundamentally separate areas, but they are highly related. Sensation refers to the information you are constantly receiving from your environment through your senses. You are bombarded with a huge amount of sensory data every minute of every day. If you just stop and think about it for a minute, frequencies of light are reflecting off all the objects around you wherever you look, near or far. There are probably a multitude of sounds entering your ears at any moment, various parts of your body are in contact with various objects, and several tastes and smells are often present. If you take your attention off this book for a moment (I know this is difficult!) and focus on each sense, one at a time, you'll begin to get some idea of the amount of "sensory input" that was beneath your level of awareness. In fact, if I do this right now I become aware of the hum from my computer, a car going by outside, a door slamming somewhere, a painting on the wall, a partly cloudy sky, the light from my desk lamp, the feel of my elbows resting on the arms of the chair, the taste of the apple I just finished eating, and so on. However, just a few seconds ago, I was not aware of any of these sensations. We are continuously filtering all this available input and using only a small percentage of it. If your sensory filtering mechanisms were suddenly to fail, the world would become so intensely confusing that you would be overwhelmed, and probably you would not be able to survive it.

The fact that the sensory world (what you see, hear, touch, taste, and smell) usually appears to you in an *organized* way is due to your abilities of *perception*. Sensations are the raw materials for perception. Your brain's perceptual processes are involved in three general activities: (1) selecting the sensations to pay attention to as discussed in the previous paragraph; (2) organizing these into recognizable patterns and shapes; and (3) interpreting this organization to explain and make judgments about the world. In other words, perception refers to how we take this jumble of sensations and create *meaning*. Your visual sensations of the page you are reading are nothing more than random black shapes on a white background. This is what is projected onto the retinas of your eyes and sent to the visual fields of your brain. However, you pay attention to them, organize them, and interpret them so that they become words and sentences that contain meaning.

Your brain has many tricks or strategies available to assist in organizing sensations in meaningful and understandable ways. In order to put Turnbull's study in proper perspective, let's take a look at several of these. The perceptual strategy you probably use the most is called *figure-ground*. A well-known example of the figure-ground relationship is pictured in Figure 1. When you look at the drawing, what do you see immediately? Some of you will see a white vase, while others will see two profiles facing one another. As you study this for awhile, you will be able to see either one and you will be able to switch back and forth between seeing the vase and seeing the profiles. You'll notice that

FIGURE 1 Figure-ground relationship–a reversible figure. Charles G. Morris, Understanding Psychology, © 1991, p. 414. Reprinted by permission of Prentice Hall, Englewood Cliffs, New Jersey

if you look at the vase (figure), the profiles (ground) seem to fade into the background. But focus on the profiles (figure) and the vase (ground) becomes the background. We appear to have a natural tendency to divide sensations into figure and ground relationships. If you think about it, this makes the world a much more organized place. Imagine trying to spot someone in a crowd of people. Without your figure-ground abilities, this task would be impossible. When soldiers wear camouflaged clothing, the distinction between figure and ground is blurred so that it becomes difficult to distinguish the figure (the soldier) from the ground (the vegetation).

Other organizational strategies we use routinely to create order and meaning out of those chaotic sensations are called "perceptual constancies." These refer to our ability to know that the characteristics of objects stay the same even though our sensations of them may change drastically. One of these, for example, is *shape constancy*. If you stand up and walk around a chair, the image of that chair projecting onto your retina (the sensation) changes with every step you take. However, you *perceive* the shape of the chair to be unchanged. Imagine how impossibly confusing a place the world would be if all objects were perceived differently each time your angle of vision changed.

Another one of these techniques is *size constancy*. This is the perceptual facility that is most related to Turnbull's article. Size constancy enables you to perceive a familiar object as being the same size, regardless of its distance from you. If you see a school bus two blocks away, the image projected onto your retina is the same as that of a small toy bus seen close up. Nevertheless, you perceive the distant bus to be its large, normal size. Likewise, if you are looking at two people standing in a field, one 10 feet from you and the other 100 feet in the distance, your sensation of the more distant person is of someone 3 feet tall. The reason you perceive that person to be of normal size is due to your ability of size constancy.

Your perceptions using any of these strategies can be tricked. This is how visual illusions work. A film director can shoot a scene in which a ship is being tossed about in a terrible storm. Even though the camera is filming a 2-foot-long model ship in a special effects tank, we perceive the ship as full size because of size constancy and the lack of any comparison objects to offer cues as to its true size. In the film spoof *Airplane*, we see a room shot from a low angle directly behind a telephone on a desk (therefore, we know this phone is about to ring with important information). The phone is so close to the camera lens that it appears huge on the screen, but we see it as a normal-size phone due to our ability of size constancy. The perceptual surprise comes when the phone rings and the actor crosses the room to answer. The phone he picks up turns out to really be as huge as it looked: about 3 feet across!

The last important point that must be made before turning to this chapter's study concerns whether these perceptual abilities are learned or inborn. Research with individuals who were blind at birth and who later gain their sight has suggested that our ability to perceive figure-ground relationships is, at least in part, innate; that is, present from birth. Perceptual constancies, on the other hand, are clearly a product of experience. When young children (age 5 and under) see cars or trains in the distance, they perceive them as toys and sometimes will ask quite adamantly to have one. By the time children reach age 7 or 8, size constancy has developed and they are able to judge sizes correctly over varying distances.

Psychologists have asked the question, what kinds of experiences allow us to acquire these abilities? And could a situation exist in which a person might grow to adulthood and not possess some of these perceptual talents? Well, Turnbull's brief report published 30 years ago shed a great deal of light on these questions.

METHOD

As mentioned at the beginning of this chapter, Turnbull is not a psychologist, but rather an anthropologist. In the late 1950s and early '60s he was in the dense Ituri Forest in the Congo (now Zaire) studying the life and culture of the BaMbuti Pygmies. Because he was an anthropologist, Turnbull's primary method of research was naturalistic observation; that is, observing behavior as it occurs in its natural setting. This is an important method of research for psychologists as well. For example, differences in aggressive behavior between young boys and girls during play could be studied through observational techniques. Examining the social behavior of non-human primates, such as chimpanzees, would also require a method involving naturalistic observation. For obvious reasons, such research is often expensive and time-consuming, yet some behavioral phenomena cannot be properly researched in any other way.

Turnbull, on one excursion, was traveling through the forest from one group of Pygmies to another. He was accompanied by a young man (about 22 years old) named Kenge, who was from one of the local Pygmy villages. Kenge always assisted Turnbull in his research as a guide, and introduced Turnbull to groups of BaMbuti who did not know him. Turnbull's observations that constitute this published report began when he and Kenge reached the eastern edge of a hill that had been cleared of trees for a missionary station. Because of this clearing, there was a distant view over the forest to the high Ruwenzori Mountains. Since the Ituri Forest is extremely thick, it was highly unusual to see views such as this.

RESULTS

Kenge had never in his life seen a view over great distances. He pointed to the mountains and asked if they were hills or clouds. Turnbull told him that they were hills, but they were larger than any Kenge had seen before in his forest. Turnbull asked Kenge if he would like to take a drive over to the mountains and see them more closely. After some hesitation—Kenge had never left the forest before—he agreed. It is interesting to note that as they began driving, a violent thunderstorm began and did not clear until they had reached their destination. This reduced visibility to about 100 yards, which prevented Kenge from watching the approaching mountains. Finally, they reached the Ishango National Park, which is on the edge of Lake Edward at the foot of the mountains. Turnbull writes:

> As we drove through the park the rain stopped and the sky cleared, and that rare moment came when the Ruwenzori Mountains were completely free of cloud and stood up in the late afternoon sky, their snow-capped peaks shining in the afternoon sun. I stopped the car and Kenge very unwillingly got out (p. 304).

Kenge glanced around and declared that this was bad country because there were no trees. Then he looked up at the mountains and was literally speechless. The life and culture of the BaMbuti were limited to the dense jungle and, therefore, their language did not contain words to describe such a sight. Kenge was fascinated by the distant snow caps and interpreted them to be a type of rock formation. As they prepared to leave, the plain stretching out in front of them also came clearly into view. The next observation makes up the central point of this article and this chapter.

Looking out across the plain, Kenge saw a herd of buffalo grazing several miles away. Remember that at such a distance, the image (the sensation) of the buffalo cast onto the retinas of Kenge's eyes was very small. Kenge turned to Turnbull and asked what kind of insect they were! Turnbull replied that they were buffalo even bigger than the forest buffalo Kenge had seen before. Kenge just laughed at what he considered to be a stupid story and asked again what those insects were. "Then he talked to himself, for want of more intelligent company, and tried to liken the distant buffalo to the various beetles and ants with which he was familiar" (p. 305).

Well, Turnbull did precisely what you or I would do in the same situation. He got back into the car and drove with Kenge to the grazing buffalo. Kenge was a very courageous young man, but as he watched the animals steadily increase in size, he moved over next to Turnbull and whispered that this was witchcraft. Finally as they approached the buffalo and he could see them for the size they truly were he was no longer afraid, but he was still unsure as to why they had been so small before, and wondered if they had grown larger or if there was some form of trickery going on.

A similar event occurred when the two men continued driving and came to the edge of Lake Edward. This is quite a large lake, and there was a fishing boat two or three miles out. Kenge refused to believe that the distant boat was something large enough to hold several people. He claimed that it was just a piece of wood, until Turnbull reminded him of the experience with the buffalo. At this, Kenge just nodded in amazement.

During the rest of the day spent outside the jungle, Kenge watched for animals in the distance and tried to guess what they were. It was apparent to Turnbull that Kenge was no longer afraid or skeptical, but was working on adapting his perceptions to these entirely new sensations. And he was learning fast. The next day, however, he asked to be returned to his home in the jungle and again remarked that this was bad country: no trees.

DISCUSSION

This brief research report dramatically illustrates how we acquire our abilities called perceptual constancies. Not only are they clearly learned as a result of experience, but these experiences are influenced by the culture and environment in which we live. In the jungle where Kenge had spent his entire life, there were no long-range views. In fact, vision was usually limited to about a hundred feet. Therefore, there was no opportunity for the BaMbuti to develop size constancy and, if you stop to think about it, there was no need for them to do so. Although it has not been directly tested, it is possible that these same groups of Pygmies may have a more highly developed ability for figure-ground relationships. The logic here is that it is extremely important for the BaMbuti to distinguish those animals (especially the potentially dangerous ones) that are able to blend into the surrounding background vegetation. This perceptual skill would seem less necessary for people living in a modern industrialized culture.

In regard to size constancy, Turnbull's observational study may offer us an explanation for why this ability is learned rather than innate. Certain perceptual skills may be necessary for our survival, but we do not all develop and grow in the same situation. Therefore, to maximize our survival potential, some of our skills are allowed to unfold over time in ways that are best suited to our physical environment.

SIGNIFICANCE OF FINDINGS

Turnbull's work fueled the fire of behavioral scientists who address the question of the relative influence of biology vs. environment (learning) on our behavior: the "nature-nurture" controversy. Obviously, Turnbull's observations of Kenge's perceptions points strongly to the nurture or environmental side of the issue. In a fascinating series of studies by Blakemore and Cooper (1970), kittens were raised in darkness except for exposure to either vertical or horizontal stripes. Later when the cats were taken out of the dark environment, the ones who had been exposed to vertical lines responded to the vertical lines on objects in the environment, but ignored horizontal lines. Conversely, the cats exposed to horizontal lines during development later appeared to only recognize the presence of horizontal figures. The cats' ability to see was not damaged, but some specific perceptual abilities had not developed. By the way, these particular deficits were permanent.

Other research, however, has suggested that some of our perceptual abilities may be present at birth; that is, given to us by nature without any learning needed. For example, one recent study exposed newborn infants (only three days old) to squares of various colors of light (red, blue, green) and to squares of gray light at the exact same brightness. All these very young infants spent significantly more time looking at the colorful squares than at the gray ones (Adams, 1987). It is unlikely that infants had the opportunity to learn that preference in three days, so these findings provide evidence that some of our perceptual abilities are innate.

The overall conclusion from research in this area is that there is not a single definitive answer regarding the source of our perceptual abilities. Turnbull and Kenge clearly demonstrated that some are learned, but others may be innate or part of our "factory-installed standard equipment." The one sure point here is that this area of research is bound to be pursued far into the future.

ADAMS, R.J. (1987) An evaluation of color preference in early infancy. *Infant Behavior and Development*, 10, 143–50.
BLAKEMORE, C., and COOPER, G.F. (1970) Development of the brain depends on physical environment. *Nature*, 228, 227–29.

WATCH OUT FOR THE VISUAL CLIFF!
Gibson, Eleanor J., and Walk, Richard D. (1960) The "visual cliff." *Scientific American*, 202, 67–71.

One of the most often told anecdotes in psychology concerns a man called S.B. (initials used to protect his privacy). S.B. had been blind his entire life until the age of 52, when a newly developed operation (the now-common corneal transplant) was performed on him and his sight was restored. However, S.B.'s new ability to *see* did not mean that he automatically *perceived* what he saw the same as the rest of us do. One important example of this became evident soon after the operation, before his clarity of vision had occurred completely. S.B. looked out his hospital window and was curious about the small objects he could see moving on the ground below. He began to crawl out on his window ledge, thinking he would lower himself down by his hands and have a look. Fortunately the hospital staff prevented him from trying this. He was on the fourth floor, and those small moving things were cars! Even though S.B. could now see, he was not able to perceive depth.

Our ability to visually sense and interpret the world around us is an area of interest to experimental psychologists. And within this lies the central question of whether such abilities are inborn or learned. As you will recall from the previous chapter, Turnbull addressed this issue in his report of the BaMbuti Pygmy Kenge's inability to perceive the true size of objects at great distances. Kenge had the ability to perceive depth per se, but because his life had been spent in dense jungle, he did not have the experiences necessary to develop the capacity for the visual skill of "size constancy." While Turnbull's discoveries were enlightening to the scientific community, the observational nature of his work did not allow for the systematic study of visual perception. In order to determine accurately if certain perceptual skills are learned or inborn, research would have to move into the laboratory.

Many psychologists believe that our most important visual skill is depth perception. You can imagine how difficult, and probably impossible, survival would be if you could not perceive depth. You would run into things, be unable to judge how far away a predator was, or step right off cliffs. Therefore, it might be logical to assume that depth perception is an inborn survival mechanism that does not require experience to develop. However, as Eleanor Gibson and Richard Walk point out in their article, "Human infants at the creeping and toddling stage are notoriously prone to falls from more or less high places. They must be kept from going over the brink by side panels on their cribs, gates on stairways, and the vigilance of adults. As their muscular coordination matures they begin to avoid such accidents on their own. Common sense might suggest that the child learns to recognize falling-off places by experience—that is, by falling and hurting himself" (p. 64).

These researchers wanted to study this visual ability of depth perception scientifically in the laboratory. To do this they conceived of and developed an experimental device they called the "visual cliff."

THEORETICAL PROPOSITIONS

If you wanted to find out at what point in the developmental process animals or people were able to perceive depth, one way to do this would be to put them on the edge of a cliff and see if they are able to avoid falling off. On its face, this is a ridiculous suggestion because of the ethical considerations of the potential injury to subjects who were unable to perceive depth (or more specifically, height). The "visual cliff" avoids this problem because it presents the subject with what appears to be a drop-off, when no drop-off actually exists. Exactly how this is done will be explained in a moment, but the importance of this apparatus lies in the fact that human or animal infants can be placed on the visual cliff to see if they are able to perceive the drop-off and avoid it. If they are unable to do this and step off the "cliff," there is no danger of falling.

Gibson and Walk took a "nativist" position on this topic, which means that they believe that depth perception and the avoidance of a drop-off appear automatically as part of our original biological equipment and are not, therefore, products of experience. The opposing view, held by empiricists, contends that such abilities are learned. Gibson and Walk's visual cliff allowed them to ask these questions: At what stage in development can a person or animal respond effectively to the stimuli of depth and height? And do these responses appear at different times with animals of different species and habitats?

METHOD

The visual cliff consisted of a table about 4 feet high with a top made from a piece of thick, clear glass. Directly under half of the table (the shallow side) is a solid surface with a red and white checkered pattern. Under the other half is the same pattern, but it is down at the level of the floor underneath the table (the deep side). At the edge of the shallow side, then, is the appearance of a sudden drop-off to the floor although, in reality, the glass extends all the way across. Between the shallow and the deep side is a center board about a foot wide. Figures 1 and 2 illustrate the visual cliff more clearly. The process of testing infants using this device was extremely simple.

The subjects for this study were 36 infants between the ages of 6 months and 14 months. The mothers of the infants also participated. Each infant was placed on the center board of the visual cliff and was then called by the mother first from the deep side and then from the shallow side.

In order to compare the development of depth perception in humans with that in other baby animals, the visual cliff allowed for similar tests with other species (without a mother's beckoning, however). These animals simply had to be placed on the center board and observed to see if they could discriminate between the shallow and deep sides and avoid stepping off "the cliff." You can imagine the rather unique situation in the psychology labs at Cornell University when the various baby animals were brought in for testing. They included chicks, turtles, rats, lambs, kids (baby goats, that is), pigs, kittens, and puppies. One has to wonder if they were all tested on the same day!

Remember, the goal of this research was to examine whether depth perception is learned or innate. What makes this method so ingenious is that it allowed that question to at least begin to be answered. After all, infants, whether human or animal, cannot be *asked* if they perceive depth, and, as mentioned above, they cannot be tested on real cliffs. In psychology, many answers are found through the development of new methods for studying the questions. And the results of Gibson and Walk's early study provide an excellent example of this.

RESULTS AND DISCUSSION

Nine children in the study refused entirely to move off of the center board. This was not explained by the researchers, but perhaps it was just infant stubbornness. When the mothers of the other 27 called to them from the shallow side, all the infants crawled off the board and crossed the glass. Only three of them, however, crept, with great hesitation, off the brink of the visual cliff when called by their mothers from the deep side. When called from the cliff side, most of the children either crawled away from the mother on the shallow side or cried in frustration at being unable to reach the mother without moving over the cliff. There was little question that the children were perceiving the depth of the cliff. "Often they would peer down through the glass of the deep side and then back away. Others would pat the glass with their hands, yet despite this tactile assurance of solidity would refuse to cross" (p. 64).

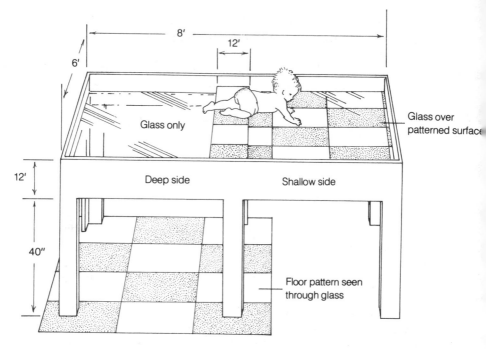

FIGURE 1   Gibson and Walk's visual cliff. From Dworetzky, Introduction to Child Development, Fourth Edition. Copyright © 1990 by West Publishing Company. Reprinted by permission.

FIGURE 2   The visual cliff in testing situation. From E. J. Gibson and R. D. Walk, "The visual cliff," Scientific American, April 1960, 65. Photo by William Vandivert. Reproduced by permission.

Do these results prove that humans' ability to perceive depth is innate rather than learned? Well, obviously it does not, since all the children in this study had at least 6 months of life experience in which to learn about depth through trial and error. However, human infants cannot be tested prior to 6 months of age because they do not have adequate locomotor abilities. It was for this reason that Gibson and Walk decided to test various other animals as a comparison. As you know, most non-human animals gain the ability to move about much sooner than do humans. The results of the animal tests were extremely interesting, in that the ability of the various animals to perceive depth developed in relation to when the species needed such a skill for survival.

For example, baby chickens must begin to scratch for their own food soon after hatching. When they were tested on the visual cliff at less than 24 hours of age they *never* made the mistake of stepping off onto the deep side.

Kids and lambs are able to stand and walk very soon after birth. From the moment they first stood up, their response on the visual cliff was as accurate and predictable as that of the chicks. Not one error was made. When one of the researchers placed a 1-day-old baby goat down on the deep side of the glass, it became frightened and froze in a defensive posture. If it was then pushed over toward the shallow side, it would relax and jump forward onto the seemingly solid surface. This indicated that the visual sense was in complete control and that the animals' ability to *feel* the solidity of the glass on the deep side had no effect on the response.

For the rats it was a different story. They did not appear to show any significant preference for the shallow side of the table. Why do you suppose this difference was found? Before you conclude that rats are just stupid, consider Gibson and Walk's much more likely explanation: A rat does not depend very much on vision to survive. In fact, its visual system is not highly developed. Since it is nocturnal, a rat locates food by smell and moves around in the dark using cues from the stiff whiskers on its nose. So when a rat was placed on the center board, it was not fooled by the visual cliff because it was not using vision to decide which way to go. To the rat's whiskers, the glass on the deep side felt the same as the glass on the shallow side and, thus, the rat was just as likely to move off the center board to the deep side as to the shallow side.

You might expect the same results from kittens. They are basically nocturnal and have sensitive whiskers. However, cats are predators, not scavengers like rats. Therefore, they depend more on vision. And, accordingly, kittens were found to have excellent depth perception as soon as they were able to move on their own: at about 4 weeks.

Although at times this research article (and this chapter) risks sounding like a children's animal story, it has to be reported that the species with the worst performance on the visual cliff was the turtle. The baby turtles chosen to be tested were of the aquatic variety, because the researchers expected that since the turtles' natural environment was water, they might prefer the deep side of the cliff. However, it appeared that the turtles were smart enough to know that they were not in water, and 76 percent of them crawled off onto the shallow side. But 24 percent went "over the edge." "The relatively large minority that chose the deep side suggests either that this turtle has poorer depth perception than other animals, or its natural habitat gives it less occasion to 'fear' a fall" (p. 67). Clearly, if you live your life in water, the survival value of depth perception, in terms of avoiding falls, would be diminished.

Gibson and Walk pointed out that all of their observations were consistent with evolutionary theory. That is, all species of animals, if they are to survive, need to develop the ability to perceive depth by the time they achieve independent movement. For humans this does not occur until around 6 months of age, but for chickens and goats, it is nearly immediate (by one day), and for rats, cats, and dogs about 4 weeks of age. The authors conclude, therefore, that this capacity is inborn, because to learn it through trial and error would cause too many potentially fatal accidents.

So, if we are so well prepared biologically, why do children take so many falls? Gibson and Walk explained that the human infants' perception of depth had matured sooner than had their skill in movement. During testing, many of the infants supported themselves on the deep side of the glass as they turned on the center board, and some even backed up onto the deep side as they began to crawl toward the mother across the shallow side. If the glass had not been there, some of the children would have fallen off the cliff!

CRITICISMS AND SUBSEQUENT RESEARCH

The most common criticism of the researchers' conclusions revolves around the question of whether they really proved that depth perception is innate in humans. As mentioned earlier, by the time infants were tested on the visual cliff, they had already *learned* to avoid such situations. A later study placed younger infants, ages 2 to 5 months, on the glass over the deep side of the visual cliff. When this happened, all of the babies showed a *decrease* in heart rate. Such a decrease is thought to be a sign of interest, not fear, which is accompanied by heart rate increases (Campos, Hiatt, Ramsay, Henderson, and Svejda, 1978). This indicates that these younger infants had not yet learned to fear the drop-off and would learn the avoidance behavior somewhat later. These findings argued against Gibson and Walk's position.

It is important to notice, however, that while there was and still is controversy over just when we are able to perceive depth (the nativists vs. the empiricists), much of the research that is done to find the answer incorporates the visual cliff apparatus developed by Gibson and Walk. Additionally, other related research using the visual cliff has turned up some fascinating findings.

One example is the work of Sorce, Emde, Campos, and Klinnert (1985). They put 1-year-old infants on a visual cliff for which the drop-off was neither shallow nor deep but in between (about 30 inches). As a baby crawled toward the cliff it would stop and look down. On the other side, as in the Gibson and Walk study, the mother was waiting. Sometimes the mother had been instructed to maintain an expression of fear on her face while other times the mother looked happy and interested. When infants saw the expression of fear they refused to crawl any further. However, most of the infants who saw their mother looking happy checked the cliff again and crawled across. When the drop-off was made flat, the infants did not check with the mother before crawling across. This method of non-verbal communication used by infants in determining their behavior is called *social referencing*.

CONCLUSION

Through the inventiveness of Gibson and Walk, behavioral scientists have been able to study depth perception in a clear and systematic way. The question of whether this and other perceptual abilities are innate or learned continues to be debated. The truth may lie in a compromise that proposes an interaction between nature and nurture. Perhaps, as various studies have indicated, depth perception is present at birth (even in the Campos, et. al., study, the interest generated by the very young infants demonstrates perception of something), but fear of falling and avoidance of danger is learned through experience, after the infant is old enough to crawl around and get into trouble.

But whatever the questions are, it is the methodological advances such as the visual cliff that allow us to begin to find the answers.

CAMPOS, J., HIATT, S., RAMSAY, D., HENDERSON, C., and SVEJDA, M. (1978) The emergence of fear on the visual cliff. In M. Lewis and L.A. Rosenblum (eds.) *The development of affect*. New York: Plenum Press.

SORCE, J., EMDE, R., CAMPOS, J., and KLINNERT, M. (1985) Maternal emotion signaling: Its effect on the visual cliff behavior of 1-year-olds. *Developmental Psychology*, 21, 195–200.

TWO

CONSCIOUSNESS

The study of consciousness, often referred to as "states of awareness," is of great interest to psychologists because it relates to the quality of your psychological interaction with your environment. Think for a moment about how your state of awareness changes as you go through your day, your night, your week, your year, and your life. You concentrate, you daydream, you sleep, you dream, maybe you've been hypnotized at some point, maybe you've used psychoactive drugs (even caffeine and nicotine count!). These conditions are all altered states of consciousness that produce various changes in your behavior.

Within the research area of consciousness, some of the most influential and interesting studies have focused on sleep, dreams, and hypnosis. After all, sleeping and dreaming are things we all do, and nearly everyone is fascinated with hypnosis for one reason or another. So, the first chapter included in this section contains two studies that changed psychology because they (1) discovered REM sleep, and (2) revealed the relationship between REM and dreaming. The second chapter allows you to experience a study by one of the leading dream researchers, which suggests that we may be able to control the content of our dreams. Third is an increasingly influential study, which views the process of dreaming as a purely physiological and random occurrence. And fourth, we discuss one of a series of recent studies arguing *against* the widespread belief that hypnosis is a unique and powerful state. This last study offers evidence demonstrating that hypnotized people are no different from awake people; just a bit more motivated.

TO SLEEP, NO DOUBT TO DREAM . . .

Aserinsky, E., and Kleitman, N. (1953) Regularly occurring periods of eye mobility and concomitant phenomena during sleep. *Science*, 118, 273–74.

Dement, William (1960) The effect of dream deprivation. *Science*, 131, 1705–7.

As you can see, this chapter is somewhat different from the others in that there are two articles being discussed. This is because the first study discovered a basic phenomenon about sleeping and dreaming that made the second study possible. The primary focus of this chapter is William Dement's work on dream deprivation, but to prepare you for that, Aserinsky's findings must be addressed first.

In 1952, Eugene Aserinsky, while a graduate student, was studying sleep. Part of his research involved observing sleeping infants. He noticed that as these infants slept, there were periodic occurrences of active eye movements. During the remainder of the night there were only occasional slow, rolling eye movements. He theorized that these periods of active eye movements might be associated with dreaming. However, infants could not tell him whether they had been dreaming or not. So, in order to test this idea, he expanded his research to include adults.

Aserinsky and his co-author, Nathaniel Kleitman, employed 20 normal adults to serve as subjects. Sensitive electronic measuring devices were connected by electrodes to the muscles around the eyes of these subjects. The leads from these electrodes stretched into the next room where the subjects' sleep could be monitored. The subjects were then allowed to fall asleep normally (subjects participated on more than one night each). During the night, subjects were awakened and "interrogated," either during periods of eye activity or during periods when little or no eye movement was observed. The idea was to wake the subjects and ask them if they had been dreaming and if they could remember the content of the dream. The results were quite revealing.

For all of the subjects combined, there were a total of 27 awakenings during periods of sleep accompanied by rapid eye movements. Of these, 20 reported detailed visual dreams. The other seven reported "the feeling of having dreamed," but could not recall the content in detail. During periods of no eye movement, there were 23 awakenings of which 19 did not report any dreaming and four felt vaguely as if they might have been dreaming, but were not able to describe the dreams. On some occasions, subjects were allowed to sleep through the night uninterrupted. It was found that they experienced between three and four periods of eye activity during the average of seven hours of sleep.

While it may not have seemed so remarkable at the time, Aserinsky had discovered what is very familiar to most of us now: REM (rapid eye movement) sleep, or dreaming sleep. From his discovery grew a huge body of research on sleep and dreaming that continues to expand today. Over the years, as research methods and physiological recording devices have become more sophisticated, we have been able to refine Aserinsky's findings and unlock many of the mysteries of sleep.

For example, we now know that, after you fall asleep, you sleep in four stages, beginning with the lightest sleep (Stage 1) and progressing predictably into deeper and deeper stages. Then after you reach the deepest stage (Stage 4), you begin to move back up through the stages; your sleep becomes lighter and lighter. As you approach Stage 1 again, you enter a very different kind of sleep called REM (see Anch, 1987, for a thorough discussion of this sleep cycle). It is during REM that you do most of your dreaming. However, contrary to popular belief, it has been found scientifically that you do not move around very much during REM. Your body is immobilized by electrochemical messages from your brain that actually paralyze your muscles. This is a survival mechanism that prevents you from acting out your dreams and possibly injuring yourself or worse!

After a short period in REM, you proceed back into the four stages of sleep called "NON-REM," or non-rapid-eye-movement sleep (NREM for short). During the night you cycle between NREM and REM about five or six times (your first REM period comes about 90 minutes after falling asleep), with NREM becoming shorter and REM becoming longer (thereby causing you to dream more toward morning). And, by the way, *everyone dreams*. While there is a small percentage of individuals who never remember dreams, research has determined that we all have them.

All of this knowledge springs from the discovery of REM by Aserinsky in the early 1950s. And one of the leading researchers who followed Aserinsky in giving us this wealth of information on sleeping and dreaming is William Dement. Beginning around the time of Aserinsky's findings, Dement was interested in studying the basic function and significance of dreaming.

THEORETICAL PROPOSITIONS

What struck Dement as most significant was the discovery that dreaming occurs every night in everyone. As Dement states in his article, "Since there appear to be no exceptions to the nightly occurrence of a substantial amount of dreaming in every sleeping person, it might be asked whether or not this amount of dreaming is in some way a necessary and vital part of our existence" (p. 1705). This led him to ask some obvious questions: "Would it be possible for human beings to continue to function normally if their dream life were completely or partially suppressed? Should dreaming be considered necessary in a psychological sense or a physiological sense or both?" (p. 1705).

Dement decided to try to answer these questions by studying subjects who had somehow been deprived of the chance to dream. At first he tried using depressant drugs to prevent dreaming, but the drugs themselves produced too great an effect on the subjects' sleep patterns to allow for valid results. So, he decided on "the somewhat drastic method" of waking subjects up every time they entered REM sleep during the night.

METHOD

This article reported on the first eight subjects in an ongoing sleep and dreaming research project. The subjects were all males ranging in age from 23 to 32. A participant would arrive at the sleep laboratory around his usual bedtime. Small electrodes were attached to the scalp and near the eyes to record brain-wave patterns and eye movements. As in the Aserinsky study, the wires to these electrodes ran into the next room so that the subject could sleep in peace in a quiet, darkened room.

The procedure for the study was as follows. For the first several nights, the subject was allowed to sleep normally for the entire night. This was done to establish a baseline for each subject's usual amount of dreaming and overall sleep pattern.

Once this information was obtained, the next step was to deprive the subject of REM or dream sleep. Over the next several nights (the number of consecutive deprivation nights ranged from three to seven for the various subjects), the experimenter would awaken the subject every time the information from the electrodes indicated that he had begun to dream. The subject was required to sit up in bed and demonstrate that he was fully awake for several minutes before being allowed to go back to sleep.

An important point mentioned by Dement was that the subjects were asked not to sleep at any other times during the dream study. This was because if subjects slept or napped, they might dream, and this could contaminate the findings of the study.

Following the nights of dream deprivation, subjects entered the "recovery phase" of the experiment. During these nights (which varied from one to six) the subjects were allowed to sleep undisturbed throughout the night. Their periods of dreaming continued to be monitored electronically, and the amount of dreaming was recorded as usual.

Next, each subject was given several nights off (something they were very glad about, no doubt!). Then six of them returned to the lab for another series of interrupted nights. These awakenings "exactly duplicated the dream-deprivation nights in number of nights and number of awakenings per night. The only difference was that the subject was awakened in the intervals between eye-movement (dream) periods. Whenever a dream period began, the subject was allowed to sleep on without interruption and was awakened only after the dream had ended spontaneously" (p. 1706). Finally, subjects again had the same number of recovery nights as they did following the dream-deprivation phase. These were called "control recovery," and were included to eliminate the possibility that any effects of dream deprivation were not due simply to being awakened many times during the night, whether dreaming or not.

One thing to keep in mind here is that these findings were published while the study was in its early stages. The reason for this early publication was the rather amazing and clearly significant results that were being obtained and it was felt that the scientific community should be notified at once.

RESULTS

Table 1 summarizes the main findings reported.

During the baseline nights, when subjects were allowed to sleep undisturbed, the average amount of sleep per night was 6 hours and 50 minutes. The average amount of time the subjects spent dreaming was 80 minutes, or 19.5 percent, as reflected in Table 1 (column 1). Dement discovered in these results from the first several nights that the amount of time spent dreaming was remarkably similar from subject to subject. In fact, the amount of variation among the dreamers was only plus-or-minus 7 minutes!

Now, the main point of this study was to examine the effects of being deprived of dreaming, or REM, sleep. The first finding to address this was the number of awakenings required to prevent REM sleep during the dream-deprivation nights. As you can see in Table 1 (column

TABLE 1 Summary of Dream-Deprivation Results

SUBJECT	1. PERCENT DREAM-TIME BASELINE	2. NUMBER OF DREAM DEPRIVATION NIGHTS	3a. NUMBER OF AWAKENINGS FIRST NIGHT	3b. LAST NIGHT	4. PERCENT DREAM-TIME RECOVERY	5. PERCENT DREAM-TIME CONTROL
1.	19.5	5	8	14	34.0	15.6
2.	18.8	7	7	24	34.2	22.7
3.	19.5	5	11	30	17.8	20.2
4.	18.6	5	7	23	26.3	18.8
5.	19.3	5	10	20	29.5	26.3
6.	20.8	4	13	20	29.0	—
7.	17.9	4	22	30	19.8 (28.1)*	16.8
8.	20.8	3	9	13	—**	—
Average	19.5	4.38	⁻1	22	26.6	20.1

*Second recovery night.
**Subject dropped out of study before recovery nights.
(adapted from p. 1707)

39

3a), on the first night, the experimenter had to awaken the subjects between seven and 22 times in order to block REM. However, as the study progressed, subjects had to be awakened more and more often in order to prevent them from dreaming. On the last deprivation night, the number of forced awakenings ranged from 13 to 30 (column 3b). On average, there were twice as many attempts to dream at the end of the deprivation nights.

The next and perhaps most revealing result was the increase in dreaming time after the subjects were prevented from dreaming for several nights. The numbers in Table 1 (column 4) reflect the first recovery night. The average total dream time on this night was 112 minutes, or 26.6 percent (compared with 80 minutes and 19.5 percent during baseline nights in column 1). Dement pointed out that there were two subjects who did not show a significant increase in REM (subjects 3 and 7). If they are excluded from the calculations, the average total dream time is 127 minutes, or 29 percent. This is a 50 percent increase over the average for the baseline nights.

While only the first recovery night is reported in Table 1, it was noted that most of the subjects continued to show elevated dream time (compared with baseline amounts) for five consecutive nights.

"Wait a minute!" you're thinking. Maybe this increase in dreaming has nothing to do with REM deprivation at all. Maybe it's just because these subjects were awakened so often. Well, you'll remember that Dement planned for your astute observation. Six of the subjects returned after several days of rest and repeated the procedure exactly except they were awakened *between* REM periods (the same number of times). This produced no significant increases in dreaming. The average time spent dreaming after the control awakenings was 88 minutes, or 20.1 percent of the total sleep time (column 5). When compared to 80 minutes, or 19.5 percent, in column 1, no significant difference was found.

DISCUSSION

Dement tentatively concluded from these findings that we need to dream. When we are not allowed to dream, there seems to be some kind of pressure to dream that increases over successive dream-deprivation nights. This was evident in his findings from the increasing number of attempts to dream following deprivation (column 3a vs. column 3b) and in the significant increase in dream time (column 4 vs. column 1). He also notes that this increase continues over several nights so that it appears to make up in quantity the approximate amount of lost dreaming. Although Dement did not use the phrase at the time, this important finding has come to be known as the "REM-rebound" effect.

There were several interesting additional points and discoveries made in this brief yet remarkable article. If you return to the table for a moment, you'll see that two subjects, as mentioned before, did not show a significant REM-rebound (subjects 3 and 7). It is always important in research incorporating a relatively small number of subjects to attempt to explain these exceptions. Dement found that the small increase in subject 7 was not difficult to explain. "His failure to show a rise on the first recovery night was in all likelihood due to the fact that he had imbibed several cocktails at a party before coming to the laboratory, so the expected increase in dream time was offset by the depressing effect of the alcohol" (p. 1706).

Subject 3, however, was more difficult to reconcile. Although he showed the largest increase in the number of awakenings during deprivation (from seven to 30), he did not have any REM rebound on any of his five recovery nights. Dement acknowledged that this subject was the one exception in his findings and theorized that perhaps he had an unusually stable sleep pattern that was resistant to change.

Finally, the eight subjects were monitored for any behavioral changes that they might experience due to the loss of REM sleep. All the subjects developed minor symptoms of anxiety, irritability, or difficulty concentrating during the REM interruption period. One subject (number 8) quit the study after only three deprivation nights "in a flurry of contrived excuses," obviously because he was feeling excessive anxiety. Two other subjects (6 and 7) insisted on stopping after four deprivation nights because of anxiety, but continued with the recovery phase of the experiment. Five of the subjects reported a clear increase in appetite during the deprivation, and three of these gained 3 to 5 pounds. None of these behavioral symptoms appeared during the period of control awakenings.

SIGNIFICANCE OF THE FINDINGS
AND SUBSEQUENT RESEARCH

Now, some 30 years after this preliminary research by Dement, we know a great deal about sleeping and dreaming. Some of this knowledge was discussed briefly earlier in this chapter. We know that most of what Dement reported in his 1960 article has stood the test of time. We all dream, and if we are somehow prevented from dreaming one night, we dream more the next night. There does indeed appear to be something basic in our need to dream. In fact, the REM-rebound effect can be seen in many animals.

One of Dement's accidental findings, one that he reported only as a minor anecdote, now has greater significance. One way that people may be deprived of REM sleep is through the use of alcohol or other drugs such as amphetamines and barbiturates. While these drugs increase your tendency to fall asleep, they suppress REM sleep and cause you to remain in the deeper stages of NREM for greater portions of the night. It is for this reason that many people are unable to break the habit of taking sleeping pills or alcohol in order to sleep. As soon as they stop, the REM-rebound effect is so strong and disturbing that they become afraid to sleep and return to the drug to avoid dreaming. An even more extreme example of this problem occurs with alcoholics who may have been depriving themselves of REM sleep for years. When they stop drinking, the onset of REM rebound may be so powerful that it can occur while they are awake. This may be an explanation for the phenomenon known as "delirium tremens," or the "D.T.s," which usually involve terrible and frightening hallucinations (Greenberg and Perlman, 1967).

Dement wanted to follow up on his preliminary findings regarding the behavioral effects of dream deprivation. In later work he deprived subjects of REM for much longer periods of time and found no evidence of harmful changes. He concluded that "A decade of research has failed to prove that substantial ill effects result even from prolonged selective REM deprivation" (Dement, 1974).

Finally, research with its origins in Dement's early work reported here suggests that there is a greater synthesis of proteins in the brain during REM sleep than during NREM sleep. Some believe that these chemical changes may represent the process of integrating new information into the memory structures of the brain and may even be the organic basis for new developments in personality (Rossi, 1973).

DEMENT, W.C. (1974) *Some must watch while some must sleep.* San Francisco: Freeman.
GREENBERG, R., and PERLMAN, C. (1967) Delirium tremens and dreaming. *American Journal of Psychiatry*, 124, 133–42.
ROSSI, E.I. (1973) The dream protein hypothesis. *American Journal of Psychiatry*, 130, 1094–7.

WHEN YOU WISH UPON A DREAM . . .
Cartwright, Rosalind D. (1974) The influence of a conscious wish
on dreams. *Journal of Abnormal Psychology*, 83, 387–93.

In the previous reading, which focused on the work of William Dement,
you learned that most of your dreaming occurs during REM sleep and
that dreaming seems to be an extremely important activity. Most people
enjoy dreaming, at least when the dreams are not nightmares, but
imagine how great it would be if you could choose the topics and
characters of your dreams before going to sleep. Is it possible? Well,
maybe. One of the leading researchers in the area of how and why you
dream is Rosalind Cartwright. The article that forms the basis of this
chapter has been quite influential in supporting the argument that you
may have the ability to control your dreams. Before discussing this
specific study, however, a brief discussion of some of the theories that
have attempted to explain dreaming seems appropriate here.

Sigmund Freud (1900) believed that dreams were windows to your
unconscious; that your greatest unfulfilled wishes and deepest fears
would be expressed in dreams. However, since these wishes and fears
were threatening to you in some way, they would be communicated
symbolically in your dreams. Freud contended that to understand the
meaning of a dream, the obvious or surface message of dreams (called
the "manifest content") had to be penetrated so that the underlying, true
message being expressed (the "latent content") could be examined and
interpreted. Freud's view of dreaming was highly influential throughout
most of this century. Many psychotherapists today, although they may
not necessarily take a strict Freudian approach, use dream interpretation
in their therapy sessions with clients. Various modern theories have
appeared recently that seek to explain dreaming in less mysterious ways.

One of these is the "mental housekeeping hypothesis" (Crick and
Mitchison, 1983). This theory says that you need to dream to clean your
cognitive structures (your mind) of information you collect over time
that is useless, overly bizarre, or redundant. To put this idea another
way, dreaming allows you to review your brain's data files and erase
what you don't need so that there is room for more input without the
files becoming too cluttered.

Another explanation of the function of dreams, and one that is
widely held, maintains that dreaming allows for a continuation or
extension of waking thought in order to resolve the problems and
difficulties you encounter in your life. According to this approach, you
are able in your dreams to experiment safely with various solutions to
personal problems and gain insight into potential solutions that might
not be available to you while awake. This theory was developed by

Rosalind Cartwright (1978), in part as a result of the experiment discussed in this chapter.

It is not easy to study dreams scientifically. Clinicians who use dreams in their psychotherapy with clients rely on a person's recollection of a dream. In research terms, this is called the "retrospective method." As you know from your own experiences with dreams, the process of trying to remember your dreams is subject to a great deal of error, and some dreams may be forgotten completely. Scientific researchers would like to be more *prospective* in their methods; that is, to be able to *predict in advance* what a dream might be about before it happens. To this end, behavioral scientists began to incorporate the research methods developed by Dement in 1957 that made it possible to retrieve the content of dreams more completely and in greater detail. This was done by awakening the sleeper while the dream was in process (as in Dement's 1960 study, discussed in the last reading). Over the years, several studies have been carried out to try to make the dreamer connect some external stimulus (such as sounds, flashing lights, or mists of water) with the dream content. However, these studies were only marginally successful, because of the difficulty of the research method and the small number of subjects used. Cartwright decided to carry out a more extensive study involving a very personally relevant suggestion *prior* to sleep to see if the topic of the suggestion would then appear in the person's dreams that night.

THEORETICAL PROPOSITIONS

Cartwright argued that if you were to make a pre-sleep wish about something that was personally relevant to you, it would be more likely to enter into your dreams in some way. She believed that the issues most relevant to people are aspects of their personality that they would like to change. Cartwright called this a "cognitive inconsistency" about the self. For example, if you see yourself as lazy, but would like to be more energetic, this would be a cognitive inconsistency. Cartwright wanted to test the idea that by bringing such a conflict to a person's attention and creating a need in the person to resolve it just prior to sleep, the probability would be increased that the inconsistency would appear in the person's dreams. She made two general predictions. The first was that dreams that follow an individual's focus on a personally relevant problem would be related to that topic. Second, she went one step further and predicted that the dream would approach the problem differently than the person would while awake. In other words, she suspected that dreams may open up a wider range of solutions than are available in normal waking thought.

METHOD

Subjects

The participants for this study were 17 paid volunteer college students, 10 males and seven females, who all claimed to be good sleepers. All the subjects slept for two nights in the sleep laboratory in order to become adapted to the new surroundings.

Selection of Target Dream-Words

Next, each subject was asked to sort a deck of 70 cards, each card containing one personal adjective (such as "shy," "selfish," "sensitive," "sarcastic," etc.). The subjects sorted the cards into seven categories ranging from 1 ("least like me") to 7 ("most like me"). After they had done this, they were given another identical deck and asked to sort them again as they would for the person they would most like to be; for their "ideal self." This allowed the researchers to find an adjective for each subject that was rated high on the "like-me" sort, but low on the "ideal-self" sort. In other words, a negative personal characteristic that the subject wanted to change was identified. This was called the "target adjective." Table 1 lists the adjectives chosen for each of the subjects. You should note that for three of the subjects (13, 16, 17), a negative characteristic with a large discrepancy on the "ideal-self" scale could not

TABLE 1   Subjects' Target Adjectives

SUBJECT	TARGET	SCORE ON "LIKE-ME" SCALE	SCORE ON "IDEAL-SELF" SCALE
1.	Defensive	7	3
2.	Lazy	7	2
3.	Sarcastic	7	4
4.	Unhappy	6	1
5.	Irritable	6	1
6.	Undecided	6	2
7.	Hostile	6	1
8.	Irritable	6	2
9.	Jealous	7	1
10.	Defensive	5	1
11.	Dependent	5	2
12.	Selfish	6	2
13.	Persevering	1	6
14.	Shy	7	1
15.	Jealous	5	1
16.	Reserved	2	6
17.	Poised	2	7

(summarized and adapted from p. 390)

be found, so a word was chosen that was rated very low on the "like-me" scale and very high on the "ideal-self" scale (just the reverse of the rest of the subjects).

A Conscious Wish

Upon arriving at the sleep lab, the subjects were wired to electrodes to monitor their sleep and so that periods of REM sleep could be observed by the experimenters. When they were in bed with the lights out, just prior to going to sleep, subjects were instructed over an intercom: "We are ready to say good night to you now. As you are falling asleep, please say over and over to yourself, 'I wish I were not so ——— (target adjective inserted here),' or in the case of subjects 13, 16, and 17, 'I wish I were more ———.' " As the subjects slept through the night, they cycled through NREM sleep and entered the usual four to six periods of REM, or dreaming, sleep. Each time they entered REM sleep, they were awakened and asked to report their dream, which they were usually able to do easily and in great detail. They were then allowed to go back to sleep and given the same instructions about focusing on the target word.

Control Words

Now, the next part of this got a little complicated. Cartwright wanted to be sure that if the target word (relating to the personal characteristic) entered the subjects' dreams, it did so because the subject *wished* for it and not simply due to chance. So, each subject's card sorts were used to select two additional words: One was chosen in the same way as the target word; that is, with a large difference between the self and the ideal. The other word, however, was selected because it was rated high on *both* the self and ideal and with no discrepancy between the two card sorts. These controls were very important methodologically for the following reasons. First, suppose subjects had dreams incorporating all three words. This would mean simply that people dream about their own personal characteristics: not a terribly interesting result. Second, what if the participants dreamed about the target word *and* the other chosen high-discrepancy word? This would indicate that when there is a large difference between who you are and who you would like to be on some trait, you dream about that more. Neither of these two control words, however, was brought to the subjects' attention prior to sleep as was the target adjective.

The reason for this was that Cartwright wanted to eliminate these other possible motivations for dreaming about a certain topic. "If only the target word is incorporated in a significant number of cases," she wrote, "it might be argued that this is one model of how dreams are formed: A tension area is brought to awareness prior to sleep" (p. 390). The only way she could attempt to prove this was to include these other two words, along with the target word, in the analysis of each subject's dreams.

Analyzing Dream Content

Two judges who were not aware of the purpose or design of the study, along with Cartwright herself, studied the transcripts of the subjects' dream reports. They looked for the presence of traits in the various characters in the dream that matched any of the three adjectives (target and two controls). Their interpretations of dream content agreed 85 percent of the time, which meant that they were quite reliable and accurate. Remember, the finding of most importance was the presence of the target word, and *not* the control words. Dreams were examined for the adjectives in the following categories:

1. The adjective describes the self in the dream.
2. The opposite of the adjective describes the self in the dream.
3. The adjective describes another character in the dream.
4. The opposite of the adjective describes another character in the dream.

One point to keep in mind before we discuss the result is that category 2 represents a direct relationship between dreaming and waking. In other words, since the subjects *wished* to be the opposite of the target adjective, dreams falling into category 2 would reflect this wish.

RESULTS AND DISCUSSION

Cartwright's results are summarized in Table 2. There are two figures in the table that represent a statistically significant proportion of the 17 subjects: the total number of subjects who dreamed about the target word, and the number who did *not* have dreams in which the opposite of the target adjective was describing the self (category 2). The first prediction made at the beginning of Cartwright's article—that dreams following a wish about a personally relevant topic would reflect that topic—was supported by the fact that 15 of the 17 subjects dreamed about the *target adjective* in some way. While some dreams relating to the *control* words were observed, the number of these was not statistically significant.

Of the 15 subjects who dreamed of the target word, only two had dreams in which the opposite of the target was describing the self. This, according to Cartwright, supported her second prediction: that the way

TABLE 2   Number of Subjects Having Dreams Incorporating the Studied Adjectives

ADJECTIVE	DESCRIBES SELF	OPPOSITE DESCRIBES SELF	DESCRIBES OTHER	OPPOSITE DESCRIBES OTHER	TOTAL*
Target	9	2**	7	5	15**
Control 1	4	4	5	3	9
Control 2	7	4	4	4	11

*This is not the total of the rows, because some subjects' dreams incorporated the adjectives in more than one way, but were only counted once.
**Statistically significant proportion of total.
(adapted from p. 391)

you explore a problem in your dreams is different from when you are awake and thinking about it. This was demonstrated even more strongly in some of the subjects' dream content. Often in the dream, not only would the undesirable target adjective be applied to the self, but the dreamer seemed to be enjoying it! For example, one subject's target word was "sarcastic." His instructions prior to going to sleep was to say over and over, "I wish I were not so sarcastic." Cartwright reported one of this person's dreams as follows.

> REM 2. I was walking through a big department store and I had just come back from lunch. I was talking to this cop who must have had $10 worth of food for lunch and he said, 'What does your mother think of all this food?,' and I said, 'I don't know, she's not with me.' The cop was . . . a real mean guy. I told him he ate like a pig. . . . I was kinda having a good time telling the cop what an animal he was. . . . (p. 392).

The conclusion drawn from this was that if you wanted to become less sarcastic, it is unlikely you would think about your sarcasm in these terms while awake.

There were also instances in category 4 (opposite describes other) when the *ideal* trait was seen in another character in the dream, but it was causing problems for that character. An example of this was a subject who wished to be less shy. When a character in one of the dreams behaved in an outgoing way, the result was embarrassment and ridicule. Again, this illustrated how, in a dream, you analyze the problem from perspectives you might not think of when you are awake.

In her discussion, Cartwright maintained that these findings demonstrated how dreaming occurs not so much to fulfill a wish in the Freudian sense, but rather to explore or review the emotional consequences of doing so. "One function of dreaming thought," she says, "appears to be to explore the emotional components of a tension area that may be different from those available to the waking self" (p. 392).

SUBSEQUENT RESEARCH

Behavioral scientists will probably never reach a consensus on the reasons for and functions of dreaming. That lack of consensus, however, serves as a positive force in the continuation of research in this area. Rosalind Cartwright was and is a powerful force in the "field of dreams" and a great deal of subsequent research owes its foundations to her work.

One recent and fascinating line of inquiry that builds on Cartwright's studies examines your ability to control your dreams, not before you go to sleep, but *while* you are dreaming! Dreams have long been considered completely unconscious and *involuntary*. However, in the early 1980s researchers demonstrated scientifically that it is possible to be fully conscious while in a state of REM. This is called "lucid dreaming" (see LaBerge, 1985, for a complete discussion). During lucid dreaming, the dreamer is often able to alter the events in the dream itself. Imagine learning to be a lucid dreamer. It could be used in psychotherapy as a way for you to experiment with possible changes in your personality or your life without risking failure, embarrassment, or pain. Also, people who have recurring nightmares could use lucid dreaming to change the outcome of the dream and perhaps eliminate their fears.

It is not difficult to see that research into dreaming, beginning with the influential work of Dement and Cartwright, may do more than explain an interesting phenomenon; it may offer ways of changing people's lives.

CARTWRIGHT, ROSALIND D. (1978) *A primer on sleep and dreaming*. Reading, Mass.: Addison-Wesley.
CRICK, F., and MITCHISON, G. (1983) The function of dream sleep. *Nature*, 304, 111–14.
FREUD, S. (1900) *The interpretation of dreams*. New York: Basic Books.
LABERGE, S. (1985) *Lucid dreaming*. New York: Ballantine.

UNROMANCING THE DREAM . . .
Hobson, J. Allan, and McCarley, Robert W. (1977) The brain as a dream-state generator: An activation-synthesis hypothesis of the dream process. *American Journal of Psychiatry*, 134, 1335–48.

The reading on the work of Aserinsky and Dement explored the apparent need for dreaming sleep in humans. Then in the previous reading, Cartwright's research led to an examination of the reasons why you dream and some of the functions dreaming might serve. The history of research on dreaming has been dominated by the belief that dreams reveal something about yourself; that they are products of your inner psychological experience of the world. This view can be traced back to Sigmund Freud's psychoanalytic theories of human nature.

As discussed briefly in the previous chapter, Freud believed that dreams are the expression of unconscious wishes for things we are unable to have while awake. Therefore, dreams offer insights into the unconscious that are unavailable in waking thought. However, the psychoanalytic approach also contends that many of these wishes are unacceptable to the conscious mind, and, if expressed openly in dreams, would disrupt sleep and create anxiety. Thus to protect the individual, the true desires contained in the dream are disguised in the dream's images by a hypothetical censor. Consequently, some assume that the true meaning of most dreams lies hidden beneath the dream's outward appearance. Freud called this surface meaning of a dream the "manifest content" and the deeper, "true" meaning the "latent content." In order to reveal the meaningful information of a dream, the manifest content must be interpreted, analyzed, and penetrated.

It is interesting to note that while the validity of a great portion of Freud's work has been drawn into serious question by behavioral scientists over the past 50 years, his conceptualization of dreams remains widely accepted by psychologists and Western culture in general (see the reading on Anna Freud for a discussion of other enduring aspects of Freud's theories). Almost everyone has had the experience of remembering an unusual dream and thinking, "I wonder what it really means!" We believe that our dreams have deep meaning.

In the late 1970s Allan Hobson and Robert McCarley, both psychiatrists and neurophysiologists at Harvard's medical school, published a new theory of dreaming that shook the scientific community so deeply that the tremors are still being felt today. What they said, in essence, was that dreams are nothing more than your attempt to interpret random electrical impulses produced automatically in your brain during REM sleep.

They proposed that while you are asleep there is a part of your brain, located in the brain stem, that is periodically *activated* and produces electrical impulses. This is a primitive, but very important, part of your brain that is related to physical movement and the processing of input from your senses while you are awake. When you are asleep, your sensory and motor abilities are shut down, but this part of your brain is not. It continues to generate what Hobson and McCarley regarded as meaningless bursts of neural static. Some of these impulses reach other parts of your brain, responsible for higher functions such as thinking and reasoning. When this happens your brain tries to *synthesize* and make some sort of sense out of the impulses. To do this, you sometimes create images, ideas, and even stories with plots. If we awaken and remember this cognitive activity, we call it a dream and invest it with all kinds of significance which, according to Hobson and McCarley, was never there to begin with.

Hobson and McCarley's original article, upon which this discussion is based, is a highly technical account of the neurophysiology of sleep and dreaming. While their work can be found in nearly all textbooks that include information about dreaming, very little of the detail is offered there, due to the complex nature of the researchers' reporting. In this chapter, their article will be explored in significantly greater detail, although for clarity and understanding, considerable distillation and simplification is unavoidable.

THEORETICAL PROPOSITIONS

Hobson and McCarley believed that modern neurophysiological evidence "permits and necessitates important revisions in psychoanalytic dream theory. The activation-synthesis hypothesis . . . asserts that many formal aspects of the dream experience may be the obligatory and relatively undistorted psychological concomitant of the regularly recurring and physiologically determined brain state called 'dreaming sleep.' " (p. 1335). What they meant by this was simply that dreams are triggered automatically by basic physiological processes, and there is no "censor" distorting the true meaning to protect you from your unconscious wishes. Moreover, they contend that the strangeness and distortions often associated with dreams are not seen as disguises, but as results of the physiology of how the brain and mind work during sleep.

The most important part of their theory was that the brain becomes activated during REM sleep and generates its own original information. This activation is then compared with stored memories in order to synthesize the activation into some form of dream content. In other words, Hobson and McCarley claim that what is referred to as REM sleep actually *causes* dreaming, instead of the opposing popular view that dreams produce REM sleep.

METHOD

In their article, Hobson and McCarley incorporated two methods of research. One method was to study and review previous studies by many researchers in the area of sleep and dreaming. In this single article, the authors cite 37 references that pertain to their hypothesis, including several earlier studies of their own. The second method they used was research on the sleep and dreaming patterns of animals. They did not try to claim that non-human animals dream, since this is something no one can know for sure (you may believe your pet dreams, but has your dog or cat ever told you what the dream was about?). However, all mammals experience stages of sleep similar to those in humans. Hobson and McCarley go one step further and claim that there is no significant difference between humans and other animals in the physiology of dreaming sleep. So they chose cats for their experimental subjects. Using various laboratory techniques, they were able to stimulate or inhibit certain parts of the animals' brains and record the effect on dreaming sleep.

RESULTS AND DISCUSSION

The various findings detailed by Hobson and McCarley were used to demonstrate different aspects of their theory. Therefore, their results will be combined with their discussion of the findings here. The evidence generated by the researchers in support of their theory can be summarized in several distinct points.

1. The part of the brain in the brain stem that controls physical movement and incoming information from the senses is at least as active during dreaming sleep (which they called the "D state") as it is when you are awake. However, while you are asleep, sensory input (information coming into your brain from the environment around you) and motor output (voluntary movement of your body) are blocked. Hobson and McCarley suggest that these physiological processes, rather than a psychological censor, may be responsible for protecting sleep.

You will remember from the last chapter that you are paralyzed during dreaming, presumably to protect you from the potential danger of acting out your dreams. Hobson and McCarley reported that this immobilization actually occurs at the spinal cord and not in the brain itself. Therefore, the brain is quite capable of sending motor signals, but the body is not able to express them. The authors suggested that this may account for the strange patterns of movement in dreams, such as your inability to run from danger or the perception that you are moving in slow motion.

2. The main exception to this blocking of motor responses is in the muscles and nerves controlling the eyes. In part, this explains why rapid eye movement occurs during D state, and may also explain how visual images are triggered during dreaming.

3. Hobson and McCarley pointed out another aspect of dreaming that emerged from a physiological analysis of the D state and that could not be explained by a psychoanalytic interpretation. This was that the brain enters REM sleep at regular and predictable intervals during each night's sleep and remains in that state for specific lengths of time. There is nothing random about this

sleep cycle. The authors interpreted this to mean that dreaming cannot be a response to waking events or unconscious wishes, because this would produce dreaming at any moment during sleep, according to the whims and needs of the person's psyche. Instead, the D state appeared to Hobson and McCarley to be a preprogrammed event in the brain that functions almost like a neurobiological clock.

4. The researchers pointed to findings by others that demonstrated that all mammals cycle through REM and NREM sleep. This sleep cycle varies according to the body size of the animal. A rat, for example, will shift between REM and NREM every six minutes, while for an elephant a single cycle takes two-and-a-half hours! One explanation for this difference may be that the more vulnerable an animal is to predators, the shorter are its periods of sound sleep during which it is less alert and thus in greater danger of attack. Whatever the reason, Hobson and McCarley took these findings as additional evidence that dreaming sleep is purely physiological.

5. Hobson and McCarley claimed to have found the trigger, the power supply, and the clock of the "dream state generator" in the brain. They reported this to be the pontine brain stem, located in the back and near the base of the brain. Measurements of neural activity (the frequency of firing of neurons) in this part of the brain in cats found significant peaks in activity corresponding to periods of REM sleep. When this part of the brain was artificially inhibited, the animals went for weeks without any REM sleep. Furthermore, reducing the activity of the pontine caused the length of time between periods of D state sleep to increase. Conversely, stimulation of the brain stem caused REM sleep to occur earlier and increased the length of REM periods. Such increases in REM have been attempted through conscious behavioral techniques, but these have been mostly unsuccessful. The authors' interpretation of these findings was that since a part of the brain completely separate from the pontine brain stem is involved in consciousness, dreaming *cannot* be driven by psychological forces.

6. The first five points summarized from Hobson and McCarley's research focused on the "activation" portion of their theory. They maintained that the "synthesis" of this activation is what produces your experience of dreaming. The psychological implications of their theory were detailed by the authors in four basic tenets:

(a) "The primary motivating force for dreaming is *not* psychological but physiological, since the time of occurrence and duration of dreaming sleep are quite constant, suggesting a preprogrammed, neurally determined genesis" (p. 1346). They did allow that dreams may have psychological meaning, but suggested that this meaning is much more basic than the psychoanalytic view imagines it to be. They further contended that dreaming should no longer be considered to have purely psychological significance.

(b) During dreaming, the brain stem is not responding to sensory input or producing motor output based on the world around you; instead it is activating itself internally. Since this activation originates in a relatively primitive part of the brain, it does not contain any ideas, emotions, stories, fears, or wishes. It is simple electrical energy. As the activation reaches the more advanced, cognitive structures of the brain, you try to make sense out of it. "In other words, the forebrain may be making the best of a bad job in producing even partially coherent dream imagery from the relatively noisy signals sent up to it from the brain stem" (p. 1347).

(c) Therefore, this elaboration of random signals into dreams is interpreted to be a *constructive* process, a synthesis, instead of a distortion process by which unacceptable wishes are hidden from your consciousness. Images are called up from your memory in an attempt to match the data generated by the brain stem's activation. It is precisely because of the randomness of the impulses, and the difficult task of the brain to try to inject them with some meaning, that dreams are often bizarre, disjointed, and seemingly mysterious.

(d) Freud's explanation for our forgetting dreams was repression. He believed, as many still do, that when the content of a dream is too disturbing for some reason, you are motivated to forget it. Hobson and McCarley, acknowledging that dream recall is poor (at least 95 percent of all dreams are not remembered), offered a pure physiological explanation that was concordant with the rest of their activation-synthesis hypothesis. They claimed that when we awaken, there is an immediate change in the chemistry of the brain. Certain brain chemicals necessary for converting short-term memories into long-term ones are suppressed during REM sleep. So unless a dream is particularly vivid (meaning that it is produced by a large amount of activation) and you awaken during or immediately after it, the content of the dream will not be remembered.

Figure 1 illustrates Hobson and McCarley's comparison between the psychoanalytic view of the dream process and their activation-synthesis model.

IMPLICATIONS AND SUBSEQUENT RESEARCH

Hobson and McCarley have continued to conduct research in support of their revolutionary hypothesis of dreaming. Clearly, their new conceptualization has not been universally accepted, but no psychological discussion of dreaming would be considered complete without its inclusion.

Twelve years after the appearance of Hobson and McCarley's original article on the activation-synthesis model, Allan Hobson published his most recent book called, simply, *Sleep*. In this work, he explains his theory of dreaming in expanded and greatly simplified terms. He also elaborates on his view about what impact the theory may have on the interpretation of dream content. And, he allows, dreams are not devoid of meaning, but should be interpreted in more straightforward ways. Hobson states quite eloquently his somewhat more compromising view as follows:

> For all their nonsense, dreams have a clear import and a deeply personal one. Their meaning would stem, I assert, from the necessity in REM sleep for the brain-mind to act upon its own information and according to its own lights. Thus, I would like to retain the emphasis of psychoanalysis upon the power of dreams to reveal deep aspects about ourselves, but without recourse to the concept of disguise and censorship or to the now

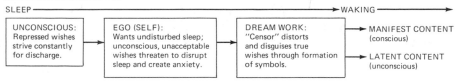

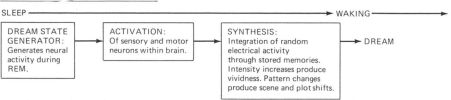

FIGURE 1 Psychoanalytic theory and activation-synthesis hypothesis compared. (adapted from p. 1346)

famous Freudian symbols. My tendency, then, is to ascribe the nonsense to brain-mind dysfunction and the sense to its compensatory effort to create order out of chaos. That order is a function of our own personal view of the world, our current preoccupations, our remote memories, our feelings, and our beliefs. That's all. (Hobson, 1979, p. 166)

Another dream researcher has taken Hobson's sentiments a step further. Foulkes (1985), a leading researcher on daydreaming, also subscribes to the notion that night dreams are generated by spontaneous brain activity during sleep. He has suggested that while dreams do not contain hidden unconscious messages, they may provide us with a great deal of psychological information. Foulkes maintains that the way your cognitive system places form and sense onto the random impulses in your brain reveals information about the importance of certain of your memories and provides insight into your thinking processes. He also believes that dreams serve several useful purposes. One of these arises from dreams you have about experiences that have not actually happened to you. These dreams may assist in preparing you to encounter new or unexpected events; something like a cognitive rehearsal, or "What would I do if . . . ?" Foulkes suggests that another possible function of dreams is that, since your dreams are usually about yourself, they may offer opportunities for you to increase your knowledge of who you are.

Whether or not you are willing to accept the rather less romantic view of dreaming developed by Hobson and McCarley's research, this is an excellent example of how psychologists or scientists in any field need to remain open to new possibilities even when the "established order" has existed for decades. There is no doubt that the activation-synthesis model of dreams has changed psychology. Of course, this does not mean that we have solved all the mysteries of sleep and dreaming, and perhaps we never will (perhaps we never should).

FOULKES, D. (1985) *Dreaming: A cognitive-psychological analysis*. Hillsdale, N.J.: Erlbaum.
HOBSON, J. ALLAN (1989) *Sleep*. New York: Scientific American Library.

ACTING AS IF YOU ARE HYPNOTIZED
Spanos, Nicholas P. (1982) Hypnotic behavior: A cognitive, social, psychological perspective. *Research Communications in Psychology, Psychiatry, and Behavior*, 7, 199–213.

The alterations in consciousness with which we are all most familiar are related to sleep and dreaming. The previous three chapters have focused on several highly influential studies relating to these topics. Another phenomenon relating to altered states of consciousness is hypnosis. Hypnosis is usually seen as a mysterious and powerful process of controlling a person's mind. The phrases and words that surround hypnosis, such as "going under" and "trance," indicate that it is commonly considered to be a separate and unique state of awareness, different from both waking and sleep. And many psychologists agree with this view. Nicholas Spanos, however, has led the opposing view that hypnosis is, in reality, nothing more than an increased state of motivation to perform certain behaviors and can be fully explained without resorting to trances or altered states.

The beginnings of hypnosis are usually traced back to the middle of the 18th century, a time when mental illness was first recognized as resulting from psychological rather than organic causes. One of the many fascinating characters who helped bring psychology out of the realm of witchcraft was Franz Anton Mesmer (1733–1815). He believed that "hysterical disorders" were a result of imbalances in a universal magnetic fluid present in the body. During strange gatherings in his laboratory, soft music would play, the lights would dim, and Mesmer, clothed like a sorcerer, would take iron rods from bottles of various chemicals and touch parts of the afflicted patients' bodies. He believed that this would transmit what he called the "animal magnetism" in the chemicals into the patients and provide relief from their symptoms. Interestingly, history has recorded that in many cases this treatment appeared to be successful. It is from Mesmer that we acquired the word "mesmerize," and many believe that his treatment included many of the techniques we now associate with hypnosis.

Throughout the history of psychology, hypnosis (named after Hypnos, the Greek god of sleep) has played a prominent role, especially in the treatment of psychological disorders, and it was a major component in Freud's psychoanalytic techniques. Ernest Hilgard has been at the forefront of recent researchers in supporting the position that hypnosis is an altered psychological state (see Hilgard, 1978). His and others' descriptions of hypnosis have included such characteristics as increased susceptibility to suggestion, involuntary performance of behaviors, improvements in recall, increased intensity of visual imagination, dissociation (the ability to be aware of some conscious events while being unaware of others), and analgesia (lowered sensitivity to pain). Until recently, the idea that hypnosis is capable of producing thoughts, ideas, and behaviors that would otherwise be impossible—that it is an altered state of consciousness—has been virtually undisputed.

However, it is often the job of scientists to look upon the status quo with a critical eye and, whenever they see fit, to debunk common beliefs. Just as Hobson and McCarley proposed a new view of dreaming that was radically different from the prevailing and popular one (see the previous chapter), social psychologist Nicholas Spanos has suggested that the major assumptions underlying hypnosis, as set forth by Hilgard and others, should be questioned. In the article that is the focus of this chapter, Spanos wrote, "The positing of special processes to account for hypnotic behavior is not only unnecessary, but also misleading. . . . Hypnotic behavior is basically similar to other social behavior and, like other social behavior, can be usefully described as strategic and goal-directed" (p. 200). In other words, Spanos contended that hypnotized subjects are actually engaging in voluntary behavior designed to produce a desired consequence. He further maintained that while such behavior may result from increased motivation, it does not involve an altered state of consciousness.

THEORETICAL PROPOSITIONS

Spanos theorized that all of the behaviors commonly attributed to a hypnotic trance state are within the normal, *voluntary* abilities of humans. He maintained that the only reason people define themselves as having been hypnotized is that they have *interpreted* their own behavior "under hypnosis" in ways that are consistent with their *expectations* about being hypnotized. Spanos views the process of hypnosis as a ritual that in Western culture carries a great deal of meaning. Subjects expect to relinquish control over their own behavior, and as the process of hypnotic induction develops, they begin to believe that their voluntary acts are becoming automatic, involuntary events. An example of this that Spanos offers is that early in the hypnotic procedure, voluntary instructions are given to the subject, such as, "relax the muscles in your legs," but later these become involuntary suggestions, such as, "your legs *feel* limp and heavy."

In collaboration with various colleagues and associates, Spanos devoted nearly a decade of research prior to this 1982 article demonstrating how many of the effects commonly attributed to hypnotic trances could be explained just as easily (or even more easily) in less mysterious ways.

METHOD

This article does not report on a specific experiment, but rather summarizes numerous studies made by Spanos and others prior to 1982, which were designed to support his position against Hilgard's contention (and the popular belief) that hypnosis is a unique state of consciousness. Most of the findings reported were taken from 16 studies in which Spanos was directly involved, and that offered alternate interpretations of hypnotically produced behavior. Therefore, as in the previous chapter on dream research, results and the discussion of them will be combined.

RESULTS AND DISCUSSION

Spanos claimed that there are two key aspects of hypnosis that lead people to believe it is an altered state of consciousness. One is that subjects interpret their behavior as being caused by something other than the self, thus making the action seem involuntary. The second aspect is the belief discussed previously that the hypnosis ritual creates expectations in the subject which in turn motivate the subject to behave in ways that are consistent with the expectations. The research Spanos reports in this article focuses on how these frequently cited claims about hypnosis have been drawn into question.

The Belief That Behavior Is Involuntary

As subjects are being hypnotized, they are usually asked to take various tests to determine if a hypnotic state has been induced. Spanos claimed that these tests are often carried out in such a way as to invite the subjects to convince themselves that something out of the ordinary is happening. These are suggestions such as, "your arm is heavy and you cannot hold it up"; "your hands are being drawn together by some force and you cannot keep them apart"; "your arm is as rigid as a steel bar and you cannot bend it"; "your body is so heavy that you cannot stand up." Spanos interpreted these test suggestions as containing two interrelated requests. One request asks subjects to do something, and the other asks them to interpret the action as having occurred involuntarily. Some subjects fail completely to respond to the suggestion. Spanos claimed that these subjects do not understand that they must *voluntarily* do something to initiate the suggested behavior and instead simply wait for their arms or body to begin to move. Other subjects respond to the suggestion, but are aware that they are behaving voluntarily. Finally there are those subjects who agree to both requests; they respond to the suggestion and interpret their response as beyond their control.

Spanos suggested that whether subjects interpret their behavior to be voluntary or involuntary depends on the way the suggestion is worded. In one of his studies, Spanos put two groups of subjects through a hypnosis induction procedure. Then to one group he made various behavior *suggestions*, such as, "your arm is very light and is rising." To the other group he gave direct *instructions* for the same behaviors, such as, "raise your arm." Afterward he asked the subjects if they thought their behaviors were voluntary or involuntary. The subjects in the suggestion group were more likely to interpret their behaviors as involuntary than were those in the direct instruction group.

Right now, while you are reading this page, hold your left arm straight out and keep it there for a couple of minutes. You will notice that it begins to feel heavy. This heaviness is not due to hypnosis; it's due to gravity! So if you are "hypnotized" and given the suggestion that your outstretched arm is becoming heavy, it would be very easy for you to attribute your action of lowering your arm to involuntary forces (you want to lower it anyway!). But what if you are given the suggestion that your arm is light and rising? If you raise your arm, it should be more difficult to interpret that action as involuntary, because you would have to ignore the contradictory feedback provided by gravity. Spanos tested this idea and found that such an interpretation was more difficult. Subjects who believed they were hypnotized were significantly more likely to define as involuntary their behavior of arm-lowering than that of arm raising. In the traditional view of hypnosis, the direction of the arm in the hypnotic suggestion should not make any difference; it should always be considered involuntary.

Suggestions made to hypnotic subjects often ask them to imagine certain situations in order to produce a desired behavior. If you were a subject, you might be given the suggestion that your arm is rigid and you cannot bend it. To reinforce this suggestion, it might be added that your arm is in a plaster cast. Spanos believed that some people may become absorbed in these "imaginal strategies" more than others, which could have the effect of leading them to believe that their response (the inability to move their arm) was involuntary. His reasoning was that if you are highly absorbed, you will not be able to focus on information that alerts you to the fact that the fantasy is not real. The more vividly you imagine the cast, its texture and hardness, how it got there, and so on, the less likely you are to remember that this is only your imagination at work. If this deep absorption happens, you might be more inclined to believe that your rigid-arm behavior was involuntary when actually it was not. In support of this, Spanos found that when subjects were asked to rate how absorbed they were in a suggested imagined scenario, the higher the absorption rating, the more likely they were to interpret their related behavior as occurring involuntarily. Spanos also noted that a person's susceptibility to hypnosis correlates with his or her general tendency to become absorbed in other activities such as books, music, or daydreaming. Consequently, these individuals are more likely to *willingly* cooperate with the kind of suggestions involved in hypnosis.

Creation of Expectations in "Hypnotic" Subjects

Spanos claims that the beliefs most people have about hypnosis are adequate in themselves to produce what is typically seen as hypnotic behavior. He further contends that these beliefs are strengthened by the methods used to induce and study hypnosis. He cites three examples of research that demonstrated how people might engage in certain behaviors under hypnosis because they think they should, rather than because of an altered state of awareness.

First, Spanos referred to a study in which a lecture about hypnosis was given to two groups of students. The lectures were identical except that one group was told that arm rigidity was a normal and spontaneous event during hypnosis. Later both groups were hypnotized. In the group that had heard the lecture including the information about arm rigidity, some of the subjects exhibited this behavior "spontaneously," without any instructions to do so. However, among the subjects in the other group, not one arm became rigid. According to Spanos, this demonstrated how people will enact their experience of hypnosis according to how they believe they are supposed to behave.

The second hypnotic event that Spanos used to illustrate his position involved research findings that hypnotized subjects claim the visual imagery they experienced under hypnosis was more intense, vivid, and real than similar imaginings when not hypnotized. Here, in essence, is how these studies typically have been done. Subjects are asked to imagine scenes or situations in which they are performing certain behaviors. Then, these *same* subjects are hypnotized and again asked to visualize the same or similar situations (the hypnotized and non-hypnotized trials can be in any order). These subjects generally report that the imagery in the hypnotized condition was significantly more intense. Spanos and his associates found, however, that when two *different* groups of subjects are used, one hypnotized and one not, their average intensity ratings of the visual imagery are approximately equal. Why the difference? The difference in the two methods is probably explained by the fact that when two different groups are tested, the subjects do not have anything to use for comparison. However, when the same subjects are used in both conditions, they can compare the two experiences and rate one against the other. So, since subjects nearly always rate the hypnotic imagery as more intense, this supports the idea that hypnosis is really an altered state, right? Well, if you ask Spanos, he would say, "Wrong!" In his view, the subjects who participate in both conditions *expect* the ritual of hypnosis to produce more intense imagery and, therefore, they rate it accordingly.

The third and perhaps most interesting demonstration of hypnosis addressed by Spanos was the claim that hypnosis can cause people to become insensitive to pain (the analgesia effect). One way that pain can be tested in the laboratory without causing damage to the subject is by using the "cold pressor test." If you are a subject in such a study, you would be asked to immerse your arm in ice water (zero degrees centigrade) and leave it there as long as you could. After the first 10 seconds or so this becomes increasingly painful, and most people will remove their arm within a minute or two. Hilgard (1978) reported that subjects who received both waking and hypnotic training in analgesia (pain reduction) reported significantly less cold-pressor pain during the hypnotized trials. His explanation for this was that during hypnosis, a person is able to dissociate the pain from awareness. In this way, Hilgard contended, a part of the person's consciousness experiences the pain, but this part is hidden from awareness by what he called an "amnesic barrier."

Again, Spanos rejected a hypnotic explanation for these analgesic findings and offered evidence from his own research to demonstrate that reduction in perceived pain during hypnosis is a result of the subjects' motivation and expectations. All of the research on hypnosis uses subjects who have scored high on measures of hypnotic susceptibility. According to Spanos, these individuals "have a strong investment in presenting themselves in the experimental setting as good hypnotic subjects" (p. 208). These subjects know that a waking state is being compared to a hypnotic state and want to demonstrate the effectiveness of hypnosis. Spanos performed a similar study involving cold-pressor pain, but with one major difference: Some subjects were told that they would first use waking analgesia techniques (such as self-distraction) and would then be tested using hypnotic pain-reduction methods, but other subjects were not told of the later hypnotic test.

Figure 1 summarizes what Spanos found. As you can see, when subjects expected the hypnosis condition to follow the waking trials, they rated the analgesic effect lower in order to, as Spanos states, "leave room" for improvement under hypnosis. Spanos claimed that this demonstrated how even the hypnotic behavior of pain insensitivity could be attributed to the subjects' need to respond to the demands of the situation rather than automatically assuming a dissociated state of consciousness.

The most important question concerning all these findings reported by Spanos is whether we should reevaluate the phenomenon called hypnosis. And what does it mean if we were to decide that hypnosis is not the powerful mind-altering force that popular culture, and many psychologists, have portrayed it to be?

FIGURE 1   Walking vs. hypnotic analgesia expectation vs. no expectation.

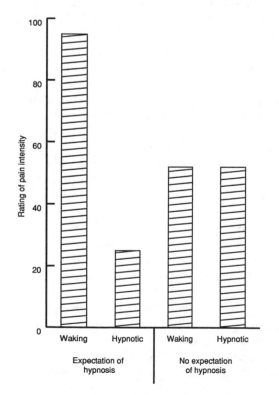

IMPLICATIONS OF THE FINDINGS

In evaluating Spanos' research, you should remember that his goal was not to prove that hypnosis does not exist, but rather to demonstrate that what we call "hypnotic behaviors" are the result of highly motivated, goal-directed social behavior, not an altered and unique state of consciousness. It is well accepted among most behavioral scientists that people cannot be hypnotized against their will. Furthermore, under hypnosis, subjects will not engage in acts they believe are antisocial, and they are not able to perform feats of superhuman strength or endurance. In this article, Spanos has demonstrated how many of the more subtle aspects of hypnosis may be explained in less mysterious and more straightforward ways than that of the "hypnotic trance."

What would be the implications of accepting Spanos' contention that hypnosis does not exist? The answer to this question is, "perhaps none." Whether the effects of hypnosis are produced by an altered state of awareness or by increased motivation does not change the fact that hypnosis is often a useful method of helping people improve something in their lives. One reason that there continues to be such widespread and unquestioning acceptance of the power of the hypnotic trance may be that humans need to feel that there is a way out, a last resort to solve their problems if all else fails—something so omnipotent that they can even change against their own resistance to such change.

Whether or not hypnosis is an altered state of consciousness remains a highly controversial issue. But whatever hypnosis is, it is not the panacea most people would like to find. Several studies have shown that hypnosis is no more effective than other methods of treatment to help people stop abusing alcohol and tobacco, improve their memory, or lose weight (see Lazar and Dempster, 1981, for a review of this research).

Spanos continues his research demonstrating his motivational theory of hypnotic behavior (see Spanos and Chaves, 1988, for a complete discussion). His work has changed psychology in that he has offered a recent, experimentally based alternative explanation for an aspect of human behavior that was virtually unchallenged for nearly 200 years.

HILGARD, E. (1978) Hypnosis and consciousness. *Human Nature*, 1, 42–51.
LAZAR, B., and DEMPSTER, C. (1981) Failures in hypnosis and hypnotherapy: A review. *The American Journal of Clinical Hypnosis*, 24, 48–54.
SPANOS, N., and CHAVES, J. (1988) *Hypnosis: The cognitive-behavioral perspective*. New York: Prometheus.

THREE

LEARNING
AND CONDITIONING

The area of psychology concerned with learning and conditioning has produced a rather well-defined body of literature explaining how animals and humans learn. Some of the most famous names in the history of psychology have devoted their entire careers to this research—names that are widely recognized even outside the behavioral sciences, such as Watson, Skinner, Pavlov, and Bandura. Picking a few of the most influential studies from this branch of psychology and from these researchers is no easy task, but the ones selected can be found in nearly every introductory psychology textbook and are representative of the mammoth contributions of these scientists.

For Pavlov, of course, we take a journey back nearly 100 years to review his work with dogs, metronomes, salivation, and the discovery of the conditioned reflex. Second, Watson, known for many contributions, is probably most famous (notorious?), for his torturous experiment with Little Albert, which demonstrated for the first time how emotions are a product of experience. For the third study in this section, we discuss Skinner's famous explanation and demonstration of superstitious behavior in a pigeon and how humans become superstitious in exactly the same way. Finally comes an examination of the well-known "Bobo Doll Study," in which Albert Bandura established that aggressive behaviors could be learned by children through their modeling of adult violence.

IT'S NOT JUST ABOUT SALIVATING DOGS!

Pavlov, Ivan P. (1927) *Conditioned reflexes*. London: Oxford
University Press.

Have you ever walked into a medical building where the odor of the
disinfectant made your teeth hurt? If you have, it was probably because
the odor triggered an association that had been conditioned in your
brain between that smell and your past experiences at the dentist. When
you hear "The Star Spangled Banner" played at the Olympic Games,
does your heart beat a little faster? This happens to most Americans.
Does the same thing happen when you hear the Italian national anthem?
Most likely it does not, because you have been conditioned to respond to
one song, but not to the other. And why do some people squint and
become nervous if you inflate a balloon near them? Well, obviously it is
because they have been conditioned to associate the expanding balloon
with something fearful (such as a loud pop). These are just a few of
countless human behaviors that exist because of a process known as
"classical conditioning."

The classical conditioning theory of learning was developed and
articulated nearly 100 years ago in Russia by one of the most familiar
names in the history of psychology, Ivan Petrovich Pavlov. Unlike most
of the research presented in this book, Pavlov's name and his basic ideas
of learning by association are widely recognized in popular culture
(there is even a Rolling Stones song that refers to "salivating like Pavlov's
dogs"). However, how he came to make his landmark discoveries and
the true significance of his work are not so widely understood.

Interestingly, while Pavlov's contribution to psychology was one of
the most important ever made, he was not a psychologist at all, but
rather a prominent Russian *physiologist* studying digestive processes. For
his research on digestion he was awarded the Nobel Prize for science.
But the discoveries that dramatically changed his career and the history
of psychology began virtually by accident. It is important to note that in
the late 1800s, psychology was a very young science and considered by
many to be less than a true science. Therefore, for Pavlov to make such
a radical turn from the more solid and respected science of physiology
to psychology was a risky career move. He wrote about the dilemma
facing a physiologist whose work might involve studying the brain:

> It is logical that in its analysis of the various activities of living matter,
> physiology should base itself on the more advanced and more exact
> sciences—physics and chemistry. But if we attempt an approach from this
> science of psychology . . . we shall be building our superstructure on a
> science that has no claim to exactness. . . . In fact, it is still open to
> discussion whether psychology is a natural science, or whether it can be
> regarded as a science at all (p. 3).

Looking back on Pavlov's discoveries, it was fortunate for the advancement of psychological science and for our understanding of human behavior that he took the risk and made the career change.

Pavlov's physiological research involved the use of dogs as subjects for studying the role of salivation on digestion. He or his assistants would introduce various food or non-food substances into a dog's mouth and observe the rate and amount of salivation. In order to measure salivation scientifically, minor surgery was performed on the dogs so that a salivary duct was redirected through an incision in the dog's cheek and connected to a tube that would collect the saliva. Throughout this research, Pavlov made many new and interesting discoveries. For example, he found that when a dog received moist food, only a small amount of saliva would be produced, compared with a heavy flow when dry food was presented. When inedible substances were placed in the dog's mouth (a marble, some sand), saliva was produced (in varying amounts depending on the substance) to assist the dog in rejecting the substance. The production of saliva under these conditions was regarded by Pavlov as a *reflex*; that is, a response that occurs automatically to a specific stimulus without conscious control or learning. If you think about it, salivation is purely reflexive for humans, too. Suppose I ask you, as you read this sentence, to salivate as fast as you can. You cannot do it. But if you are hungry and find yourself sitting in front of your favorite food, you will salivate whether you want to or not!

So, Pavlov experimented with various stimuli to determine just how "intelligent" these salivary glands were. As the research continued, he began to notice certain events that were totally unexpected. The dogs began to salivate *before* any food reached their mouths and even before the odor of food was present. After a while the dogs were salivating at times when no digestive stimulus was present at all. Somehow, the reflexive action of the salivary glands had been altered through the animals' experience in the lab: "Even the vessel from which the food has been given is sufficient to evoke an alimentary reflex [salivation] complete in all its details; and, further, the secretion may be provoked even by the sight of the person who has brought the vessel, or by the sound of his footsteps" (p. 13).

This was the crossroads for Pavlov. He had observed digestive responses occurring to stimuli seemingly unrelated to digestion, and pure physiology could not provide an explanation for this. The answer had to be found in psychology.

THEORETICAL PROPOSITIONS

Pavlov theorized that the dogs had learned from experience in the lab to expect food following the appearance of certain signals. While these "signal stimuli" do not naturally produce salivation, the dogs came to associate them with food, and thus responded to them with salivation. Consequently, Pavlov determined that there must be two kinds of reflexes.

Unconditioned reflexes are inborn and automatic, require no learning, and are generally the same for all members of a species. Salivating when food enters the mouth, jumping at the sound of a loud noise, and the dilation of your pupils when the lights are turned off are examples of unconditioned reflexes. *Conditioned reflexes*, on the other hand, are acquired through experience or learning and may vary a great deal among individual members of a species. A dog salivating at the sound of footsteps, or you feeling pain in your teeth when you smell medical disinfectant, are conditioned reflexes.

Unconditioned reflexes are formed by an unconditioned stimulus (UCS) producing an unconditioned response (UCR). In Pavlov's studies, the UCS was food and the UCR was salivation. Conditioned reflexes consist of a conditioned stimulus (CS), such as the footsteps, producing a conditioned response (CR), salivation. You will notice that the response in both of these examples is salivation, but when the salivation results from hearing footsteps, it is conditioning that prompts it.

The question Pavlov wanted to answer was this: Since conditioned reflexes are not inborn, exactly how are they acquired? He proposed that if a particular stimulus in the dog's environment was often present when the dog was fed, this stimulus would become associated in the dog's brain with food; it would *signal* the approaching food. Prior to being paired with the food, the environmental stimulus did not produce any important response. In other words, to the dogs, it was a neutral stimulus (NS). When the dogs first arrived at the lab, the assistant's footsteps might have produced a response of curiosity (Pavlov called it the "what is it?" response), but hearing the footsteps certainly would not have caused the dogs to salivate. The footsteps, then, were a neutral stimulus. However, over time, as the dogs heard the same footsteps just prior to being fed every day, they would begin to associate the sound with food. Eventually, according to the theory, the footsteps alone would cause the dogs to salivate. So, according to Pavlov, the process by which a neutral stimulus becomes a conditioned stimulus could be diagrammed as follows:

Step 1.		UCS ------------------------> UCR
		(food) (salivation)
Step 2.	NS +	UCS ------------------------> UCR
	(footsteps)	(food) (salivation)
Step 3.	(Repeat step 2 several times)	
Step 4.		CS ------------------------> CR
		(footsteps) (salivation)

Now that he had a theory to explain his observations, Pavlov began a series of experiments to prove that it was correct. For some reason, it is commonly believed that Pavlov conditioned dogs to salivate at the sound of a bell. But as you will see, his early experiments involved a metronome.

METHOD AND RESULTS

Pavlov's first problem was that there were too many sources of stimulation in his laboratory. It was extremely important that he be able to isolate one single stimulus to determine if the dogs could be conditioned to respond to it. He tried to limit these influences by allowing only one experimenter to come in contact with a particular dog. However, this was inadequate because that one person would unintentionally provide numerous subtle stimuli, such as blinking of the eyes or standing a certain way, that made an exact interpretation of the dog's behavior very difficult.

Fortunately, Pavlov was able to build a special laboratory at the Institute of Experimental Medicine in Petrograd (which became Leningrad and has now returned to its original name of St. Petersburg) with funds donated by "a keen and public-spirited Moscow businessman." This soundproof lab allowed for complete isolation of the subjects from the experimenters and from all extraneous stimuli during the experimental procedures. Therefore, a specific stimulus could be administered and responses could be recorded without any direct contact between the experimenters and the animals.

After the necessary research environment had been established, the procedure was quite simple. Pavlov chose food as the unconditioned stimulus. As explained previously, food will elicit the unconditioned response of salivation. Then Pavlov needed to find a neutral stimulus that was, for the dogs, completely unrelated to food. For this he used the sound of the metronome. Over several conditioning trials, the dog was exposed to the ticking of the metronome and then was immediately presented with food. "A stimulus which was neutral of itself had been superimposed upon the action of the inborn alimentary reflex. We observed that, after several repetitions of the combined stimulation, the sounds of the metronome had acquired the property of stimulating salivary secretion." (p. 26). In other words, the metronome had become a conditioned stimulus for the conditioned response of salivation.

Pavlov and his associates elaborated on this preliminary finding by using different unconditioned and neutral stimuli. For example, the odor of vanilla (NS) was presented to the subjects prior to a mild acid solution (similar to lemon juice) being placed in the dog's mouth (the

UCS). The acid, of course, caused heavy salivation (UCR). After 20 repetitions of the combination, the vanilla alone produced salivation. For a visual test, an object would begin to rotate just prior to the presentation of food. After only five pairings, the rotating object by itself (CS) caused the dogs to salivate (CR).

One additional important finding was that if the neutral stimulus (the vanilla or the rotating object) was presented to the subject *after* the unconditioned stimulus, no conditioning takes place. A demonstration of this was made in Pavlov's lab when the acid solution was placed in the dog's mouth and then, five seconds later, the odor of vanilla presented. After 427 of these pairings the vanilla did not become a conditioned stimulus.

Of course, the importance and application of Pavlov's work extends far beyond salivating dogs. His theories of classical conditioning explained a major portion of human behavior and helped to launch psychology as a true science.

SIGNIFICANCE OF THE FINDINGS

The theory of classical conditioning (also called Pavlovian conditioning) is universally accepted and has remained virtually unchanged since its conception through Pavlov's work. It is used to explain and interpret a wide range of human behavior, including where phobias come from, why you dislike certain foods, the source of your emotions, how advertising works, why you feel anxiety before a job interview or an exam, and what arouses you sexually. Several later studies dealing with some of these applications will be discussed here.

Classical conditioning focuses on reflexive behavior: those behaviors that are not under your voluntary control. Any reflex can be conditioned to occur to a previously neutral stimulus. You can be classically conditioned so that your left eye blinks when you hear a doorbell, your heart rate increases at the sight of a flashing blue light, or you experience sexual arousal when you eat strawberries. The doorbell, blue light, and strawberries were all neutral in relation to the conditioned responses until they somehow were paired with and became associated with unconditioned stimuli for eye blinking (a puff of air into the eye), heart rate increase (a sudden loud noise), and sexual arousal (romantic caresses).

To experience firsthand the process of classical conditioning, here is an experiment you can perform on yourself. All you will need is a bell, a mirror, and a room that becomes completely dark when the light is switched off to serve as your temporary laboratory. The pupils of your eyes dilate and constrict reflexively according to changes in light intensity. You have no voluntary control over this, and you did not have to learn how to do it. If I say to you, "please dilate your pupils now," you would be unable to do so. However, when you walk into a dark theater, they dilate immediately. Therefore, a decrease in light would be considered an unconditioned stimulus for pupil dilation, the unconditioned response. In your "lab," ring the bell and immediately after, turn off the light. Wait in the total darkness about 15 seconds and turn the light back on. Wait another 15 seconds and repeat the procedure: bell . . . light off . . . wait 15 seconds . . . light on. . . . Repeat this pairing of the neutral stimulus (the bell) with the unconditioned stimulus (the darkness) 20 to 30 times, making sure that the bell only rings just prior to the sudden darkness. Now, with the lights on, watch your eyes closely in the mirror and ring the bell. You will see your pupils dilate slightly even though there is no change in light! The bell has become the conditioned stimulus and pupil dilation the conditioned response.

RELATED RESEARCH

There are two other studies presented in this book that rest directly on Pavlov's theory of classical conditioning. In the next chapter, Watson conditioned little Albert to fear a white rat (and other furry things) by employing the same principles Pavlov used to condition salivation in dogs. By doing so, Watson demonstrated how emotions, such as fear, are formed. Later, Joseph Wolpe (see the reading on Wolpe in the chapter on psychotherapy) developed a therapeutic technique for treating intense fears (phobias) by applying the concepts of classical conditioning. His work was based on the idea that the association between the conditioned stimulus and the unconditioned stimulus must be broken in order to reduce the fearful response.

The examples and uses for Pavlov's theory in the literature on learning and conditioning are far too numerous to summarize here. Instead, a few of the more notable findings will be discussed.

A common problem that plagues ranchers around the world is that of predator animals, usually wolves and coyotes, killing and eating their livestock. In the early 1970s, studies were conducted that attempted to apply Pavlovian conditioning techniques to solve the problem of the killing of sheep by coyotes and wolves without the need for killing the predators (see Gustafson, Garcia, Hawkins, and Rusiniak, 1974). Wolves and coyotes were given pieces of mutton containing small amounts of lithium chloride (UCS), a chemical that if ingested makes an animal sick. When the animals ate the meat, they became dizzy with severe nausea and vomiting (UCR). After recovering, these same hungry predators were placed in a pen with live sheep. The wolves and coyotes began to attack the sheep (CS), but as soon as they smelled their prey, they stopped and stayed as far away from the sheep as possible. When the gate to the pen was opened, the wolves and coyotes actually ran (CR) from the sheep! Based on this and other related research, it is now common practice for ranchers to use this method of classical conditioning to keep wolves and coyotes away from their herds.

Another application of Pavlov's discoveries is in advertising. In fact, the entire advertising industry has at its foundation the principles of classical conditioning. Most television commercials and magazine advertisements are trying to pair a product with something that produces a positive response. Each advertiser's hope is that when you are trying to choose among, say, 30 brands of beer at the market, you will see their brand, experience a pleasant emotion based on your association between their beer and "Here's to good friends," or "It doesn't get any better than this," or "For all you do," and, therefore, be more likely to buy it. There has been research to support the effectiveness of this marketing strategy. One study exposed subjects to either pleasant or unpleasant music while they were looking at advertisements for competing products. Results indicated that the products paired with the pleasant music were preferred over those paired with the unpleasant music, even though all the products were essentially the same (Gorn, 1982).

Finally, a relatively new and potentially vital line of research involving classical conditioning is in the field of behavioral medicine. Recent research has found that the activity of the immune system can be altered by using Pavlovian principles. Ader and Cohen (1985) gave mice water flavored with saccharine (mice love this water). They then paired the saccharine water with an injection of a drug that weakened the immune system of the mice. Later, when these conditioned mice drank the saccharine water, they showed signs of *immunosuppression*, a weakening of the immune response. Currently research is underway to discover if the reverse is also possible. Laboratory rats have been exposed to the strong odor of camphor and then injected with a drug that enhances the immune response. Early results have shown that the camphor odor alone becomes a conditioned stimulus for increased immune functioning.

If the same strategy is effective for humans, and there is reason to believe it would be, it may be possible one day soon to strengthen your resistance to illness (a conditioned response) by exposing yourself to a non-medical conditioned stimulus. For example, imagine you feel the beginnings of a cold or the flu, so you slide your special classically conditioned "immune response enhancement music disk" into your CD player. As the music fills the room, your resistance rises as a conditioned response to this stimulus and stops the disease in its tracks.

CONCLUSION

It is clear from these few examples how extensive Pavlov's influence has been on the field of psychology. There are few scientists who have had as much impact in any single discipline. Classical conditioning is one of the fundamental theories on which modern psychology rests. Without Pavlov's contributions, behavioral scientists still may have uncovered most of these principles over the decades. It is unlikely, however, that such a cohesive, elegant, and well-articulated theory of the conditioned reflex would ever have existed if Pavlov had not made the decision to risk his career and venture into the untested, uncharted, and highly questionable science of 19th-century psychology.

ADER, R., and COHEN, N. (1985) CNS-immune system interactions: Conditioning phenomena. *Behavioral and Brain Sciences*, 8, 379–94.
GORN, G. (1982) The effect of music in advertising on choice behavior: A classical conditioning approach. *Journal of Marketing*, 46, 94–101.
GUSTAFSON, C.R., GARCIA, J., HAWKINS, W., and RUSINIAK, K. (1974) Coyote predation control by aversive conditioning. *Science*, 184, 581–83.

LITTLE EMOTIONAL ALBERT
Watson, J.B., and Raynor, R. (1920) Conditioned emotional responses. *Journal of Experimental Psychology*, 3, 1–14.

Have you ever wondered where your emotional reactions come from? If you have, you're not alone. The source of emotions has fascinated behavioral scientists throughout psychology's history. Part of the evidence for this fascination can be found here in this book; there are five studies included that relate directly to emotional responses (see also Schachter and Singer, 1962; Ekman and Oster, 1979; Harlow, 1958; Seligman and Meier, 1967). This study by Watson and Raynor on conditioned emotional responses was a strikingly powerful piece of research when it was published over 70 years ago, and it continues to exert influence today. You would be hard-pressed to pick up a textbook on general psychology or on learning and behavior without finding a summary of their findings.

The historical importance of this study is not solely due to the research findings, but also to the new psychological territory it pioneered. If we could be transported back to the turn of the century and get a feel for the state of psychology at the time, we would find it nearly completely dominated by the work of Sigmund Freud (see the reading on A. Freud). Freud's *psychoanalytic* view of human behavior was based on the idea that we are motivated by unconscious instincts and repressed conflicts from early childhood. In simplified Freudian terms, behavior, and specifically emotion, is generated *internally* through biological and instinctual processes.

In the 1920s a new movement in psychology known as behaviorism, spearheaded by Pavlov and Watson, began to take hold. The behaviorist viewpoint was radically opposed to the psychoanalytic school and proposed that behavior is generated *outside* the person through various environmental or situational stimuli. Therefore, Watson theorized, emotional responses exist in us because we have been *conditioned* to respond emotionally to certain stimuli in the environment. In other words, we *learn* our emotional reactions. In fact Watson believed that all human behavior was a product of learning and conditioning, as he proclaimed in his famous statement of 1913:

> Give me a dozen healthy infants, well-formed, and my own special world to bring them up in, and I'll guarantee to take any one at random and train him to become any type of specialist I might select—doctor, lawyer, artist, merchant-chief, and, yes, beggarman and thief (Watson, 1913).

This was, for its time, an extremely revolutionary view. Most psychologists, as well as public opinion in general, were not ready to accept these new ideas. This was especially true for emotional reactions, which seemed to be somehow generated from within. So Watson set out to demonstrate that emotions could be experimentally conditioned.

THEORETICAL PROPOSITIONS

Watson theorized that if a stimulus that automatically produces a certain emotion in you (such as fear) is repeatedly experienced at the same moment as something else, such as a rat, the rat will become associated in your brain with the fear. In other words, you will eventually become conditioned to be afraid of the rat. He maintained that we are not *born* to fear rats, but that such fears are learned through conditioning. This formed the theoretical basis for his most famous experiment, involving a subject named "little Albert B."

METHOD AND RESULTS

The subject, Albert B., was recruited for this study at the age of 9 months from a hospital where he had been raised, as an orphan, from birth. He was judged by the researchers and the hospital staff to be very healthy, both emotionally and physically. In order to see if Albert was afraid of certain stimuli, he was presented with a white rat, a rabbit, a monkey, a dog, masks with and without hair, and white cotton wool. Albert's reactions to these stimuli were closely observed. Albert was interested in the various animals and objects and would reach for them and sometimes touch them, but he never showed the slightest fear of any of them. Since they produced no fear, these are referred to as "neutral stimuli."

The next phase of the experiment involved determining if a fear reaction could be produced in Albert by exposing him to a loud noise. All humans, and especially all infants, will exhibit fear reactions to loud, sudden noises. Since no learning is necessary for this response to occur, the loud noise is called an "unconditioned stimulus." In this study, a steel bar 4 feet in length was struck with a hammer behind Albert. This noise startled and frightened him and made him cry.

Now the stage was set for testing the idea that the emotion of fear could be conditioned in Albert. The actual conditioning test was not done until the child was 11 months old. There was hesitation on the part of the researchers to create fear reactions in a child experimentally, but the decision was made to proceed (based on reasoning to be discussed in conjunction with the overall questionable ethics of this study, found later in this chapter).

As the experiment began, the researchers presented Albert with the white rat and the frightening noise at the same time. At first, Albert was interested in the rat and reached out to touch it. As he did this, the metal bar was struck, which startled and frightened Albert. This process was repeated three times. One week later the same procedure was followed. After a total of seven pairings of the noise and the rat, the rat was presented to Albert alone, without the noise. Well, as you've probably guessed by now, Albert reacted with extreme fear to the rat. He began to cry, turned away, rolled over on one side away from the rat, and began to crawl away so fast that the researchers had to rush to catch him before he crawled off the edge of the table! A fear response had been conditioned to an object that had not been feared only one week earlier.

The researchers then wanted to determine if this learned fear would transfer to other objects. In psychological terms, this transfer is referred to as "generalization." If Albert showed fear to other similar objects, then the learned behavior is said to have generalized. The next week, Albert was tested again and was still found to be afraid of the rat. Then to test for generalization, an object similar to the rat (a white rabbit) was presented to Albert. In the author's words: "Negative responses began at once. He leaned as far away from the animal as possible, whimpered, then burst into tears. When the rabbit was placed in contact with him, he buried his face in the mattress, then got up on all fours and crawled away, crying as he went" (p. 6). Remember, Albert was not afraid of the rabbit prior to conditioning, and had not even been conditioned to fear the rabbit specifically.

Little Albert was presented over the course of this day of testing with a dog, a white fur coat, a package of cotton, and Watson's own head of gray hair. He reacted to all of these items with fear. One of the most well-known tests of generalization that made this research as infamous as it is famous occurred when Watson presented Albert with a Santa Claus mask. The reaction? Yes . . . fear!

After another five days Albert was tested again. The sequence of presentations on this day are summarized in Table 1.

Another aspect of conditioned emotional responses Watson wanted to explore was whether the learned emotion would transfer from one situation to another. If Albert's fear responses to these various animals and objects occurred only in the experimental setting and nowhere else, the significance of the findings would be greatly reduced. To test this, later on the day outlined in Table 1, Albert was taken to an entirely different room with brighter lighting and more people present. In this new setting, Albert's reactions to the rat and rabbit were still clearly fearful, although somewhat less intense.

The final test that Watson and Raynor wanted to make was to see if Albert's newly learned emotional responses would persist over time. Well, Albert had been adopted and was scheduled to leave the hospital in the near future. Therefore, all testing was discontinued for a period of 31 days At the end of this time he was once again presented with the Santa Claus mask, the white fur coat, the rat, the rabbit, and the dog. After a month, Albert was still very afraid of all these objects.

TABLE 1   Sequence of Stimulus Presentations To Albert On Fourth Day of Testing

STIMULUS PRESENTED	REACTION OBSERVED
1. Blocks	Played with blocks as usual
2. Rat	Fearful withdrawal (no crying)
3. Rat + Noise	Fear and crying
4. Rat	Fear and crying
5. Rat	Fear, crying, and crawling away
6. Rabbit	Fear, but less strong reaction than on former presentations
7. Blocks	Played as usual
8. Rabbit	Same as 6
9. Rabbit	Same as 6
10. Rabbit	Some fear, but also wanted to touch rabbit
11. Dog	Fearful avoidance
12. Dog + Noise	Fear and crawling away
13. Blocks	Normal play

Watson and his colleagues had planned to attempt to "recondition" little Albert and eliminate these fearful reactions. However, Albert left the hospital on the day these last tests were made and, as far as anyone knows, no reconditioning ever took place.

DISCUSSION AND SIGNIFICANCE OF FINDINGS

Watson had two fundamental goals in this study and in all his work: (a) to demonstrate that all human behavior stems from learning and conditioning; and (b) to demonstrate that the Freudian conception of psychology, that our behavior stems from unconscious processes, was wrong. This study, with all its methodological flaws and serious breaches of ethical conduct (to be discussed on the next page) succeeded to a large extent in convincing a great portion of the psychological community that emotional behavior could be conditioned through simple stimulus-response techniques. This finding helped, in turn, to launch one of the major schools of thought in psychology: behaviorism. Here, something as complex, personal, and human as an emotion was shown to be subject to conditioning, just as a rat in a maze learns to find the food faster and faster on each successive try.

A logical extension of this is that other emotions, such as anger, joy, sadness, surprise, or disgust, may be learned in the same manner. In other words, the reason you are sad when you hear that old song, nervous when you have a job interview or a public speaking engagement, happy when spring arrives, or afraid when you hear a dental drill is that you have developed an association in your brain between these stimuli and specific emotions through conditioning. Other more extreme emotional responses, such as phobias and sexual fetishes, may also develop through similar sequences of conditioning. These processes are the same as what Watson found with little Albert, although usually more complex.

Watson was quick to point out that his findings could explain human behavior in rather straightforward and simple terms, compared with the psychoanalytic notions of Freud and his followers. As Watson and Raynor explained in their article, a Freudian would explain thumb-sucking as an expression of the original pleasure-seeking instinct. Albert, however, would suck his thumb whenever he felt afraid. As soon as his thumb entered his mouth, he ceased being afraid. Therefore, Watson interpreted thumb-sucking as a conditioned device for blocking fear-producing stimuli.

An additional attack on Freudian thinking made in this article concerned how Freudians in the future, given the opportunity, might analyze Albert's fear of a white fur coat. Watson and Raynor claimed that Freudian analysts "will probably tease from him the recital of a dream which, upon their analysis, will show that Albert at 3 years of age attempted to play with the pubic hair of the mother and was scolded violently for it." Their main point was that they had demonstrated with little Albert that emotional disturbances in adults cannot always be attributed to sexual traumas in childhood, as the Freudian view was commonly interpreted.

QUESTIONS AND CRITICISMS

As you have been reading this, you have probably been concerned or even angered over the treatment by the experimenters of this innocent child. This study clearly violates current standards of ethical conduct in research involving humans. It would be highly unlikely that any *human-subjects committee* at any research institution would approve this study today. Seventy years ago, however, such ethical standards did not formally exist and it is not unusual to find reports in the early psychological literature of what now appear to be questionable research methods. It must be pointed out that Watson and his colleagues were not sadistic or cruel people and that they were engaged in a new, unexplored area of research. They acknowledged considerable hesitation in proceeding with the conditioning process, but decided that it was justifiable since, in their opinion, some such fears would arise anyway when Albert left the sheltered hospital environment. Even so, is it ever appropriate to frighten a child to this extent, regardless of the importance of the potential discovery? Today nearly all behavioral scientists would agree that it is not.

Another important point regarding the ethics of this study was the fact that Albert was allowed to leave the research setting and was never "reconditioned" to remove his fears. Watson and Raynor contend in their article that such emotional conditioning may persist over a person's lifetime. If they were correct on this point, it is extremely difficult, from an ethical perspective, to justify allowing someone to grow into adulthood fearful of all these objects (and who knows how many others!).

On a related point, several researchers have criticized Watson's assumption that these conditioned fears would persist indefinitely (Harris, 1979). Others claim that Albert was not conditioned as effectively as the authors maintained (Samelson, 1980). It has frequently been demonstrated that behaviors acquired through conditioning can be lost because of other experiences or simply because of the passage of time. Imagine, for example, that when Albert turned 5, he was given a pet white rabbit for a birthday present. At first, he might have been afraid of it (no doubt baffling his adoptive parents). But as he continued to be exposed to the rabbit without anything frightening occurring (such as that loud noise), very likely he slowly became less and less afraid until the rabbit no longer caused a fear response. This is a well-established process in learning psychology called "extinction," and it happens routinely as part of the constant learning and unlearning, conditioning and unconditioning processes we experience throughout our lives.

HARRIS, B. (1979) What ever happened to little Albert? *American Psychologist*, 34, 151–60.
SAMELSON, F. (1980) Watson's Little Albert, Cyril Burt's twins, and the need for a critical science. *American Psychologist*, 35, 619–25.
WATSON, J.B. (1913) Psychology as the behaviorist views it. *Psychological Review*, 20, 158–77.

KNOCK WOOD!
Skinner, Burrus Frederick (1948) Superstition in the pigeon. *Journal of Experimental Psychology*, 38, 168–72.

In this chapter we examine one study from a huge body of research carried out by one of the most influential and most widely known psychologists ever, B.F. Skinner. Deciding how to present Skinner and which of his studies to explore was a difficult task. It is clearly impossible to represent adequately in one short chapter his contributions to the history of psychological research. After all, Skinner is considered by most to be the father of radical behaviorism, is the inventor of the famous (or infamous) "Skinner Box," and is the author of over a dozen books and over 70 scientific articles. This article, with the somewhat humorous-sounding title "Superstition in the pigeon," has been selected from all of his work because it allows for a clear discussion of Skinner's basic theories, provides an interesting example of his approach to studying behavior, and offers a "Skinnerian" explanation of a behavior with which we are all familiar: superstition.

Skinner was called a *radical* behaviorist because he believed that all behavior in either human or non-human animals is caused, shaped, and maintained by its consequences. To put it in basic terms: If, in a given situation, you behave in some way and your behavior is followed by a rewarding event (such as food, praise, or money), you will tend to behave that way again. On the other hand, if you do something that produces an unpleasant event (such as pain or embarrassment), you will be less likely to do that again in identical or similar situations. Rewarding events are called "reinforcement" and unpleasant events are called "punishment." Skinner called this learning process *operant conditioning*. It may be diagrammed as follows:

```
                                 | -------->Reinforcement = Learning
Situation --- > Behavior ----> Consequence --- > |
                                 | -------->Punishment = No learning
```

Within this conceptualization, Skinner also was able to explain how behaviors are lost or unlearned. Once a behavior has been reinforced and the reinforcement is then discontinued, the behavior will slowly decrease until it disappears completely. This unlearning process is called "extinction."

If you think about it, these ideas are not new to you. The process we all use to train our pets follows these same rules. You tell a dog to sit, it sits, and you reward it with a "dog yummy." After a while the dog will sit when told to, even without the immediate reward of a dog yummy. You have applied the principles of operant conditioning. This is a very powerful form of learning and is effective with all animals, even old dogs learning new tricks and, yes, even cats! Also, if you want a pet to stop doing something, all you have to do is remove the reinforcement, and the behavior will stop. For example, if your dog is begging at the dinner table, there is a reason for that (regardless of what you may think, dogs are not born to beg at the table!). You have conditioned this behavior in your dog through reinforcement. If you want to "put that behavior on extinction," the reinforcement must be totally discontinued. Eventually, the dog will stop begging. By the way, if one member of the family "cheats" during extinction and secretly gives the "beggar" some food once in a while, extinction will never happen.

Beyond these fundamentals of learning, Skinner maintained that *all* human behavior is created and maintained in precisely the same way. It's just that with humans, the exact behaviors and consequences are not always so easy to identify. Skinner was well-known for arguing that if a human behavior was interpreted by others (such as cognitive or humanistic psychologists) to be due to our highly evolved consciousness or intellectual capabilities, it was only because psychologists had been unable to pinpoint the reinforcers that had created and were maintaining the behavior. If this feels like a rather extreme position to you, remember that Skinner's position was called *radical* behaviorism and was always surrounded by controversy.

Skinner often met skepticism and defended his views by demonstrating experimentally that behaviors considered to be the sole property of humans could be learned by lowly creatures such as pigeons or rats. One of these demonstrations involved the seemingly human activity of "insight," or working on a problem until a solution presented itself in a flash of finger-snapping illumination. Skinner set up an experiment in which a pigeon solved a problem of the food dish being too high to reach in a way that appeared to be the same as human insight. Of course it was really operant conditioning—as it is, Skinner argued, for humans as well.

Another challenge accepted by Skinner was the contention by others that superstitious behavior is uniquely human. The argument was that superstition requires human cognitive activity (thinking, knowing, reasoning). A superstition is a *belief* in something, and we do not usually attribute such "beliefs" to animals. Well, Skinner said in essence that superstitious behavior could be explained as easily as any other action by using the principles of operant conditioning. He performed an experiment to prove it.

THEORETICAL PROPOSITIONS

Think back to a time when you have behaved superstitiously. Did you knock on wood, avoid walking under a ladder, avoid stepping on cracks, carry a lucky coin or other charm, shake the dice a certain way in a board game, change your behavior because of your horoscope? It is probably safe to say that everyone has done something out of superstition at some time, even if some of them might not want to admit it. Skinner said that the reason people do this is that they believe or presume that there is a connection between the superstitious behavior and some reinforcing consequence, even though, in reality, there is not. This connection exists because the behavior (such as shaking the dice that certain way) was *accidentally* reinforced (such as a good roll) once, twice, or several times. Skinner called this "non-contingent" reinforcement, a reward that is not contingent on any particular behavior. You *believe* that there is a causal relationship between the behavior and the reward, when no such relationship exists.

"And if you think this is some exclusive human activity," Skinner might have said, "I'll make a superstitious pigeon!"

METHOD

In order to understand the method used in this experiment, a brief description of what has become known as the "Skinner Box" is necessary. The principle behind the Skinner Box (or *conditioning chamber*, as Skinner called it) is really quite simple. It consists of a cage or box that is empty except for a dish or tray into which food may be dispensed. This allows a researcher to have control over when the animal receives reinforcement, such as pellets of food. The early conditioning boxes also contained a lever which, if pressed, would cause some food to be dispensed. If a rat (rats were used in Skinner's earliest work) was placed in one of these boxes, it would eventually, through trial and error, learn to press the lever for food. Alternately, the experimenter could, if desired, control the food dispenser and reinforce a specific behavior. Later it was found that pigeons also made ideal subjects in conditioning experiments, and conditioning chambers were designed with disks to be pecked instead of bars to be pressed.

One of these conditioning cages was used in the study discussed here, but with one important change. In order to study superstitious behavior, the food dispenser was rigged to drop food pellets into the tray at intervals of 15 seconds, *regardless of what the animal was doing at the time.* You can see that this produced non-contingent reinforcement. In other words, the animal received a reward every 15 seconds, no matter what it did.

Subjects in this study were eight pigeons. These birds were fed less than their normal daily amount for several days, so that when tested they would be hungry and therefore highly motivated to perform behaviors for food (this increased the power of the reinforcement). Each pigeon was placed into the experimental cage for a few minutes each day and just left to do whatever a pigeon does. During this time, reinforcement was being delivered automatically every 15 seconds. After several days of conditioning in this way, two independent observers recorded the birds' behavior in the cage.

RESULTS

As Skinner reports:

> In six out of eight cases the resulting responses were so clearly defined that two observers could agree perfectly in counting instances. One bird was conditioned to turn counter-clockwise about the cage, making two or three turns between reinforcements. Another repeatedly thrust its head into one of the upper corners of the cage. A third developed a tossing response as if placing its head beneath an invisible bar and lifting it repeatedly. Two birds developed a pendulum motion of the head and body in which the head was extended forward and swung from right to left with a sharp movement followed by a somewhat slower return. The body generally followed the movement and a few steps might be taken when it was extensive. Another bird was conditioned to make incomplete pecking or brushing movements directed toward but not touching the floor (p. 168).

None of these behaviors had been observed in the birds prior to the conditioning procedure. As you can see, the new behavior had nothing to do with the pigeon receiving food. Nevertheless, they behaved *as if* a certain action would produce the food: they became superstitious.

Skinner next wanted to see what would happen if the time interval between reinforcements was extended. With one of the head-bobbing birds, the interval between the delivery of food pellets was slowly increased to one minute. When this occurred the pigeon's movements became more energetic until finally the stepping became so pronounced that it appeared the bird was performing a kind of dance during the minute between reinforcement (such as a "pigeon food dance").

Finally, the new behavior of the birds was put on extinction. This meant that the reinforcement in the test cage was discontinued. When this happened the superstitious behaviors gradually decreased until they disappeared altogether. However, it was noted that in the case of the "hopping" pigeon with a reinforcement interval that had been increased to a minute, over 10,000 responses were recorded before extinction occurred!

DISCUSSSION

Clearly, what Skinner ended up with here was six superstitious pigeons. However, he explains his findings more carefully and modestly: "The experiment might be said to demonstrate a sort of superstition. The bird behaves as if there were a causal relation between its behavior and the presentation of food, although such a relation is lacking" (p. 171).

Of course, the next step would be to apply these findings to humans. I am sure it is not difficult for you to think of analogies in human behavior, nor was it for Skinner. He described "the bowler who has released a ball down the alley but continues to behave as if he were controlling it by twisting and turning his arm and shoulder as another case in point" (p. 171). You know, rationally, that behaviors such as these don't really have any effect on a bowling ball that is already halfway down the alley. As Skinner points out in the case of the pigeons in this study, the food was going to appear no matter what the bird did.

An additional and interesting point made by Skinner in this article was that it is not completely correct to conclude that there is no relationship between the twisting and turning of the bowler and the direction of the ball. What is true is that after the ball has left the bowler's hand, the "bowler's behavior has no effect on the ball, but the behavior of the ball has an effect on the bowler" (p. 171). In other words, it is a fact that on some occasions, the ball might happen to move in the direction of the bowler's body movements. That movement of the ball, coupled with the consequence of a strike or a spare, is enough to *accidentally* reinforce the twisting behavior and maintain the superstition.

Finally, the reason that superstitions are so resistant to extinction was demonstrated by the pigeon that hopped 10,000 times before giving up the behavior. When any behavior is only reinforced once in a while, it becomes very difficult to extinguish. This is because the expectation stays high that the superstitious behavior might work to produce the reinforcing consequences. You can imagine that if the connection was present every time and then disappeared, the behavior would stop quickly. However, for humans, the instances of that accidental reinforcement usually occur at large time intervals, so the superstitious behavior often may persist for a lifetime.

CRITICISMS AND SUBSEQUENT RESEARCH

As mentioned before, Skinner's behaviorist theories and research were always the subject of great and sometimes heated controversy. Other prominent theoretical approaches to human behavior argued that the strict behavioral view was unable to account for many of the psychological processes that are fundamental to humans. Carl Rogers, the founder of the "humanistic" school of psychology, and well-known for his debates with Skinner, summed up this criticism:

> In this world of inner meanings, humanistic psychology can investigate issues which are meaningless for the behaviorist: purposes, goals, values, choice, perceptions of self, perceptions of others, the personal constructs with which we build our world . . . the whole phenomenal world of the individual with its connective tissue of meaning. Not one aspect of this world is open to the strict behaviorist. Yet that these elements have significance for man's behavior seems certainly true (Rogers, 1964, p. 119).

Behaviorists would argue in turn that all of these human characteristics are open to behavioral analysis. The key to this is a proper interpretation of the behaviors and consequences that constitute them (see Skinner, 1974, for a complete discussion of these issues).

On the specific issue of superstitions, however, there appears to be less controversy and a rather wide acceptance of the learning processes involved in their formation. An experiment performed by Bruner and Revuski (1961) demonstrated how easily superstitious behavior develops in humans. Four high school students each sat in front of four telegraph keys. They were told that each time they pressed the correct key, a bell would sound, a red light would flash, and they would earn a nickel. The correct response was key number three. However, as in Skinner's study, key number 3 would produce the desired reinforcement only after a delay interval of 10 seconds. During this interval the students would try other keys in various combinations. Then, at some point following the delay, they would hit the third key again and receive the reinforcement. The results were the same for all the students. After a while they had each developed a pattern of key responses (such as 1, 2, 3, 4, 1, 2, 3) that they repeated over and over between each reinforcement. Pressing the 3-key was the only reinforced behavior; the other presses in the sequence were completely superstitious. Not only did they behave superstitiously, but all the students believed that the other key presses were necessary to "set up" the reinforced key. They were not aware of their superstitious behavior.

CONCLUSION

Superstitions are everywhere. You probably have some, and you surely know others who have them. One study of high school and college athletes found that 40 percent of them engaged in superstitious behavior before or during games (Buhrmann and Zaugg, 1981). A famous story of superstitious behavior was told by hockey player Phil Esposito (of the Boston Bruins and the New York Rangers). Prior to each game he would wear the same black turtleneck, drive through the same tollbooth on the way to the stadium, and get dressed in his uniform in exactly the same sequence. Years earlier, when he had first done all these things, he had been the team's high scorer. He behaved as if there were a causal connection between these behaviors and his performance on the ice, when no such connection actually existed. That's exactly how Skinner defined superstition.

Some superstitions are such a part of a culture that they produce societywide effects. You may be aware that most high-rise buildings do not have a 13th floor. Well, that's not exactly true. Obviously there is a 13th floor, but there is no floor that is *called* "13." This is probably not because architects and builders are an overly superstitious bunch, but it is rather due to the difficulty of renting or selling space on the 13th floor. Another recent example is that Americans are so superstitious about $2 bills that the U.S. Treasury has a pile of 4 million of these bills that people refuse to use!

Are superstitions psychologically unhealthy? Most psychologists believe that even though superstitious behaviors, by definition, do not produce the consequences that you think they do, they can serve useful functions. Often such behaviors can produce a feeling of strength and control when a person is facing a difficult situation. It is interesting to note that people who are employed in dangerous occupations tend to have more superstitions than others do. This feeling of increased power and control that is sometimes created by superstitious behavior can often lead to reduced anxiety, greater confidence and assurance, and improved performance.

BRUNER, A., and REVUSKI, S. (1961) Collateral behavior in humans. *Journal of the Experimental Analysis of Behavior*, 4, 349–50.

BUHRMANN, H., and ZAUGG, M. (1981) Superstitions among basketball players: An investigation of various forms of superstitious beliefs and behavior among competitive basketball players at the junior high school to university level. *Journal of Sport Behavior*, 4, 163–74.

ROGERS, C.R. (1964) Toward a science of the person. In F.W. WANN (ed.), *Behaviorism and phenomenology: Contrasting bases for modern psychology*. Chicago: Phoenix Books.

SKINNER, B.F. (1974) *About behaviorism*. New York: Knopf.

SEE AGGRESSION . . . DO AGGRESSION!

Bandura, Albert, Ross, Dorothea, and Ross, Sheila A. (1961) Transmission of aggression through imitation of aggressive models. *Journal of Abnormal and Social Psychology*, 63, 575–82.

Aggression, in its overabundance of forms, is arguably the greatest social problem facing this country and the world today. Consequently, it is also one of the most heavily researched topics in the history of psychology. Over the years, the behavioral scientists who have been in the forefront of this research have been the social psychologists, whose focus is on human interaction. One goal of social psychologists has been to define aggression. This may, at first glance, seem like a relatively easy goal, but such a definition turns out to be rather elusive. For example, which of the following behaviors would you define as aggression: A boxing match? A cat killing a mouse? A soldier shooting an enemy? Setting rat traps in your basement? A bullfight? The list of behaviors that may or may not be included in a definition of aggression goes on. As a result, if you were to consult 10 different social psychologists, you would probably get 10 different definitions of aggression.

Many researchers have gone beyond trying to agree on a definition to the more important process of examining the *sources* of human aggression. The question they pose is this: Why do people engage in acts of aggression? Throughout the history of psychology, many theoretical approaches have been proposed to explain the causes of aggression. Some of these contend that you are biologically preprogrammed for aggression, such that violent urges build up in you over time until they demand to be released. Other theories look to situational factors, such as repeated frustration, as the main determinants of aggressive responses. A third view, and one that may be the most widely accepted, is that aggression is *learned*.

One of the most famous and influential experiments ever conducted in the history of psychology demonstrated how children learn to be aggressive. This study, by Albert Bandura and his associates Dorothea Ross and Sheila Ross, was carried out in 1961 at Stanford University. Bandura is considered to be one of the founders of a school of psychological thought called "social learning theory." Social learning theorists believe that learning is the primary factor in the development of personality, and that this learning occurs through interactions with other people. For example, as you are growing up, important people such as your parents and teachers reinforce certain behaviors and ignore or punish others. Even beyond direct rewards and punishments, however, Bandura believed that behavior can be shaped in important ways through simply observing and imitating (or modeling) the behavior of others.

As you can see from the title of this chapter's study, Bandura, Ross, and Ross were able to demonstrate this modeling effect for acts of aggression. This research has come to be known throughout the field of psychology as "the Bobo doll study," for reasons that will become clear shortly. The article began with a reference to earlier research findings which demonstrated that children readily imitated the behavior of adult models while they were in the presence of the model. One of the things Bandura wanted to address in the new study was whether such imitative learning would generalize to settings in which the model was not with the child.

THEORETICAL PROPOSITIONS

The researchers proposed to expose children to adult models who behaved in either aggressive or non-aggressive ways. The children would then be tested in a new situation without the model present to determine to what extent they would imitate the acts of aggression they had observed in the adult. Based on this experimental manipulation, Bandura and his associates made four predictions.

1. Subjects who observed adult models performing acts of aggression would imitate the adult and engage in similar aggressive behaviors, even if the model was no longer present. Furthermore, this behavior would differ significantly from subjects who observed non-aggressive models or no models at all.

2. Children who were exposed to the non-aggressive models would not only be less aggressive than those who observed the aggression, but also significantly less aggressive than a control group of children who were exposed to

no model at all. In other words, the non-aggressive models would have an aggression-inhibiting effect.

3. Because children tend to identify with parents and other adults of their same sex, subjects would "imitate the behavior of the same-sex model to a greater degree than a model of the opposite sex" (p. 575).

4. "Since aggression is a highly masculine-typed behavior in society, boys should be more predisposed than girls toward imitating aggression, the difference being most marked for subjects exposed to the male model" (p. 575).

METHOD

This article by Bandura, Ross, and Ross outlined the methods used in the experiment with great organization and clarity. Although somewhat summarized and simplified, these methodological steps are presented here.

Subjects

The researchers enlisted the help of the director and head teacher of the Stanford University Nursery School in order to obtain subjects for their study. Thirty-six boys and 36 girls, ranging in age from 3 years to almost 6 years, participated in the study as subjects. The average age of the children was 4 years and 4 months.

Experimental Conditions

Twenty-four children were assigned to the control group, which meant that they would not be exposed to any model. The remaining 48 subjects were first divided into two groups: one exposed to aggressive models and the other exposed to non-aggressive models. These groups were divided again into male and female subjects. Finally, each of these groups were divided so that half of the subjects were exposed to same-sex models and half to opposite-sex models. This created a total of eight experimental groups and one control group. A question you might be asking yourself is this: What if the children in some of the groups are already more aggressive than others? Bandura guarded against this potential problem by obtaining ratings of each subject's level of aggressiveness. The children were rated by an experimenter and a teacher (both of whom knew the children well) on their levels of physical aggression, verbal aggression, and aggression toward objects. These ratings allowed the researchers to match all the groups in terms of average aggression level.

The Experimental Procedure

Each child was exposed individually to the various experimental procedures. First, the experimenter brought the child to the playroom. On the way, they encountered the adult model who was invited by the experimenter to come and "join in the game." The child was seated in one corner of the playroom at a table containing highly interesting activities. There were potato prints (this was 1961, so for those of you who have grown up in the high-tech age, a potato print is a potato cut in half and carved so that, like a rubber stamp, it will reproduce geometric shapes when inked on a stamp pad), and stickers of brightly colored animals and flowers that could be pasted onto a poster. Next, the adult model was taken to a table in a different corner containing a tinker toy set, a mallet, and an inflated Bobo doll 5 feet tall. The experimenter explained that these toys were for the model to play with and then left the room.

For both the aggressive and non-aggressive conditions, the model began assembling the tinker toys. However, in the aggressive condition, after a minute, the model attacked the Bobo doll with violence. For all the subjects in the aggressive condition, the sequence of aggressive acts performed by the model was identical.

> The model laid Bobo on its side, sat on it, and punched it repeatedly in the nose. The model then raised the Bobo doll, picked up the mallet, and struck the doll on the head. Following the mallet aggression, the model tossed the doll up in the air aggressively, and kicked it about the room. This sequence of physically aggressive acts was repeated three times, interspersed with verbally aggressive responses such as, 'Sock him in the nose . . . ,' 'Hit him down . . . ,' 'Throw him in the air . . . ,' 'Kick him . . . ,' 'Pow . . . ,' and two non-aggressive comments, 'He keeps coming back for more' and 'He sure is a tough fella' (p. 576).

All this took about 10 minutes, after which the experimenter came back into the room, said goodbye to the model, and took the child to another game room.

In the non-aggressive condition, the model simply played quietly with the tinker toys for the 10-minute period and completely ignored the Bobo doll. Bandura and his collaborators were careful to ensure that all experimental factors were identical for all the subjects except for the factors being studied: the aggressive vs. non-aggressive model, and the sex of the model.

Arousal of Anger or Frustration

Following the 10-minute play period, all subjects from the various conditions were taken to another room that contained very attractive toys, such as a fire engine, a jet fighter, a complete doll set including wardrobe, a doll carriage, and so on. The researchers believed that in order to test the subjects for aggressive responses, the children should be somewhat angered or frustrated, which would make such behaviors more likely to occur. To accomplish this, they allowed the subjects to begin playing with the attractive toys, but after a short time told them that the toys in this room were reserved for the other children. The subjects were also told, however, that they could play with some other toys in the next room.

Test For Imitation of Aggression

The final experimental room was filled with both aggressive and non-aggressive toys. Aggressive toys included a Bobo doll (of course!), a mallet, two dart guns, and a tether ball with a face painted on it. The non-aggressive toys included a tea set, crayons and paper, a ball, two dolls, cars and trucks, and plastic farm animals. Each subject was allowed to play in this room for 20 minutes. During this period judges behind a one-way mirror rated each child's behavior on several measures of aggression.

Measures of Aggression

A total of eight different responses were measured in the subjects' behavior. In the interest of clarity, only the four most revealing measures will be summarized here. First, all acts that imitated the physical aggression of the model were recorded. These included sitting on Bobo, punching it in the nose, hitting it with the mallet, kicking it, and throwing it into the air. Second, imitation of the models' verbal aggression was measured by counting the subjects' repetition of the phrases, "Sock him," "Hit him down," "Pow," etc. Third, other mallet aggression (that is, hitting objects other than the doll with the mallet) were recorded. Fourth, non-imitative aggression was documented by tabulating all subjects' acts of physical and verbal aggression that had *not* been performed by the adult model.

RESULTS

The findings from these observations are summarized in Table 1. If you examine the results carefully, you will discover that three of the four hypotheses presented by Bandura, Ross, and Ross in the introduction were supported.

The children who were exposed to the violent models tended to imitate the exact violent behaviors they observed. There were an average of 38.2 instances of imitative physical aggression for each of the male

TABLE 1 Average Number of Aggressive Responses From Children in Various Treatment Conditions

| TYPE OF AGGRESSION | TYPE OF MODEL | | | | |
	AGGRESSIVE MALE	NON-AGGRESSIVE MALE	AGGRESSIVE FEMALE	NON-AGGRESSIVE FEMALE	CONTROL GROUP
Imitative Physical Aggression					
Boys	25.8	1.5	12.4	0.2	1.2
Girls	7.2	0.0	5.5	2.5	2.0
Imitative Verbal Aggression					
Boys	12.7	0.0	4.3	1.1	1.7
Girls	2.0	0.0	13.7	0.3	0.7
Mallet Aggression					
Boys	28.8	6.7	15.5	18.7	13.5
Girls	18.7	0.5	17.2	0.5	13.1
Non-imitative Aggression					
Boys	36.7	22.3	16.2	26.1	24.6
Girls	8.4	1.4	21.3	7.2	6.1

(adapted from p. 579)

subjects, and 12.7 for the female subjects who had been exposed to the aggressive models. Additionally, the models' verbally aggressive behaviors were imitated an average of 17 times by the boys and 15.7 times by the girls. These specific acts of physical and verbal aggression were virtually never observed in the subjects exposed to the non-aggressive models or in the control subjects who were not exposed to any model.

As you will recall, Bandura and his associates predicted that non-aggressive models would have a violence-inhibiting effect on the children. In order for this hypothesis to be supported, the results should show that the subjects in the non-aggressive conditions averaged significantly fewer instances of violence than those in the no-model control group. In Table 1, if you compare the non-aggressive model columns with the control group averages, you'll see that the findings were mixed. For example, boys and girls who observed the non-aggressive male exhibited far less non-imitative mallet aggression than controls, but boys who observed the non-aggressive female aggressed more with the mallet than did the boys in the control group. As the authors readily admit, these results were so inconsistent in relation to the aggression-inhibiting effect of non-aggressive models that they were inconclusive.

The predicted gender differences, however, were strongly supported by the data in Table 1. Clearly, boys' violent behavior was influenced more by the aggressive male model than by the aggressive female model. The average total number of aggressive behaviors by boys was 104 when they had observed a male aggressive model, compared with 48.4 when a female model had been observed. Girls, on the other hand, while their scores were less consistent, averaged 57.7 violent behaviors in the aggressive female model condition, compared with 36.3 when they observed the male model. The authors point out that in same-sex aggressive conditions, girls were more likely to imitate verbal aggression while boys were more inclined to imitate physical violence.

Finally, boys were significantly more physically aggressive than girls in nearly all the conditions. If all the instances of aggression in Table 1 are tallied, there were 270 violent acts by the boys, compared with 128.3 by the girls.

DISCUSSION

Bandura, Ross, and Ross claimed that they had demonstrated how specific behaviors, in this case violent ones, could be learned through the process of observation and imitation without any reinforcement provided to either the models or the observers. They concluded that children's observation of adults engaging in these behaviors sends a message to the child that this form of violence is permissible, thus weakening the child's inhibitions against aggression. The consequence of this observed violence, they contended, is an increased probability that a child will respond to future frustrations with aggressive behavior.

The researchers also addressed the issue of why the influence of the male aggressive model on the boys was so much stronger than the female aggressive model was on the girls. They explained that in our culture, as in most, aggression is seen as more typical of males than females. In other words, it is a masculine-typed behavior. So, a man's modeling of aggression carried with it the weight of social acceptability and was, therefore, more powerful in its ability to influence the observer.

SUBSEQUENT RESEARCH

At the time this experiment was conducted, the researchers probably had no idea how influential it would become. By the early 1960s, television had grown into a powerful force in American culture and consumers were becoming concerned about the effect of televised violence on children. This has been and continues to be hotly debated. In the past 30 years there have been no less than three congressional hearings on the subject of television violence, and the work of Bandura and other psychologists has been included in these investigations.

These same three researchers conducted a follow-up study two years later that was intended to examine the power of aggressive models who are on film, or who are not even real people. Using a similar experimental method involving aggression toward a Bobo doll, Bandura, Ross, and Ross designed an experiment to compare the influence of a live adult model with the same model on film and to a cartoon version of the same aggressive modeling. The results demonstrated that the live adult model had a stronger influence than the filmed adult, who, in turn, was more influential than the cartoon. However, all three forms of aggressive models produced significantly more violent behaviors in the children than was observed in children exposed to non-aggressive models or control subjects (Bandura, Ross, and Ross, 1963).

On an optimistic note, Bandura found in a later study that the effect of modeled violence could be altered under certain conditions. You will recall that in his original study, no rewards were given for aggression to either the models or the subjects. But what do you suppose would happen if the model behaved violently and was then either reinforced or punished for the behavior while the child was observing? Bandura (1965) tested this idea and found that children imitated the violence more when they saw it rewarded, but significantly less when the model was punished for aggressive behavior.

Critics of Bandura's research on aggression have pointed out that aggressing toward an inflated doll is not the same as attacking another person, and that children know the difference. Building on the foundation laid by Bandura and his colleagues, other researchers have examined the effect of modeled violence on real aggression. In a study using Bandura's Bobo doll method (Hanratty, O'Neil, and Sulzer, 1972), children observed a violent adult model and were then exposed to high levels of frustration. When this occurred, they often aggressed against a live person (dressed like a clown), whether that person was the source of the frustration or not.

Another study randomly assigned children to two groups. One group watched a portion of a television show ("The Untouchables") that contained violence such as shootings, knifings, and fights, while the other group saw an exciting sports show. Besides the difference in program viewing content, the two groups were treated exactly the same. Later, the children from both groups were given the opportunity to aggress toward another child by pressing a button marked "hurt" (the button wasn't really connected to anything, of course). Those who had been exposed to the violent program were more likely to press the button and hold it down longer than those who viewed the sports (Liebert and Baron, 1972).

CONCLUSION

The research by Bandura, Ross, and Ross discussed in this chapter made two crucial contributions to psychological thought. First, it demonstrated quite dramatically how children can acquire new behaviors simply by observing adults. Social learning theorists believe that much if not most of human personality is formed through this modeling process. Second, this research laid the groundwork for decades of research and dozens of studies on the effects on children of viewing violence in person or in the media. While the controversy and debate continue, the body of literature that has grown out of Bandura's work, taken together, supports the view that there is a link between violence in the media and violent behavior among children.

BANDURA, A. (1965) Influence of models' reinforcement contingencies on the acquisition of imitative responses. *Journal of Personality and Social Psychology*, 1, 589–95.
BANDURA, A., ROSS, D., and ROSS, S. (1963) Imitation of film mediated aggressive models. *Journal of Abnormal and Social Psychology*, 66, 3–11.
HANRATTY, M., O'NEIL, E., and SULZER, J. (1972) The effect of frustration on the imitation of aggression. *Journal of Personality and Social Psychology*, 21, 30–34.
LIEBERT, R., and BARON, R. (1972) Some immediate effects of televised violence on children's behavior. *Developmental Psychology*, 6, 469–75.

FOUR

INTELLIGENCE, COGNITION, AND MEMORY

The branch of psychology most concerned with the topics in this section is known as "cognitive psychology." Cognitive psychologists study human mental processes. Our intelligence, our ability to think and reason in complex ways, and our ability to store and retrieve symbolic representations of our experiences all combine to make humans uniquely different from other animals. And, of course, how we do these things greatly affects our behavior. However, studying these mental processes is much more difficult than studying observable behavior, so a great deal of creativity and ingenuity has been necessary.

The studies included here have changed the way psychologists view our internal mental behavior. The first article discusses the famous "Pygmalion study," which demonstrated that not only performance in school, but actual IQ scores of children, can be influenced by the *expectations* of others, such as teachers. The second study, a very early one for this field, addressed how our minds work when we form impressions of other people, even without actually meeting or even seeing them. Third, we again travel to a far-off culture with a study that offered new insights into how we group objects together into categories. And fourth is an examination of recent research that revealed how our memories don't work exactly as we think they do, and the implication of this for eyewitness testimony.

WHAT YOU EXPECT IS WHAT YOU GET
Rosenthal, Robert, and Jacobson, Lenore (1966) Teachers'
   expectancies: Determinates of pupils' I.Q. gains. *Psychological
   Reports*, 19, 115–18.

We are all familiar with the idea of the self-fulfilling prophecy. One way
of describing this concept is to say that if we expect something to
happen in a certain way, our expectation will tend to make it so.
Whether self-fulfilling prophecies really do occur in a predictable way in
everyday life is open to scientific study, but psychological research has
demonstrated that in some areas they are a reality.

   The question of the self-fulfilling prophecy in scientific research
was first brought to the attention of psychologists in 1911 in the famous
case of "Clever Hans," the horse of Mr. von Osten (Pfungst, 1911).
Clever Hans was a horse that was famous for being able to read, spell,
and solve math problems by stomping out answers with his front hoof.
Naturally there were many skeptics, but when Hans' abilities were tested
by a committee of experts, they were found to be genuinely performed
without prompting from Mr. von Osten. But how could any horse
(except possibly for Mr. Ed!) possess such a degree of human
intelligence? Well, a psychologist, O. Pfungst, performed a series of
careful experiments and found that Hans was indeed receiving subtle
unintentional cues from his questioners. For example, after asking a
question, people would look down at the horse's hoof for the answer. As
the horse approached the correct number of hoofbeats, the questioners
would very slightly raise their eyes or head in anticipation of the horse
completing his answer. The horse had been conditioned to use these
subtle movements from the observers as signs to stop stomping, and this
usually resulted in the correct answer to the question.

   So, you might ask, how is a trick horse related to psychological
research? Well, the Clever Hans findings pointed out the possibility that
observers often have specific expectations or biases that may cause them
to send covert and *unintentional* signals to a subject being studied. These
signals, then, may cause the subject to respond in ways that are
consistent with the observers' bias and, consequently, confirm their
expectations. What all this finally boils down to is that an experimenter
may think a certain behavior results from his or her scientific treatment
of one subject or one group of subjects compared with another. Actually
it results from nothing more than the experimenter's own biased
expectations. If this occurs, it renders the experiment invalid. This
threat to the validity of a psychological experiment is called the
experimenter expectancy effect.

Robert Rosenthal, considered the leading researcher on this methodological issue, has demonstrated the experimenter expectancy effect in actual laboratory psychological experiments. In one study, psychology students in a learning and conditioning course unknowingly became subjects themselves. Some of the students were told they would be working with rats that had been specially bred for high intelligence, as measured by their ability to learn mazes quickly. The rest of the students were told that they would be working with rats bred for dullness in learning mazes. The students then proceeded to condition their rats to perform various skills, including maze learning. The students who had been assigned the "maze-bright" rats reported significantly faster learning times than those reported by the students with the "maze-dull" rats. In reality, the rats given to the students were standard lab rats and were *randomly* assigned (Rosenthal and Fode, 1963). These students were not cheating or purposefully slanting their results. The influences they exerted on their animals were apparently unintentional and unconscious.

Other research has demonstrated similar effects in the judgments people make of each other. For example, imagine you are shown several photographs of people and are asked to rate each person on a scale of + 10 to − 10 regarding the person's recent success or failure in life. Prior to your ratings, you are given general information about your group of photographs that leads you to expect them to be, on average, experiencing either success or failure. In actual studies such as this, the biasing information created ratings of the photographs that were in line with the induced expectation. However, prior to the experiment, all the photographs had been rated as neutral (a score of zero) by previous groups of subjects without induced expectations.

As a result of these lines of research, the threat of experimenter expectancies to scientific research has been well established. Properly trained researchers using careful procedures (such as the "double-blind" method, in which the experimenters who come in contact with the subjects are unaware of the hypotheses of the study) are usually able to avoid these expectancy effects.

Beyond this, however, Rosenthal was concerned about how such biases and expectancies might occur outside the laboratory in places such as the school classroom. Since teachers in public schools do not generally have the opportunity to learn about the dangers of expectancies, how great an influence might this have on the students' potential performance? After all, teachers have historically been given students' I.Q. scores beginning in the first grade. Could this information set up biased expectancies in the teachers' minds and cause them to *unintentionally* treat "bright" students (as judged by high I.Q. scores) differently from those seen as less bright? And if so, is this fair? Those questions formed the basis of Rosenthal and Jacobson's study on what they later called the "Pygmalion effect" in the classroom.

THEORETICAL PROPOSITIONS

Rosenthal labeled this expectancy effect, as it occurs in natural interpersonal settings outside the laboratory, "the Pygmalion effect." In the Greek myth, a sculptor (Pygmalion) fell in love with his sculpted creation of a woman. We are more familiar with the modern Shaw play *Pygmalion* (*My Fair Lady* is the musical version) about the blossoming of Eliza Doolittle because of the teaching, encouragement, and *expectations* of Henry Higgins. Rosenthal suspected that when an elementary school teacher is provided with information (such as I.Q. scores) that creates certain expectancies about students' potential, either strong or weak, the teacher might unknowingly behave in ways that subtly encourage or facilitate the performance of the students seen as more likely to succeed. This, in turn, would create the self-fulfilling prophecy of actually causing those students to excel, perhaps at the expense of the students for whom lower expectations exist. In order to test these theoretical propositions, Rosenthal and his colleague Jacobson obtained the assistance of an elementary school (called Oak School) in a predominantly lower-middle-class neighborhood in a large town.

METHOD

With the cooperation of the Oak School administration, all the students in grades 1 through 6 were given an I.Q. test (called the "Tests of General Ability," or TOGA) near the beginning of the academic year. This test was chosen because it was a non-verbal test for which a student's score did not depend primarily upon school-learned skills of reading, writing, and arithmetic. Also, it was a test with which the teachers in Oak School probably would not be familiar. The teachers were told instead that the students were being given the "Harvard Test of Inflected Acquisition." Such deception was necessary in this case in order for expectancies to be created in the minds of the teachers, a necessary ingredient for the experiment to be successful. It was further explained to the teachers that the Harvard test was designed to serve as a predictor of academic "blooming" or "spurting." In other words, teachers believed that students who scored high on the test were ready to enter a period of increased learning abilities within the next year. This predictive ability of the test was also, in fact, not true.

At Oak School there were three classes at each of the six grade levels. All of the 18 teachers (16 women, two men) for these classes were given a list of names of students in their classes who had scored in the top 20 percent on the Harvard test and were therefore identified as potential academic bloomers during the academic year. But here's the key to this study: The children on the teachers' top-10 lists had been assigned to this experimental condition purely at *random*. The only difference between these children and the others (the controls) was that they had been identified *to their teachers* as the ones who would show unusual intellectual gains.

Near the end of the school year, all children at the school were tested again with the same I.Q. test (the TOGA), and the degree of change in I.Q. was calculated for each child. The differences in I.Q. changes between the experimental group and the controls could then be examined to see if the expectancy effect had been created in a real-world setting.

RESULTS

Figure 1 summarizes the results of the comparisons of the I.Q. increases for the experimental vs. the control groups. For the entire school, the children for whom the teachers had expected greater intellectual growth

FIGURE 1   I.Q. score gains grades 1 through 6.

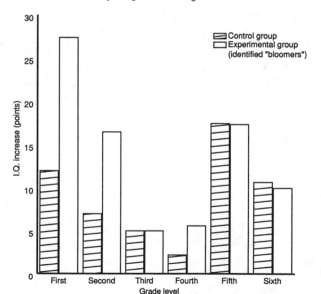

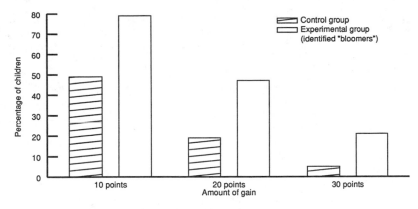

FIGURE 2 Percentage of first- and second-grade students with major gains in I.Q. scores.

averaged significantly greater improvement than did the control children (12.2 and 8.2 points, respectively). However, if you examine Figure 1 it is clear that this difference was accounted for by the huge differences in grades 1 and 2. Possible reasons for this will be discussed shortly. Rosenthal and Jacobson offered another useful and revealing way to organize the data for these first and second graders. Figure 2 illustrates the percentage of the children in each group who obtained increases in I.Q. of at least 10, 20, or 30 points.

Two major findings emerged from this early study. First, the expectancy effect previously demonstrated in formal laboratory settings also appears to function in less formal real-world situations. Second, the effect was very strong in the early grades, and almost non-existent for the older children. What does all this mean?

DISCUSSION

As Rosenthal suspected from his past research, the teachers' expectations of their students' behavior became a self-fulfilling prophecy. "When teachers expected that certain children would show greater intellectual development, those children did show greater intellectual development" (Rosenthal and Jacobson, 1968, p. 85). Remember that the data reported are averages of three classes and three teachers for each grade level. It is difficult to think of other explanations for the differences in I.Q. gains besides the teachers' expectations.

However, it is important to try to explain why the self-fulfilling prophecy was not demonstrated in the higher grade levels. Both in the article that is the focus of this chapter and in later writings, Rosenthal and Jacobson offered several possible reasons for this finding.

1. Younger children are generally thought of as being more malleable or "transformable." If this is true, then the younger children in the study may have

experienced greater change simply because they were *easier* to change than the older children were. Related to this is the possibility that even if younger children are not more malleable, teachers may have *believed* that they were. This belief alone may have been enough to create differential treatment and produce the results that were reported.

2. Younger students in an elementary school tend to have less well-established reputations. In other words, if the teachers had not yet had a chance to form an opinion of a child's abilities, the expectancies created by the researchers would have carried more weight.

3. Younger children may be more easily influenced by and more susceptible to the subtle and unintentional processes that teachers use to communicate performance expectations to them.

"Under this interpretation, it is possible that teachers react to children of all grade levels in the same way if they believe them to be capable of intellectual gain. But perhaps it is only the younger children whose performance is affected by the special things the teacher says to them; the special ways in which she says them; the way she looks, postures, and touches the children from whom she expects greater intellectual growth" (Rosenthal and Jacobson, 1968, p. 83).

4. Teachers of these lower grades may differ from upper-grade teachers in ways that produce greater communication of their expectations to the children. Rosenthal and Jacobson did not speculate as to exactly what these differences might be if indeed they exist.

SIGNIFICANCE OF FINDINGS AND
SUBSEQUENT RESEARCH

The real importance of Rosenthal and Jacobson's findings at Oak School relate to the potential long-lasting effects of teachers' expectations on the scholastic performance of students. This, in turn, feeds directly into one of the most controversial topics in psychology and education today: the question of the fairness of I.Q. tests. We'll return to this discussion shortly, but first it is of interest to explore some later research that examined the ways in which teachers unconsciously communicate their higher expectations to the students whom they believe possess greater potential.

A study conducted by Chaiken, Sigler, and Derlega (1974) involved videotaping teacher-student interactions in a classroom situation in which the teachers had been informed that certain children were extremely bright (these "bright" students had been chosen at random from all the students in the class). Careful examination of the videos indicated that teachers favored the identified "brighter" students in many subtle ways. They smiled at these students more often, made more eye contact, and had more favorable reactions to these students' comments in class. These researchers go on to report that students for whom these high expectations exist are more likely to enjoy school, receive more constructive comments from teachers on their mistakes, and work harder to try to improve. What this and other studies indicate is that teacher expectancies, while their influence is not the only determinant of a child's performance in school, can affect more than just I.Q. scores.

Imagine for a moment that you are an elementary school teacher with a class of 20 students. On the first day of class you receive a class roster on which is printed the I.Q. scores for all of your students. You notice that five of your pupils have I.Q. scores over 145, well into the genius range. Do you think that your treatment and expectations of those children during the school year would be the same as your other students? What about your expectations of those students compared with another five students with I.Q. scores in the low to normal range? If you answered that your treatment and expectations would be the same, I'd be willing to bet that you'd be wrong. As a matter of fact, they probably *shouldn't* be the same! The point is that if your expectations became self-fulfilling prophecies, it might be unfair to some of the students. Now consider another, more crucial point. Suppose the I.Q. scores you received on your class roster were wrong. If these erroneous scores created expectations that benefited some students over others, it would clearly be unfair and probably would be unethical. This is one of the major issues fueling the I.Q. controversy that rages today.

For many years there have been charges that the standard I.Q. tests used to assess the intelligence of children contain a racial, ethnic, or cultural bias. The argument is that since the tests were designed primarily by white, upper-middle-class males, they contain ideas and information to which other ethnic groups are not exposed. Children from various minority subcultures within the United States traditionally score lower on these tests than white children do. Since it would be ridiculous to assume that these non-white children possess less basic intelligence than white children, the reason for these differences in scores must lie in the tests themselves. Traditionally, however, teachers in grades K through 12 are given this I.Q. information on all their students. If you stop and think about this fact in relation to the research by Rosenthal and Jacobson, you'll see what a potentially dangerous situation may have been created. Besides the fact that children have been categorized in school according to their I.Q. scores (advanced placement, remedial classes, etc.), teachers' *unintended* expectations, based on this possibly biased information, may have been creating unfair self-fulfilling prophecies. The arguments supporting this idea are convincing enough that several states have instituted a moratorium on I.Q. testing and the use of I.Q. scores until such testing can be shown to be bias-free. And at the core of these arguments has been the research addressed in this chapter.

CHAIKEN, A., SIGLER, E., and DERLEGA, V. (1974) Non-verbal mediators of teacher expectancy effects. *Journal of Personality and Social Psychology*, 30, 144–49.
PFUNGST, O. (1911) *Clever Hans (the horse of Mr. von Osten): A contribution to experimental, animal, and human psychology*. New York: Holt, Rinehart & Winston.
ROSENTHAL, R., and FODE, K. (1963) The effect of experimenter bias on the performance of the albino rat. *Behavioral Science*, 8, 183–89.
ROSENTHAL, R., and JACOBSON, L. (1968) *Pygmalion in the classroom: Teacher expectations and pupils' intellectual development*. New York: Holt, Rinehart & Winston.

MAKING A GOOD IMPRESSION
Asch, Solomon E. (1946) Forming impressions of personality.
Journal of Abnormal and Social Psychology, 41, 258–90.

Solomon Asch was one of the most influential researchers in the history of psychology. You will note that he is the only behavioral scientist with two studies included in this book. (Asch is considered by most to have been a social psychologist and his classic work on conformity is included in that section.) However, his important contributions in the area of impression formation, while certainly a social psychological event, are being included here under cognitive psychology. This is perhaps, as you will see, more appropriate.

As you read the previous paragraph, you performed several mental tasks. One of them was that you formed an impression of Solomon Asch's personality. Your impression may not be very well developed due to the small amount of information you received, but if you were asked to describe him you probably would include certain characteristics such as intelligent, versatile, and scholarly. Forming impressions of others appears to be a natural and unavoidable cognitive activity for us. Furthermore, we form these impressions quickly and easily (right or wrong!) and often with incredibly small amounts of information. Think about it: Suppose I tell you there is someone I want you to meet, and I say this person is sociable, responsible, and manipulative. What kind of person comes to mind? Is it someone you like? Someone you would rather avoid? How do you think you would respond to this person when you meet? Probably you would be able to answer all these questions, and yet the only information you have is three adjectives. As Asch says in his article:

> We look at a person and immediately a certain impression of his character forms itself in us. A glance, a few spoken words are sufficient to tell us a

story about a highly complex matter. We know that such impressions form
with remarkable rapidity and great ease. . . . This remarkable capacity we
possess to understand something of the character of another person . . . is
a precondition of social life. In what manner are these impressions
established? Are there lawful principles regulating their formation?
(p. 258)

Asch recognized that we usually have at least several characteristics from
which to form an impression of a person. However, you do not perceive
others as being made up of several distinct traits. Instead, you have a
general, *unified* impression of the whole person. What Asch wanted to
find out was how you mentally or cognitively organize these various
discrete characteristics in order to produce this single unified
impression.

THEORETICAL PROPOSITIONS

Consider a person who possesses five distinct characteristics, labeled a, b,
c, d, and e. Asch summarized two general theories that might be used to
explain how you combine these characteristics and come up with an
impression. The first suggests that you simply add them up:

$$a + b + c + d + e = Impression$$

The problem with this conceptualization is that it implies that you think
about people in terms of these separate traits, when, as explained
previously, you actually take a much more integrated view.

The second theory applies this more unified concept by proposing
that, instead of adding separate traits together, you sort of throw them
all into a pot and stir them together. In this view, the characteristics are
seen in relation with one another within the person's personality:

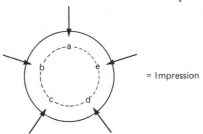

According to Asch, this second explanation appeared to most
psychologists as the more acceptable because of the need for unity in
your perception of another person.

Asch's study, however, was not so concerned with the actual
organization of personality characteristics within a person, but with the

process you use when you form a unified impression. In other words, he wanted to find out how you combine and order the parts to produce the whole. Keep in mind that he was not looking at the emotional components of an impression, but rather the cognitive ones. As Asch put it, "something must be perceived and discriminated in order that it may be loved or hated" (p. 260). The ingenious method Asch developed to study this process caused this research to become known as the "warm-cold" study.

METHOD

This article by Asch contained reports of 10 experiments. However, the present discussion will be limited to the two studies (I and III) that have had the greatest influence on psychological science and have been referred to the most often in subsequent research and publications.

Asch had observed in previous research that various characteristics you see in others do not carry equal weight in the process of forming impressions of them. The qualities that are the most influential are called "central," while those that are less important are "peripheral" characteristics. To examine the existence and relative influence of these two types of traits, Asch presented lists of descriptive characteristics to subjects and asked them to describe their impression of the person to whom the qualities belonged.

The subjects in this research were university students. In the first experiment there were 90 subjects in group A and 76 in group B. They were asked to listen carefully to a list of adjectives describing human qualities, and to try to form an impression of the person described. The groups heard the following lists:

> Group A: Intelligent, skillful, industrious, *warm*, determined, practical, cautious
>
> Group B: Intelligent, skillful, industrious, *cold*, determined, practical, cautious

As you can see, both lists were identical except for the change of a single word: "warm" vs. "cold."

The subjects were then asked to write a brief sketch of the person described and select the term from each of 18 pairs of opposite adjectives that they believed best fit the person. The adjective list to which the subjects responded is shown in Table 1.

In the second experiment being discussed here (experiment III), the same procedure was followed, but with two changes. First, there were only 20 subjects in group A and 26 in group B. For this

TABLE 1 Adjective Checklist Given to Subjects

1. Generous—Ungenerous	10. Ruthless—Humane
2. Shrewd—Wise	11. Good-looking—Unattractive
3. Unhappy—Happy	12. Persistent—Unstable
4. Irritable—Good-natured	13. Frivolous—Serious
5. Humorous—Humorless	14. Restrained—Talkative
6. Sociable—Unsociable	15. Self-centered—Altruistic
7. Popular—Unpopular	16. Imaginative—Hard-headed
8. Unreliable—Reliable	17. Strong—Weak
9. Important—Unimportant	18. Dishonest—Honest

(from p. 262)

experiment, this was a relatively minor change. The important difference was the lists of traits used:

> Group A: Intelligent, skillful, industrious, *polite*, determined, practical, cautious
>
> Group B: Intelligent, skillful, industrious, *blunt*, determined, practical, cautious

These subjects did not write sketches (at least none were reported), but they responded to the same checklist as in experiment I.

Remember, everything was the same for the two groups in both studies except for the change in a single word in the list of traits. What Asch wanted to discover was how much effect that one word would have on the overall impression created in the minds of the subjects.

RESULTS

The results of these experiments were measured by the subjects' written sketches of the people described and the percentage of subjects in the various groups who selected each term from the 18 pairs of adjectives listed.

Here are two examples of sketches from subjects in the two groups (from p. 263 of the article).

> *Group A (warm):* A person who believes certain things to be right, wants others to see his point, would be sincere in an argument, and would like to see his point won.
>
> *Group B (cold):* A rather snobbish person who feels that his success and intelligence set him apart from the run-of-the-mill individual. Calculating and unsympathetic.

It is clear that the description for the group A subject was much more favorable than that for the group B subject. This difference was typical of the sketches in general. Table 2 summarizes the percentages of subjects who checked the positive adjective in each pair for both experiments.

This table contains a great deal of data, and it may seem somewhat confusing at first. But on careful examination of the WARM and COLD columns, you can see that the percentage of subjects assigning certain positive qualities to the person described was strikingly greater in the WARM condition. Subjects who heard the word "warm" in the description judged the person to be generous, wise, happy, good-natured, humorous, sociable, popular, humane, altruistic, and imaginative. Subjects hearing the word "cold" judged the person to be the opposite on all 10 of these adjective pairs.

It is interesting to note that the "warm-cold" difference did not affect judgments on the remaining eight pairs of adjectives. A person described as warm was *not* judged to be significantly more reliable, important, good-looking, persistent, serious, restrained, strong, or honest.

Now take a look at the POLITE and BLUNT columns. When these words were substituted for "warm" and "cold" in the same list of traits,

TABLE 2   Percentage of Subjects Choosing Positive Word in Pair

	WORD CONDITION		WORD CONDITION	
	WARM vs. COLD		POLITE vs. BLUNT	
ADJECTIVE	N = 90	N = 76	N = 20	N = 26
1. Generous	91	8	56	58
2. Wise	65	25	30	38
3. Happy	90	34	75	65
4. Good-natured	94	17	87	56
5. Humorous	77	13	71	48
6. Sociable	91	38	71	48
7. Popular	84	28	84	68
8. Reliable	94	99	95	100
9. Important	88	99	94	96
10. Humane	86	31	59	77
11. Good-looking	77	69	93	79
12. Persistent	100	97	100	100
13. Serious	100	99	100	100
14. Restrained	77	89	82	77
15. Altruistic	69	18	29	46
16. Imaginative	51	19	30	31
17. Strong	98	95	100	100
18. Honest	98	94	87	100

(adapted from p. 263)

all these extreme differences in judgment disappeared! If you look closely, you will still find some differences, but they are much less pronounced, appear on fewer adjective pairs, and sometimes are even slightly reversed (such as wise, humane, or altruistic). If you look right down the list and compare the differences in these columns with the "warm-cold" columns you'll see that "polite" and "blunt" just did not carry the same weight.

With these findings, Asch had discovered something about how people's minds work when they make judgments about others. Let's discuss what this discovery was.

DISCUSSION

As Asch explains in his article, what these results demonstrated was that the change of a single word in a description of someone can produce a change in the entire impression formed. In addition, the changes produced by this single adjective change are widespread, but not universal. Certain characteristics appear to be connected to the "warm-cold" dimension, but others are not. In terms of the way you think about another individual, "warm" activates the qualities of generosity, wisdom, happiness, and sociability, among others; but "warm" is not particularly related to traits such as reliability, attractiveness, or honesty. Even though you probably never thought about it before, this makes sense, doesn't it? It also makes these little words seem quite powerful. By the way, we do seem to know that these words are powerful even though we are not really conscious of it (well, now *you* are). Asch asked subjects to rank all the words on the list in order of their importance in determining their impression. For group A, 49 percent ranked "warm" either first or second out of seven. In group B, 48 percent ranked "cold" as either first or second.

Asch further clarified the mental processes that function when you form impressions of others when he substituted "polite" and "blunt" into the list of characteristics. These words, although probably used just as commonly as "warm" and "cold" to describe people, did not contain the same degree of power in influencing the overall impression. The relative weakness of these characteristics was recognized by the subjects when they were asked to rank their importance, as in the first study. In the three *lowest* possible rankings of importance, 90 percent placed "polite," and 54 percent placed "blunt."

Two main points emerged from this work by Asch. One was that some qualities of individuals function as *central* characteristics, while others are seen as *peripheral* traits. These two types of traits function very differently in your cognitive process of impression formation.

The second point relates to the theories of impression formation discussed at the beginning of this chapter. What Asch discovered was how traits interact with each other in your thought processes. It was almost as if these various characteristics developed social relationships in the subjects' brains. Some traits are in power, and when they say "jump" many of the other traits jump. On the other hand, some traits are minor players without much power of their own, but are readily influenced by the dominant ones. Asch suggested that perhaps the best theoretical model of impression formation would conceive of each trait interacting with one or more of the others. We do not simply add up the individual traits to arrive at an impression, but we total all the various interactions among them. According to Asch, this cognitive process would look something like this:

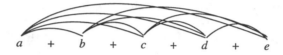

$$a \quad + \quad b \quad + \quad c \quad + \quad d \quad + \quad e$$

SUBSEQUENT RESEARCH AND CRITICISMS

You should have been thinking of one important criticism of this research already. In fact, Asch himself pointed it out in his discussion. These experiments involved descriptions of people, not people themselves. Asch acknowledges that observations of actual people might involve other processes not present in these studies. The loss of realism in laboratory research is always a potential problem. It is for this reason that a related study conducted by Harold Kelly a few years later proved very interesting (Kelly, 1950).

Kelly replicated Asch's research in a real-life setting. Students in psychology courses were told that they were going to have a guest lecturer. Half the students were given a description of the guest that used the same list of traits as in Asch's study, including the word "warm," while the other half had the same description but with the word "cold." Then the guest actually came in and led a discussion for about 20 minutes. Afterward, the students were asked to rate the person on several qualities. Even though the students heard the *same* lecturer lead the *same* discussion (and the lecturer was not aware of the purpose of the experiment), their impressions were very different. Table 3 illustrates the different ratings the two groups gave to the speaker on several dimensions similar to those used by Asch. Moreover, and perhaps even more important, students in the "warm" condition interacted with the speaker in a more friendly way, laughed more at his jokes, and asked more questions during the discussion. What this means is that not only are our impressions altered by slight changes in central

TABLE 3   Students' Ratings of Guest Lecturer

ADJECTIVE	"WARM"	"COLD"
1. Self-centered	6.3	9.6
2. Irritable	9.4	12.0
3. Unsociable	5.6	10.4
4. Unpopular	4.0	7.4
5. Formal	6.3	9.6
6. Humorless	8.3	11.7

(adapted from Kelly, 1950)

characteristics, but this, in turn, also alters our behavior toward the person of whom we have formed the impression.

Another criticism that should be mentioned here was proposed much more recently. Zanna and Hamilton (1972) argued that there are two dimensions on which we describe people, "intellectual traits" and "social traits." They contended that Asch's initial list given to the subjects (containing either "warm" or "cold") was made up primarily of *intellectual* traits (intelligent, skillful, industrious, etc.) with the exception of "warm" or "cold," which are social qualities. However, the traits on the adjective checklist that showed large differences were *social* characteristics and would *automatically* be strongly influenced by "warm" vs. "cold," simply because of the relationships between the words.

While this criticism has merit, Asch's work greatly influenced the growth of one of today's most productive fields in the behavioral sciences: *cognitive psychology*. One of the theoretical foundations upon which cognitive psychology rests is the concept of the *schema*. A "schema" is defined as a basic unit of knowledge that develops from past experiences, provides a framework for judging future experiences, and influences how you perceive and react to people and events. Schemas are the way you organize information about the world (see Fiske and Taylor, 1984, for a complete discussion of the concept of schema). Over 45 years ago, Asch's look into your brain's method of organization in forming impressions of others helped to open the door for the present-day science of cognitive psychology.

FISKE, S.T., and TAYLOR, S. (1984) *Social cognition*. Reading, Mass.: Addison-Wesley.
KELLY, H. (1950) The warm-cold variable in first impressions of persons. *Journal of Personality*, 18, 431–39.
ZANNA, M.P., and HAMILTON, D.L. (1972) Attribute dimensions and patterns of trait inferences. *Psychonomic Science*, 27, 353–54.

AS A CATEGORY, IT'S A NATURAL!

Rosch, Eleanor H. (1973) Natural categories. *Cognitive Psychology*, 4, 328–50.

In the Shirley Temple movie *Stand Up and Cheer*, the great film actor and dancer who went by the name of Stepin Fetchit sat on the porch steps examining one of his old, beat-up pieces of footwear, and lamented philosophically, "Why's a shoe called a shoe?" His character often wondered why things were called what they were called and psychologists, in various ways, have wondered the same thing. There is a relatively new branch of psychology that focuses its research on human mental processes such as language, thinking, analyzing, knowing, and remembering. This is the field of *cognitive psychology*.

One of the fundamentals of cognitive psychology is the idea of *concepts*. Concepts are mental representations of your experience of the world that allow you to classify objects (shoes, furniture, vegetables, animals, professions, etc.) according to the characteristics they have in common. Concepts are extremely useful because they allow you to group objects into categories for efficient processing of information. For example, you know that a certain piece of furniture is a chair because it fits your concept of a chair. Therefore, it is not necessary for you to learn that a specific chair is called a chair each time you see an unfamiliar style, so long as it fits into your category for chairs. So, now you are thinking of a chair. What features comprise your "chair concept"? You probably think of a chair as having legs, a seat, and a back to lean against. Even though some chairs violate your rules (recliners and rocking chairs don't really have legs), they still fit into your category well enough. However, if you were to encounter a bean-bag "chair" without knowing what it was, you probably would not call it a chair.

The question that has most interested cognitive psychologists is this: Where do our categories for objects come from? The traditional or "classical" view that was widely accepted prior to 1970 held that categories are a function of the language we speak. In other words, categories exist because we have words for them. For example, we have a category for animals that lay eggs, fly, have feathers, and chirp; the category is "bird." The classical view maintained that if we did not have a word for bird, the category or concept for bird would not exist. Therefore, concepts and categories should vary from culture to culture due to variations in language. And there is evidence of this. A frequently cited example is that the Eskimo language has 12 words for "snow," whereas in English there are only one or two. Obviously, Eskimos need greater flexibility in communicating about snow because of the climate in which they must survive, and this is reflected in their language. In the language of the South Pacific islands, there may be no word at all for snow and, therefore, according to the classical theory, such a concept would not exist.

For many years, this theory of the origin of concepts was taken for granted by scientists throughout the social sciences of psychology, anthropology, linguistics, and sociology. During the early 1970s, Eleanor Rosch, at the University of California at Berkeley, published a series of studies that challenged the classical view and turned the field of cognitive psychology upside down. She is considered to have revolutionized the study of categorization. She proposed that categories do not necessarily arise from the language, but exist naturally on their own, in relation to humans' biological abilities of perception. Her landmark study, presented here, involved two separate experiments and some rather technical procedures. For the sake of clarity and space limitations, only a summary of the first experiment reported in the article will be detailed here.

THEORETICAL PROPOSITIONS

Rosch theorized that if the classical theory were correct, all objects belonging to a certain category would have equal status in that category; that is, fit into it equally well. She observed, however, that this is not the case. Instead, some members of a category are perceived by us to be better examples of the category than others. As an example of this, consider again the category of "bird." Now, quickly, picture a bird in your mind. You probably pictured something like a robin, a blue jay, a wren, or a sparrow. It is quite unlikely that you thought of a goose, a chicken, an ostrich, or a penguin. According to Rosch, this is because a robin fits your *prototype* of a bird better than a chicken does. In other words, a robin exhibits all or most of the features that describe our category of bird and is, therefore, judged higher in "birdiness." Conversely, an ostrich has few of the features (doesn't fly, doesn't chirp, is too big) and so does not fit the prototype for a bird well at all.

What Rosch argued was that most categories do not have clear boundaries as to what fits and what does not, but category borders are "fuzzy." We decide if an object fits into the category by comparing it to our category prototype. She also believed that categories can be psychologically real even when there are no words in a person's language with which to name them. To test this theory, Rosch traveled to New Guinea where there is a society of people called the "Dani." The Dani to this day exist as a Stone Age culture and communicate in a language that does not include certain concepts that exist in all modern cultures.

Rosch's early studies, including the one discussed here, were on categories relating to color. In English-speaking countries there are 11 major color categories: red, yellow, green, blue, black, gray, white, purple, orange, pink, and brown. It has been found in other research that speakers of English are able to agree on certain "focal colors": those that are the best examples for each color category. For example, fire-engine red is the *focal color* for the category of red (you could say it is the *most* red) and it is identified as red much more easily than are other "reddish" or off-red colors.

In the Dani language, however, there are only two color categories: "mili," which describes dark, cool colors, and "mola," used for light, warm colors. Rosch theorized that if the classical view was correct, and language determines concepts, the Dani should only possess two conceptual categories for colors. What she decided to do was to teach the Dani new words for eight focal colors or eight non-focal colors. She hypothesized that focal color categories were *psychologically* real for the Dani natives, even though names for them had never existed in their language. If this was true, names for focal colors should be able to be learned by the Dani faster and easier than names for non-focal colors.

METHOD

Subjects

The subjects for her study were young Dani males who were all pretested to be sure that no one was color-blind. They were also tested to confirm that their knowledge of color terms was restricted to "mili" (dark) and "mola" (light). Interestingly, the Dani do not measure age, so based on size and general physical maturity the researchers judged all the subjects to be at least 12 to 15 years of age. The participants volunteered to be subjects and were told that they would be paid after they had completed the learning part of the procedure. They were divided into several groups of 12 subjects each, but only the two most important experimental groups will be discussed here.

Color Stimuli

Glossy color chips, similar to those you might obtain from a paint store, were used as the stimuli for the colors to be learned. These chips, however, were developed scientifically to represent specific colors of exacting wavelengths. The color categories used were pink, red, yellow, orange, brown, green, blue, and purple. For one group of subjects, the colors were the focal, prototype hue for each color (such as fire-engine red). These were the colors that Rosch theorized to be universally represented by natural categories. For the other group, the hues of the eight color chips fell in between focal colors so that you, as an English-speaker, might call them "red-brown" or "yellow-green." These were called ambiguous or "non-focal colors."

Procedure

The first problem was to assign names in Dani for the various colors. This was not as easy as it might sound because the names needed to be words that were all equally frequent, familiar, and meaningful to the subjects. Rosch discovered that among the Dani there are many names for what they call "sibs." A sib was described by Rosch as a family group similar to a clan. These names appeared to meet her requirements and so were used to represent the different color categories to be learned by the subjects. To avoid bias, a subject's own sib name was not used as a color category.

Each subject was told that the task involved learning a new language that would be taught to him by the experimenter. At the beginning of the first day the colors were presented to the subject, and the name assigned to each color was spoken by the researcher and repeated by the subject. Then the colors were shuffled and presented again. Each time the subject named the color correctly he was praised or, if he was incorrect, he was told the correct name. Over a period of five to 12 days the subjects were tested on their learning of the color categories and their progress recorded until all the subjects were able to name all the colors without error.

Upon completion of the learning period, an additional task was performed by all subjects to determine if this new ability was truly understood as a general concept and would transfer to new situations, or was limited only to the specific colors learned. To test for this, each subject was shown a group of various colors and asked to identify eight of them that had *not* been part of the training categories. The success rate of this "transfer" task was calculated for the subjects in both groups.

RESULTS

If humans possess by nature the ability to perceive certain categories of colors, then the results of the Dani's learning task should demonstrate faster learning for the focal color categories than for the non-focal colors. Figure 1 summarizes the learning progress of the two groups over the testing period. The average number of errors over the entire learning period was 8.54 for the prototype color group, compared with 18.96 for the ambiguous color group. This difference was highly

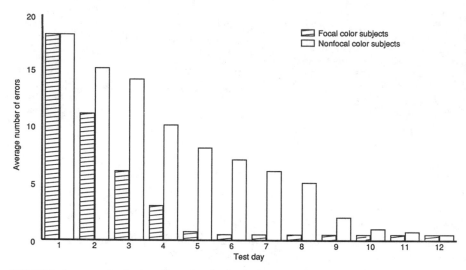

FIGURE 1   Average rate of color category learning for the focal color and non-focal color subjects.

statistically significant. If you consult Figure 1, you can see that the group presented with the colors we consider central to a particular color category was able to learn the names of the colors in only five days, compared with 11 days for the group trying to learn the non-focal color categories.

It was important to demonstrate that the skill of recognizing color categories had been acquired in such a way that it would transfer to new situations; that it was a "usable" concept. On the task in which subjects were asked to identify colors that were not part of the learning period, correct responses would be expected only about 12 percent of the time (percentage correct due to chance alone) if the concept did not transfer. The subjects in Rosch's study correctly identified the colors not used with 90 percent accuracy.

One additional informal finding reported by Rosch was that four of the subjects in the non-focal color group became very frustrated during the learning period and wanted to quit before learning all the color names. It took a great deal of persuasion to convince them to continue until they had completed the task. This problem was not encountered with the other group, which generally seemed to enjoy the experimental process.

Well, all this may seem like a long way to go for rather simple findings, but, as mentioned at the beginning of this chapter, the results from this and additional studies by Rosch and others had a profound effect on our knowledge of how the brain works. First we will summarize Rosch's discussion of her findings, then we will get a brief glimpse of the huge amount of subsequent related research.

DISCUSSION

Rosch had found a way to test a theory that, on the surface, would seem nearly impossible to test. Can you think of a concept or category of objects that does not exist for speakers of English (or any other language) in the way color categories are missing from the Dani language? Well, there may be some, but they are difficult to find and even more difficult to test. The notion to locate and study a culture that does not acknowledge color categories was ingenious in itself. But the weight of her contributions lies in what she discovered.

The main finding was that people from a culture that did not possess concepts for colors could learn colors that constituted hypothesized prototypes faster than they could learn non-prototype colors. This finding indicated that certain concepts exist in the brains of all humans, regardless of the language they speak or whether they have ever used the concepts themselves. Since these concepts appear to be part of the biological structure of humans, Rosch called them "natural categories" (the title of her article). The reason this study had such an impact on psychological research was that suddenly the nearly universally accepted idea that language produces concepts had been changed to the radically opposing view that linguistic concepts *follow* and form around these naturally occurring categories.

Rosch concludes her article by suggesting further implications of her findings:

> In short, the evidence which has been presented regarding the structure and learning of color . . . categories may have implications beyond the domain of color: (a) there may be other domains which are organized into natural categories and (b) even in non-perceptual categories, artificial prototypes (the best examples of non-perceptual categories), once developed, may affect learning and processing of categories in that domain in a manner similar to the effects of natural prototypes (p. 349).

What this meant, in short, was that possibly most of what you perceive is analyzed and categorized by you according to how well or poorly it matches an appropriate prototype (natural or not), rather than how well it meets the criteria of a formal linguistic definition. A great deal of subsequent research by Rosch and others has shown this to be the case.

SUBSEQUENT RESEARCH

Nearly all of the research since Rosch's early study has supported the existence of natural categories and the use of prototypes in concept formation. Rosch and her colleagues as well as others have expanded on the early findings reported in this chapter to demonstrate its broader implications.

For example, it has been experimentally demonstrated that concepts do not have the clear, distinct boundaries that might exist if we used a strict linguistic definition to categorize objects, but rather, as mentioned earlier in this chapter, they are indeed *fuzzy* (see Rosch, 1975). For example, if we return once again to our example of your concept of "bird," would you include a kiwi bird? How about a bat? You may have formal knowledge that a kiwi is a bird (even though it doesn't fly, or chirp, or sit in trees), but when you think of a *bird*, a kiwi rarely comes to mind (well, maybe now it will!). On the other hand, you may know that technically a bat is not a bird, and yet it flies, makes a sort of a chirping sound, and may live in trees. So you might, on some level, conceive of bats as birds. As another example, consider your category for "fruit." What fruits are you thinking of? Apples and oranges are usually the ones named first. What about a tomato? A tomato may be a fruit, but it is a poor example of one because it is quite distant in resemblance to your prototypical fruit. Remember, cognitive psychologists are interested more in *how* you think than whether you are technically correct. (By the way, a kiwi is not only a bad example of a bird, it is also a bad example of a fruit!)

Various research techniques designed to reveal how people conceptualize the world around them have been developed since Rosch first demonstrated the existence of natural categories with the Dani in New Guinea (for a complete discussion, see Rosch, 1978, and Lakoff, 1987). One method simply asks subjects (from any culture) to use a number scale (such as from one to 10) to rate how well an object fits into a certain category (meaning how well it matches your prototype for that category). So for the category "dog," a German shepard might rate 10, while a basenji might get a 3 (this has nothing to do with the quality of the breed, just how "doggy" we think they are).

Another research technique uses reaction time to measure how well something fits into a mental category. The way this works is you see or hear a statement (such as, "A turkey is a bird") and then press a button for true or false as fast as you can. Findings from this research demonstrate that the closer the category example matches your prototype, the faster you will respond. "A turkey is a bird" will produce a significantly slower reaction time than "A robin is a bird."

A third method involves asking subjects to produce examples of category members either by listing them or making line drawings. In a given amount of time, the subjects will produce a far greater number of the more representative members of a category. For example, if you are asked to draw pieces of furniture, you will probably draw a chair, a couch, and a table before you will draw a lamp or a bookcase.

In conclusion, it should be noted that although Rosch's discovery of natural categories and prototype theory revolutionized psychology's view of our use of concepts, it does not mean we have abandoned strict linguistic definitions. What seems to be true is that we will invoke such definitions when that level of precision is necessary. The category of fruit provides an excellent example. If someone asks you, "Would you like a piece of fruit?", you do not think "fruit: the ripened seed-bearing structure of a plant." Instead you immediately access your prototype for *fruit*, which is something like an apple or an orange. You would be quite surprised if you answered "Yes!", and someone tossed you a pine cone! However, there are times when your formal definition of fruit might be useful: Suppose you are on a nature walk and come upon an unusual plant with strange objects growing on it. Even though the objects on this plant bear little resemblance to your fruit prototype, your *formal definition* would allow you to say, "Look! This plant is bearing fruit."

LAKOFF, G. (1987) *Women, fire, and dangerous things: What categories reveal about the mind.* Chicago: University of Chicago Press.
ROSCH, E.H. (1975) Cognitive representations of semantic categories. *Journal of Experimental Psychology: General*, 104, 192–233.
ROSCH, E.H. (1978) Principles of categorization. In E. ROSCH and B. LLOYD (eds.) *Cognition and categorization.* Hillsdale, N.J.: Erlbaum.

THANKS FOR THE MEMORIES!
Loftus, Elizabeth F. (1975) Leading questions and the eyewitness report. *Cognitive Psychology*, 7, 560–72.

PERRY MASON: Hamilton, I believe that my client is telling the truth when she says she was nowhere near the scene of the crime.

HAMILTON BURGER: Perry, why don't we let the jury decide?

PERRY MASON: Because I don't believe there is going to be a trial. You haven't got a case. All you have is circumstantial evidence.

HAMILTON BURGER: Well, Perry, I suppose this is as good a time as any to tell you. We have someone who saw the whole thing, Perry. We have an *eyewitness*!

And as the mysterious music crescendos, we know that this is going to be another difficult case for Perry. Even though we are reasonably certain he will prevail in the end, the presence of a single eyewitness to the crime has changed a weak case into a nearly airtight one for the district attorney. Why do eyewitness reports provide such strong evidence in criminal cases? The reason is that attorneys, judges, juries, and the general public believe that the way in which the person remembers an event must be the way it actually happened. In other words, memory is thought of as a process of *re-creating* an event. We commonly make assumptions concerning the reliability of human memory, which psychologists who study memory (cognitive psychologists) have now drawn into question.

One of the leading researchers in the area of memory is Elizabeth Loftus at the University of Washington. She has found that when an event is recalled it is not accurately re-created. Instead, what is recalled is a memory that is a reconstruction of the actual event. Loftus' research has demonstrated that *reconstructive memory* is a result of your use of new and existing information to fill in the gaps in your recall of an experience. She maintains that your memories are not stable, as we commonly believe, but that they are malleable and changeable over time. So if you tell someone a story from your vacation five years ago, you think you are re-creating the experience just as it happened, but you probably are not. Instead, you have reconstructed the memory using information from many sources, such as the previous times you've told it, other experiences from the same or later vacations, perhaps a movie you saw last year that was shot in the same place as your vacation, and so on. You know this is true if you have ever recounted an experience in the presence of another person who was with you at the time. It is surprising how much your stories can disagree about an event you both witnessed at the same time!

Usually, these alterations in memory are harmless. However, in legal proceedings, when a defendant's fate may rest on the testimony of an eyewitness, memory reconstructions can be crucial. For this reason, most of Loftus' research in the area of memory has been connected to legal eyewitness testimony. In her early research, she found that very subtle influences, such as how a question is worded, can alter a person's memory for a witnessed event. For example, if witnesses to an automobile accident are asked, "Did you see *a* broken headlight?" or "Did you see *the* broken headlight?", the question using the word "the" produced more positive responses than the question using the word "a," even when there had been no broken headlight. The use of "the" presupposes the presence of a broken headlight and this, in turn, causes witnesses to "add" a new feature to their memories of the event.

The article that is the focus of this chapter is one of the most often cited studies by Loftus because it reports on four related studies that took her theory one major step further. In these studies, she demonstrated that the wording of questions asked of eyewitnesses could alter their memories of events when they were asked other questions about the events at a later time. Keep in mind that this research influenced *both* memory theory and criminal law.

THEORETICAL PROPOSITIONS

This research focused on the power of questions containing presuppositions to alter a person's memory of an event. Loftus defines a *presupposition* as a condition that must be true in order for the question to make sense. For example, suppose you have witnessed an automobile accident and I ask you, "How many people were in the car that was speeding?" The question presupposes that the car was speeding. But what if the car was not actually speeding? Well, you might answer the question anyway because it was not a question about the speed of the car. Loftus proposed, however, that because of the way the question was worded, you might add the speeding information to your memory of the event. Consequently, if you are asked other questions later you will be more likely to say the car was speeding.

Based on her previous research, Loftus hypothesized that if eyewitnesses are asked questions that contain a false presupposition about the witnessed event, the new false information may appear subsequently in additional reports by the witness. Because three of the four studies included in this article involved recall tests after an interval of a week, Loftus was implicitly predicting that the reconstructed memory involving the false information would persist over time.

METHOD AND RESULTS

For each of the four experiments reported, the method and results will be summarized together.

Experiment 1, Method

In the first study 150 students in small groups saw a film of a five-car chain-reaction accident that occurs when a driver runs through a stop sign into oncoming traffic. The accident takes only 4 seconds and the entire film runs less than a minute. After the film, the subjects were given a questionnaire containing 10 questions. For half of the subjects, the first question was, "How fast was Car A [the car that ran the stop sign] going when it ran the stop sign?" For the other half of the subjects, the question read, "How fast was Car A going when it turned right?"

The remaining questions were of little interest to the researchers until the last one, which was the same for both groups: "Did you see a stop sign for Car A?"

Results

In the group that had been asked about the stop sign, 40 subjects (53 percent) said they saw a stop sign for Car A, while only 26 (35 percent) in the "turned right" group claimed to have seen it. This difference was found to be statistically significant.

Experiment 2, Method

The second study Loftus reported was the first in this series to involve a delayed memory test and was the only one of the four not to use an automobile accident as the witnessed event. For this study, 40 subjects were shown a three-minute segment from the film *Diary of a Student Revolution*. The clip showed a class being disrupted by eight demonstrators. After they viewed the film, the subjects were given questionnaires containing 20 questions relating to the film clip. For half of the subjects, one of the questions asked, "Was the leader of the four demonstrators who entered the classroom a male?" For the other half, the question asked, "Was the leader of the 12 demonstrators who entered the classroom a male?" All remaining questions were identical for the two groups.

One week after this initial test, the subjects from both groups returned and answered 20 new questions about the film (without seeing it again). The one question that provided the results of the study was, "How many demonstrators did you see entering the classroom?" Remember, both groups of subjects saw the same film and answered the same questions, except for the reference to 12 vs. four demonstrators.

Results

The group that had received the question presupposing 12 demonstrators reported seeing an average of 8.85. Those who had received the question asking about four demonstrators averaged 6.40. This was also a significant difference. Some of the subjects recalled the correct number of eight. However, this experiment showed that, on average, the wording of one question altered the way subjects remembered the basic characteristics of a witnessed event.

Experiment 3, Method

This experiment was designed to see if false presuppositions inherent in questions could cause witnesses to reconstruct their memory of an event to include objects that were not even there. One hundred and fifty subjects (university students) watched a short video of an accident involving a white sports car and then answered 10 questions about the content of the video. One question included for half of the subjects was, "How fast was the white sports car going when it passed the barn while traveling along the country road?" The other half of the subjects were asked, "How fast was the white sports car going while traveling along the country road?" As in the previous study, the subjects returned a week later and answered 10 new questions about the accident. The question addressing the issue under study was, "Did you see a barn?"

Results

Of those subjects who had previously answered a question in which a barn was mentioned, 13 (17.3 percent) of them answered "yes" to the test question a week later, compared with only 2 (2.7 percent) in the no-barn group. Once again, there was a statistically significant difference.

Experiment 4, Method

The final experiment reported in this article was a somewhat more elaborate study designed to meet two goals. First, Loftus wanted to further demonstrate the memory reconstruction effects found in Experiment 3. Second, she wondered if perhaps just the mention of an object, even if it was not included as part of a false presupposition, might be enough to cause the object to be added to memory. For example, you are asked directly, "Did you see a barn?" when there was no barn in the film. You will probably answer "No." But if you are asked again a week later, might that barn have crept into your memory of the event? This was the idea Loftus tested in the fourth experiment.

Three groups of 50 subjects viewed a three-minute film shot from the inside of a car that ends with the car colliding with a baby carriage pushed by a man. The three groups then received booklets containing questions about the film. These booklets differed as follows:

> Group D: The direct question group received booklets containing 40 "filler" questions and five key questions directly asking about non-existent objects; for example, "Did you see a barn in the film?"
>
> Group F: The false presupposition group received the same 40 filler questions and five key questions that contained presuppositions about the same non-existent objects, such as, "Did you see a station wagon parked in front of the barn?"
>
> Group C: The control group received only the 40 filler questions.

One week later all the subjects returned and answered 20 new questions about the film. Five of the questions were the exact same key questions as were asked of the direct-question group a week before. So group D saw those five questions twice. The measurement used was the percentage of subjects in each group who claimed to remember the non-existent objects.

Results

Table 1 summarizes the findings for all three groups. Remember, there was no school bus, truck, center line on the road, woman pushing the carriage, or barn in the film. Combining all the questions, the overall percentages of those subjects answering "yes" to the direct questions one week later were: 29.2 percent for the false-presupposition group, 15.6 percent for the direct-question group, and 8.4 percent for the control group. The differences between the direct-question group and the false-presupposition group for each item as well as for all the items combined were statistically significant. However, while there is a trend to indicate a similar effect of the direct questions over controls, these differences were not large enough to reach statistical significance.

DISCUSSION

Based on these and other studies, Loftus argued that an accurate theory of memory and recall must include a process of reconstruction that occurs when new information is integrated into the original memory of an event. To simply assume that recall involves only a re-creation of an event, with varying degrees of accuracy, cannot explain the findings of these studies. To illustrate, Figure 1 compares the traditional view of recall with the reformulated process proposed by Loftus. As you can see, the extra step of integrating new information into memory has been added. This new information, in turn, causes your representation of the original memory to be altered or reconstructed. Later, if you are asked a question about the event, your recall will not be of the actual original event, but of your reconstruction of it. Loftus contended that this reconstruction process was the reason that barns, school busses, trucks, women pushing baby carriages, and center lines in roads were all conjured up in subjects' memories when they were not part of the original experience. The false presupposition in the questions asked provided a subtle form of new information that was unintentionally integrated into the original memory of the event.

In applying this to eyewitnesses in criminal investigations, Loftus pointed out that often witnesses are questioned more than once. They might be asked questions by police at the scene of the crime, interviewed

TABLE 1   Appearance of Non-Existent Objects in Subjects' Recall of Filmed Accident Following Direct Questions and False Presuppositions

DIRECT QUESTION	FALSE PRESUPPOSITION	PERCENT OF "YES" RESPONSES TO DIRECT QUESTION ONE WEEK LATER		
		C	D	F
Did you see a school bus in the film?	Did you see the children getting on the school bus?	6	12	26
Did you see a truck in the beginning of the film?	At the beginning of the film, was the truck parked beside the car?	0	8	22
Did you see a center line on the country road?	Did another car cross the center line on the country road?	8	14	26
Did you see a woman pushing the carriage?	Did the woman pushing the carriage cross into the road?	26	36	54
Did you see a barn in the film?	Did you see a station wagon parked in front of the barn?	2	8	18

C = control group
D = direct-question group
F = false-presupposition group
(from p. 568)

by the prosecuting attorney assigned to the case, and again examined if they testify in court. During these various sessions of questions it is not unlikely that false presuppositions will be made, probably unintentionally. There are innumerable ways in which this might happen. Common, innocent-sounding questions such as "What did the guy's gun look like?" or "Where was the getaway car parked?" have been shown to increase the chances that witnesses will remember a gun or a getaway car whether or not they were actually there (Smith and Ellsworth, 1987). So, while the witness, the attorneys, the judge, and the jury are making the assumption that the witness is recreating what was actually seen, Loftus contends that what is being remembered by the witness is a "regenerated image based on the altered memorial representation" (p. 571).

CONCLUSIONS

Elizabeth Loftus is considered by most to be the leading researcher in the areas of memory reconstruction and eyewitness inaccuracy. Her research in these areas continues (see Loftus and Hoffman, 1989). Her

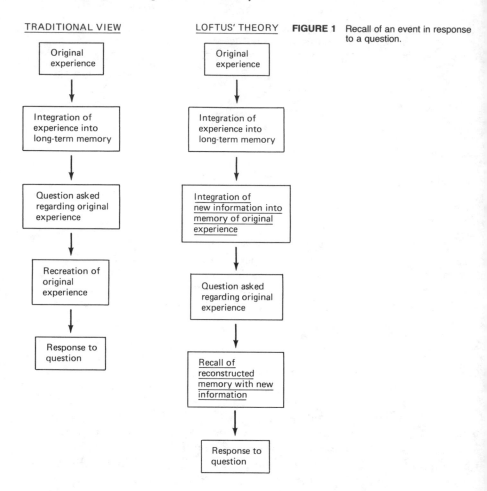

TRADITIONAL VIEW   LOFTUS' THEORY   **FIGURE 1** Recall of an event in response to a question.

findings over the years have held up quite well to challenges and have been supported by other researchers in the field.

This is not to say that her work is without criticism. Several researchers have argued that the integration of new information may *lead* a witness to incorrect answers, but that the original correct memory is not lost and may be accessed under the right conditions (see Bekerian and Bowers, 1983). Others have suggested that, if asked to think very carefully, eyewitnesses are actually able to discriminate between objects they actually saw and suggestions that were made to them after the original event (Lindsay and Johnson, 1989).

There is little doubt, however, that in the course of criminal prosecutions, eyewitness reports are subject to many sources of error such as post-event information integration. It is because of the body of research by Loftus and others that the power and reliability of eyewitnesses in judicial proceedings is being seriously questioned. Loftus herself is one of the most sought-after expert witnesses (usually for the defense) to demonstrate to juries the care they must use when evaluating the testimony of eyewitnesses.

BEKERIAN, D., and BOWERS, J. (1983) Eyewitness testimony: Were we misled? *Journal of Experimental Psychology: Learning, Memory and Cognition*, 9, 139–45.

LINDSAY, D., and JOHNSON, M. (1989) The eyewitness suggestibility effect and memory of source. *Memory and Cognition*, 17, 349–58.

LOFTUS, E., and HOFFMAN, H. (1989) Misinformation and memory: The creation of new memories. *Journal of Experimental Psychology: General*, 118, 100–104.

SMITH, V., and ELLSWORTH, P. (1987) The social psychology of eyewitness accuracy: Leading questions and communicator expertise. *Journal of Applied Psychology*, 72, 294–300.

FIVE

HUMAN
DEVELOPMENT

This subfield of psychology is concerned with the changes everyone goes through from birth to death. That's all. This is one of the largest and most complex specialties in the behavioral sciences. Although we grow up to be unique individuals, a great deal of our development is similar and predictable, and occurs according to certain relatively fixed schedules. Included among the most influential areas of research in developmental psychology are the processes of attachment or bonding between infant and mother, the development of intellectual abilities, and the changes relating to the aging process.

Some of the most famous and influential research ever conducted in pscyhology is discussed in this section. The work by Dr. Harry Harlow with monkeys demonstrated the importance of early infant attachments in later psychological adjustment. The sweeping discoveries of Jean Piaget formed the entire foundation of what we know today about cognitive development. A small sample of his research is included here in detail so that the ingenuity of his methods and clarity of his findings may be glimpsed. Also discussed is an influential study by Robert Zajonc about environmental influences on intelligence. In addition, since human development is a lifelong process, a well-known project by Ellen Langer and Judith Rodin (often referred to as "the plant study") is included to illustrate how everyone, no matter how old, needs to feel in control of their own lives, activities, and destinies.

DISCOVERING LOVE
Harlow, Harry F. (1958) The nature of love. *American Psychologist,* 13, 673–85.

Sometimes it seems that research psychologists have gone too far. How can something such as *love* be studied scientifically? Well, however you define love, you'll have to agree that it influences a huge amount of our behavior. If we make that assumption, then it follows that psychologists would have to be interested in what it is, where you get it, and how it works.

Harry Harlow, a developmental psychologist, is considered by many to have made the greatest contribution since Freud in studying how our early life experiences affect adulthood. Most psychologists agree that your experiences as an infant with closeness, touching, and attachment to your mother (or primary caregiver) have an important influence on your abilities to love and be close to others later in life. After all, if you think about it, what was your first experience with love? It was the bond between you and your mother beginning at the moment of your birth. But what exactly was it about that connection that was so crucial? The Freudians believed that it was the focus around the importance of the breast and the instinctive oral tendencies during the first year of life (the famous "oral stage"). Later, the behaviorists countered that notion with the view that all human behavior is associated with our so-called primary needs, such as hunger, thirst, and avoidance of pain. Since the mother can fill these needs, the infant's closeness with her is constantly reinforced by the fact that she provides food for the infant. Consequently, the mother becomes associated with pleasurable events and, therefore, love develops. In both of these conceptualizations, love was seen as something secondary to other instinctive or survival needs. However, Harlow discovered that love and affection may be primary needs that are just as strong or even stronger than those of hunger or thirst.

One way to begin to uncover the components of the love between an infant and mother would be to place infants in situations where the mother does not provide for all of the infant's needs and where various components of the environment can be scientifically manipulated. According to previous theories, we should be able to prevent or change the quality and strength of the bond formed between the infant and mother by altering the mother's ability to meet the infant's primary needs. For ethical reasons, however, it is obvious that such research could not be done on humans. Since Harlow had been working with rhesus monkeys for several years in his studies of learning, it was a simple process to begin his studies of love and attachment with these subjects. Biologically, rhesus monkeys are very similar to humans.

Harlow also believed that the basic responses of the rhesus monkey relating to bonding and affection in infancy (such as nursing, contact, clinging, etc.) are the same for the two species. Whether such research with non-human subjects is ethical will be addressed later in this chapter.

THEORETICAL PROPOSITIONS

In Harlow's previous studies, infant monkeys were raised carefully by humans in the laboratory so that they could be bottle-fed better, receive well-balanced nutritional diets, and be protected from disease more effectively than if they were raised by their monkey mothers. Harlow noticed that these infant monkeys became very attached to the cloth pads (cotton diapers) that were used to cover the bottoms of their cages. They would cling to these pads and would become extremely angry and agitated when the pads were removed for cleaning. This attachment was seen in the baby monkeys as early as one day old and was even stronger over the monkeys' first several months of life. Apparently, as Harlow states, "the baby, human or monkey, if it is to survive, must clutch at more than a straw" (p. 675). If a baby monkey was in a cage without this soft covering, it would thrive very poorly even though it received complete nutritional and medical care. When the cloth was introduced, the infant would become healthier and seemingly content. Therefore, Harlow theorized that there must be some basic need in these infant monkeys for close contact with something soft and comforting in addition to primary biological needs such as hunger and thirst. In order to test this theory, Harlow and his associates decided to "build" different kinds of experimental monkey mothers.

METHOD

The first surrogate "mother" they built consisted of a smooth wooden body covered in sponge rubber and terry cloth. It was equipped with a "breast" in the chest area that delivered milk and contained a light bulb inside for warmth. They then constructed a different kind of surrogate mother that was less able to provide soft comfort. This mother was made of wire mesh shaped about the same as the wooden frame, so that an infant monkey could cling to it in a similar way as to the cloth mother. This wire mother also came equipped with a working nursing "breast" and also was able to provide heat. In other words, the wire mother was identical to the cloth mother in every way except for the ability to offer what Harlow called "contact comfort."

These manufactured mothers were then placed in separate cubicles that were attached to the infant monkeys' living cage. Eight infant monkeys were randomly assigned to two groups. For one group, the cloth mother was equipped with the feeder (a nursing bottle) to provide milk and for the other group, the wire mother was the milk provider. I'm sure you can already see what Harlow was testing here. He was attempting to *separate* the influence of nursing from the influence of contact comfort on the monkeys' behavior toward the "mother." The monkeys were then placed in their cages and the amount of time they spent in direct contact with each mother was recorded for the first five months of their lives. The results were striking, but we'll get to those shortly.

Following these preliminary studies, Harlow wanted to explore the effects of attachment and contact comfort in greater detail. Common knowledge tells us that when children are afraid, they will seek out the comfort of their mothers (or other primary caregivers). To find out how the young monkeys with the wire and cloth mothers would respond in such situations, Harlow placed in their cages various objects that caused a fearful reaction in them, such as a wind-up drum-playing toy bear. (To a baby monkey this bear, which is as big as the monkey itself, is very frightening.) The responses of the monkeys in these situations was observed and recorded carefully.

Another study Harlow developed was called the "open field test" and involved placing young monkeys in a small, unfamiliar room containing various objects (wooden blocks, blankets, containers with lids, a folded piece of paper) that, under normal conditions, monkeys like to play with and manipulate. The monkeys who were raised with both the cloth and wire mothers were placed in the room with either the cloth mother present, no mother present, or the wire mother present. The idea here was to examine the tendency of the young monkeys to adapt to and explore this strange situation with or without the presence of the mother.

Finally, Harlow wanted to find out if the attachments formed between the monkeys and their surrogate mothers would persist after periods of separation. When the monkeys reached 6 months of age and were on solid food diets, they were separated for short periods from the mother, and then reunited in the open-field situation.

RESULTS

In the original experiment you will remember that all the monkeys had access to both the cloth mother and the wire mother. For half the monkeys the cloth mother provided the milk and for the other half the wire mother did so. By now you've probably guessed that the monkeys preferred the cloth mother (wouldn't you?), but what was so surprising was the extreme strength of this preference even among those monkeys who received their milk from the wire mother. Contrary to the popular theories at the time of this research, the fulfilling of biological needs such as hunger and thirst was of almost no importance in the monkeys' choice of a mother. The huge influence of *contact comfort* in producing an attachment between infant and mother monkey was clearly demonstrated. Figure 1 graphically illustrates this effect. After the first few days of adjustment, all the monkeys, regardless of which mother had the milk, were spending nearly all their time each day on the cloth mother. Even those monkeys who were fed by the wire mother would only leave the comfort of the cloth mother to nurse briefly and then return to the cloth-covered surrogate immediately.

The two groups of monkeys that were raised with only a cloth or wire mother further demonstrated the importance of contact comfort. While both groups of these infants ate the same amount and gained

FIGURE 1 Amount of time spent each day on the cloth and wire mothers.

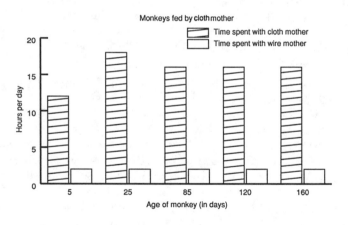

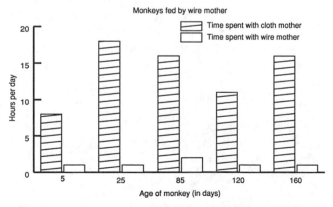

weight at the same rate, the infants in the wire mother condition did not digest the milk as well and experienced frequent bouts of diarrhea. This suggests that the lack of the soft mother was psychologically stressful to these infants.

The results of the frightening-object tests provided additional evidence of the young monkeys' attachment to the cloth mother. Whenever the monkeys found themselves faced with something frightening they would run to the cloth mother and cling to it for comfort and protection. As the monkeys' age increased, this response became even stronger. Again, it made no difference whether a monkey had received its milk from the wire or the cloth mother; when afraid, they all sought the security of the soft, cloth-covered surrogate.

You may have noticed in humans that when children feel safe and secure because of the presence of a parent, they are more curious and more willing to explore their environment. Often, they will investigate everything around them, provided they are able to see the parent. Harlow's strange-situation or open-field tests were designed to simulate this behavior in the monkeys in relation to the surrogate mothers. When placed into this strange room, all the monkeys immediately rushed to the cloth mother, clutched it, rubbed their bodies against it, and manipulated its body and face. After a while these infants "began to use the mother surrogate as a source of security, a base of operations. . . . They would explore and manipulate a stimulus and then return to the mother before adventuring again into the strange new world" (p. 679).

However, when the infant monkeys were placed into the same room without the soft mother, their reactions were completely different. They would freeze with fear and engage in emotional behaviors such as crying, crouching, and thumb-sucking. Sometimes they would run to the part of the room where the mother usually was and then run from object to object, screaming and crying. When the wire mother was present they behaved exactly the same as in the no-mother condition. This was once again true of all the monkeys, regardless of the nursing condition (cloth vs. wire) in which they had been raised.

Getting back to the last part of the study mentioned previously, the monkeys were separated from the mother for various periods of time after they stopped nursing and were on solid-food diets (about 5 to 6 months of age). In the longest separation (30 days) the monkeys were reunited with the cloth mother in the same open-field situation. When this reunion occurred, the monkeys rushed to the mother, climbed on it, clutched it tightly, and rubbed their heads and faces on its body. They then played with the surrogate mother, which included biting and tearing at the cloth cover. The main difference was that the monkeys did not leave the mother to explore and play with the objects in the room as they had done before. Apparently, according to Harlow, the need for contact comfort was greater than the natural tendency for exploration. It should be pointed out, however, that these reunions only lasted about three minutes and that such exploration may have occurred if the sessions had been extended.

DISCUSSION

As Harlow points out quite clearly, the studies reported in this article demonstrate the overwhelming importance of *contact comfort* in the development of attachment between infant monkeys and their mothers. In fact, this factor in bonding appears to be considerably more important than the mother's ability to provide life-sustaining milk to the infant.

One of the many reasons this research changed psychology is that the findings went against the grain of the popular beliefs of the behaviorists at that time, who focused on the reinforcement qualities of feeding as the driving force behind the infant-mother bond. However, as Harlow stated about his findings, "the primary function of nursing as an affectional variable is that of ensuring frequent and intimate body contact of the infant with the mother. Certainly, man cannot live by milk alone" (p. 677).

There is little question that Harlow believed that his results could be applied to humans, a question that will be briefly discussed shortly. In fact, he offered the possibility of his findings' practical applications to humans. He contended that as socioeconomic demands on the family increase, women would be entering the workplace with increasing frequency. This was of concern to many at the time of Harlow's research, since it was widely believed that the mother's presence for nursing was necessary for attachment and proper child-rearing. He went on to state that, since the key to successful parenting is contact comfort and not the "mammalian capabilities" of women, the American male is able to participate on equal terms in the rearing of infants. This view may be widely accepted today, but when Harlow wrote this in 1958, it was revolutionary.

CRITICISMS AND CONTRIBUTIONS

Harlow's claims notwithstanding, do you think it's appropriate to view humans as having the same attachment (or love) processes as monkeys? There has been some research to support the view that the attachment of human babies to their caregivers does indeed go well beyond simply fulfilling biological needs. It has been shown that greater skin-to-skin contact between a mother and her very young infant enhances attachment (Klaus and Kennell, 1976). However, the attachment process develops much more slowly in humans: over the first six months compared with the first few days for monkeys. In addition, only approximately 70 percent of children appear to be securely attached to an adult at 1-year-old (Sroufe, 1985).

There are many people, past and present, who would offer criticisms of Harlow's work based on the ethics of performing such experiments on infant monkeys. The question raised is this: Do we as humans have the right to subject monkeys (or any animal) to potentially harmful situations for the sake of research? In the case of Harlow's research there are sensible arguments on both sides. One of the ways science judges the ethics of such research is by examining the potential benefits to people and society. Whether you feel that this study was ethical or not, the findings have affected humans in several positive ways. Some of these relate to issues of institutionalized children, adoption, and child abuse.

Unfortunately, many children in our culture are forced to spend portions of their lives in institutional settings, either because their parents are unable to keep and care for them (orphanages), or because of their own various illnesses and other physical difficulties (hospital settings). Harlow's research has influenced the kind of care we try to provide for those children. There is now general acceptance that basic biological care in institutional settings is inadequate, and that infants need to be in physical contact with other humans. Therefore, institutionalized children are handled and held by staff members, nurses, and volunteers as much as possible. Also, when not precluded by medical conditions, these children are often placed in situations where they can see and touch each other, thereby gaining additional contact comfort. While such attempts at filling attachment needs will never replace real parental care, they are clearly a vast improvement over simple custodial care.

The work of Harlow offered encouragement and optimism for non-maternal caregivers to be effective parents. Since it appeared that nursing was secondary to contact comfort in the development and adjustment of infants, the actual mother of a child was no longer seen as the only proper person to provide care. Now, as mentioned above, fathers could feel more adequate to assume a larger role in the process. But beyond this, other non-parental caregivers, such as baby sitters or day-care center workers, when necessary, could be seen as acceptable options. Moreover, these discoveries greatly enhanced the prospect of adoption, since it was recognized that an adoptive parent could offer a child just as much contact comfort as a biological parent could.

Finally, Harlow's studies shed light on the terrible problem of child abuse. One surprising aspect of such abusive relationships is that in nearly all cases, the abused child seems to love and to be firmly attached to the abusive parent. According to a strict behaviorist interpretation, this is difficult to understand. But if attachment is the strongest basic need, as Harlow suggested, then this would far outweigh the effects of the abusive punishment. Harlow actually tested this in later studies. He designed surrogate mother monkeys that were able to reject their infants. Some emitted strong jets of air, while others had blunt spikes that would pop out and force the baby monkeys away. The way the monkeys would respond to this treatment would be to move a small distance away until the rejection ended. They would then return and cling to the mother as tightly as ever (Rosenblum and Harlow, 1963).

CONCLUSION

It would be a mistake to assume that Harlow had a monopoly on the definition of the nature of love. It is unmistakable, however, that his discoveries changed the way we view the connection between infant and mother. Perhaps, if this research has permeated, at least a little, into our culture, some good has come from it. For example, Harlow tells the story of a woman who, after hearing Harlow present his research, came up to him and said, "Now I know what's wrong with me! I'm just a wire mother" (p. 677).

KLAUS, M.H., and KENNELL, J.H. (1976) *Maternal infant bonding*. St. Louis: Mosby.
ROSENBLUM, L.A. and HARLOW, H. (1963) Approach-avoidance conflict in the mother surrogate situation. *Psychological Reports*, 12, 83–85.
SROUFE, A. (1985) Attachment classification from the perspective of the infant-caregiver relationships and infant temperament. *Child Development*, 56, 1–14.

OUT OF SIGHT, BUT NOT OUT OF MIND
Piaget, Jean (1954) The development of object concept. *The construction of reality in the child*. New York: Basic Books Inc., 3–96.

The question this chapter focuses on is this: How did you progress from an infant, with a few elementary thinking skills, to the adult you are now, with the ability to reason and analyze the world in many complex ways involving language, symbols, and logic? Your first reaction to this question may very likely be to say, "Well, I acquired these intellectual abilities through learning: the process of interacting with my environment and the teaching I received from adults as I developed." While this explanation seems intuitively correct to most people, many developmental psychologists believe that there is much more to acquiring intellectual abilities than simple learning. The prevailing view about intellectual development is that it is a process of maturation, much like physical development, that occurs in a predictable fashion from birth through adulthood.

Do you look at an infant and see a person who, with enough learning, is capable of adult physical behaviors? Of course not. Instead you know that there is a process of physical maturation that will enable the child to behave in increasingly complex ways over time. Until the child achieves a given level of development, all the learning in the world cannot produce certain behaviors. For example, consider the behavior of walking. You probably think of walking as a learned behavior. But imagine trying to teach a 6-month-old to walk. You could place the infant on an Olympic schedule of eight hours of practice every day, and the child will not learn to walk. This is because the child has not yet reached the physical *maturity* to be able to perform the behavior of walking.

Intellectual, or cognitive, development is seen by most researchers in much the same way. There are certain levels of thinking and reasoning ability that cannot be understood until an appropriate stage of cognitive development has been reached, no matter how much learning takes place. Psychology owes its realization and understanding of this conceptualization of cognitive development to the work of the Swiss psychologist, Jean Piaget.

Piaget is one of the most influential figures in the history of psychology. His work not only revolutionized developmental psychology, but is the foundation of all subsequent investigations in the area of the formation of the intellect. Piaget was originally trained as a biologist, and studied the inborn ability of animals to adapt to new environments. While Piaget was studying at the Sorbonne in Paris, he accepted a job (to earn extra money) at the Alfred Binet Laboratory, where the first intelligence tests had been developed. He was hired to standardize a French version of a reasoning test that had been developed in English. The reason such tests are standardized is so that each child who takes the test will receive the same questions. In this way, any differences in scores can be attributed to the child and not to variations in the test. It was during his employment in Paris that Piaget began to formulate his theories about cognitive development.

THEORETICAL PROPOSITIONS

The work at the Binet Laboratory was tedious and not very interesting to Piaget at first. But then he began to notice some interesting patterns in the answers given by children at various ages to the questions on the test. Children at similar ages appeared to be making the same mistakes. That is, they were using the same reasoning to reach the same answers. And what fascinated Piaget was not the correct answers, but the thinking that produced the *wrong* answers. Based on these observations, he theorized that older children had not just learned more than the younger ones, but were *thinking differently* about the problems. This led him to question the current prevailing definition of intelligence, based on a test score, in favor of one that involved a more complete understanding of the cognitive strategies used by children at various ages (Ginzburg and Opper, 1979).

Piaget devoted the next 50 years of his life and career to studying intellectual development in children. His work led to his famous theory of cognitive development, which for decades was a virtually undisputed explanation for how humans acquire their complex thinking skills. His theory holds that *all humans* develop through four stages of cognitive development that always occur in the same sequence and at approximately the same ages. For the sake of brevity, these are summarized in Table 1.

As important as his theory itself were the techniques Piaget used to study the thinking abilities in children. At the Binet Laboratory, he realized that if his new conceptualization of intelligence were to be explored, new methods had to be developed. Instead of the usual, overly rigid standardized tests, he proposed an interview technique that allowed the child's answers to influence the direction of the questioning. In this way the processes underlying the child's answers could be best explored.

One of the most remarkable aspects of Piaget's research is that in reaching many of his conclusions, he studied his own children, Lucienne, Jacqueline, and Laurent. By today's scientific standards, this method would be highly questionable because of the rather extreme possibility of bias and lack of objectivity. However, as there are always exceptions to rules, Piaget's findings from his children have been successfully applied to all children universally.

Obviously there is insufficient space in this single chapter to explore more than a small fraction of Piaget's work. Therefore, we will focus on his discovery of a key intellectual skill called "object permanence." This ability provides an excellent example of one of Piaget's most important findings as well as ample opportunity to experience his methods of research.

Object permanence refers to your ability to know that an object exists even when it is out of reach of your senses. If someone walks over to you now and takes this book out of your hands and runs into the other room, do you think that the book or the book-snatcher has ceased to exist? No; you have a *concept* of the book and the person in your mind even though you cannot see, hear, or touch them. However,

TABLE 1 Piaget's Stages of Cognitive Development

STAGE	AGE RANGE	MAJOR CHARACTERISTICS
Sensori-motor	0–2 years	• All knowledge is acquired through senses and movement (such as looking and grasping) • Thinking is at the same speed as physical movement • Object permanence develops
Preoperational	2–7 years	• Thinking separates from movement and increases greatly in speed • Ability to think in symbols • Non-logical, "magical" thinking • Animism: all objects have thoughts and feelings • Egocentric thinking: unable to see world from others' points of view
Concrete operations	7–11 years	• Logical thinking develops, including classifying objects and mathematical principles, but only as they apply to real, concrete objects • Conservation of liquid, area, volume • Ability to infer what others may be feeling or thinking
Formal operations	11 and up	• Logical thinking extends to hypothetical and abstract concepts • Can reason using metaphors and analogies • Can explore values, beliefs, philosophies • Can think about past and future • Not all people use formal operations to the same degree, and some not at all

according to Piaget, this was not always true for you. He demonstrated that your cognitive ability to conceive of objects as permanent was something you and everyone else developed beginning at about 8 months of age. The reason this ability is important is that without it, problem-solving and internal thinking are impossible. Therefore, before a child can leave the sensori-motor stage (0 to 2 years; see Table 1) and enter the preoperational period (2 to 7 years), object permanence must be mastered.

METHOD AND RESULTS

The process of developing the cognitive skill of object permanence was studied by Piaget using his unstructured evaluation methods. For infants and very young children, these techniques often took the form of games that he would play with his children. Through observing their problem-solving ability and the errors they made in the games, Piaget identified six substages of development that occur during the sensori-motor period and are involved in the formation of the object concept. For you to experience the flavor of his research, these six stages will be summarized here with examples of Piaget's interactions with his children from his own observational journals.

STAGE 1. (Birth to 1 month) This stage is concerned primarily with reflexes relating to feeding and touching. There is no evidence of object permanence during this first month of life.

STAGE 2. (1 to 4 months) During stage 2, while there is still no sign of an object concept, there are behaviors that Piaget interprets as preparing the infant for this ability. The child begins to repeat purposely behaviors that center on the infant's own body. For example, if an infant's hand accidentally comes in contact with its foot it might reproduce the same movements over and over again to cause the event to be repeated. Piaget called these "primary circular reactions." Also, at this stage, infants are able to follow moving objects with their eyes. Often, if an object leaves the child's visual field his or her gaze will remain fixed on the spot where it disappeared as if expecting it to return. While this may seem to indicate a concept of the permanence of the object, Piaget claimed it did not because the child would not actively search for the vanished object, if the object fails to reappear, the child will turn its attention to other visible objects. Piaget called this behavior "passive expectation." The following interaction between Piaget and his son, Laurent, illustrates this.

Observation 2. Laurent at 0;2 [zero years, two months]. I look at him through the hood of his bassinet and from time to time I appear at a more or less constant point; Laurent then watches that point when I am out of his sight and obviously expects me to reappear. (p. 9)

The child limits himself to looking at the place where the object vanished: Thus he merely preserves the attitude of the earlier perception and if nothing reappears, he soon gives up. If he had the object concept . . . he would actively search to find out where the thing could have been put. . . . But this is precisely what he does not know how to do, for the vanished object is not yet a permanent object which has been moved; it is a mere image which reenters the void as soon as it vanishes, and emerges from it for no objective reason (p. 11).

STAGE 3. (4 to 10 months) It is during this stage that children begin to purposefully and repeatedly manipulate objects they encounter in their environment (secondary circular reactions). The child begins to reach for and grasp things, to shake them, bring them closer to look at or place in the mouth, and to acquire the ability of rapid eye movements to follow quickly moving or falling objects. Late in this stage, the first signs of object permanence appear. For example, children begin to search for objects that are obscured from view if a small part of the object is visible.

Observation 23. At 0;9 I offer [Lucienne] a celluloid goose which she has never seen before; she grasps it at once and examines it all over. I place the goose beside her and cover it before her eyes, sometimes completely, sometimes revealing the head. Two very distinct reactions. . . . When the goose disappears completely, Lucienne immediately stops searching even when she is on the point of grasping it. . . . When the beak protrudes, not only does she grasp the visible part and draw the animal to her, but . . . she sometimes raises the coverlet beforehand in order to grasp the whole thing! . . . Never, even after having raised the coverlet several times on seeing the beak appear, has Lucienne tried to raise it when the goose was completely hidden! Here . . . is proof of the fact that the reconstruction of a totality is much easier than search for an invisible object. (p. 29–30)

Still, however, Piaget maintains that the object concept is not fully formed. To the child at this stage, the object does not have an independent existence, but is tied to the child's own actions and sensory perceptions. In other words, "it would be impossible to say that the half-hidden objective is conceived as being masked by a screen; it is simply perceived as being in the process of disappearing" (p. 35).

STAGE 4. (10 to 12 months) During the later weeks of stage 3 and early in stage 4 children have learned that objects continue to exist even when they are no longer in sight. A child will search actively and creatively for an object that has been completely hidden from view. While on the surface this may indicate a fully developed object concept, Piaget found that this cognitive ability is still incomplete because the child still lacks the ability to understand "visible displacements." To understand what Piaget meant by this, consider the following example (you can try this yourself!). If you sit with an 11-month-old and hide a toy completely under a towel (call this place A), the child will search for and find it. The object obviously continued to exist for the child and did not "enter the void." However, if you then openly hide the toy under a blanket (place B), the child will probably go back to searching where it was previously found, in place A. Furthermore, you can repeat this process over and over and the child will continue to make the same error, called the "A not B effect."

Observation 40. At 0;10 Jacqueline is seated on a mattress. . . . I take her parrot from her hands and hide it twice in succession under the mattress, on her left, in A. Both times Jacqueline looks for the object immediately and grabs it. Then I take it from her hands and move it very slowly before her eyes to the corresponding place on her right, under the mattress, in B. Jacqueline watches the movement very attentively, but at the moment when the parrot disappears in B she turns to her left and looks where it was before, in A. (p. 51)

Piaget's interpretation of this error in stage 4 was not that children are absentminded, but that the object concept is not the same for them as it is for you or me. To 10-month-old Jacqueline, her parrot is not an individual, permanent, separate thing that exists independently of her actions. When it was hidden and successfully found in A it became a "parrot-in-A," a thing that was defined not only by its "parrotness," but also by its hiding place. In other words, the parrot is just a piece of the overall picture in the child's mind and not a separate object.

STAGE 5. (12 to 18 months) Beginning around the end of the first year of life, the child gains the ability to follow visible sequential displacements and searches for an object where it was last visibly hidden. When this happens, Piaget claimed that the child had entered stage 5 of the sensori-motor period.

Observation 54. Laurent, at 0;11, is seated between two cushions, A and B. I hide the watch alternately under each; Laurent constantly searches for the object where it has just disappeared, that is sometimes in A, sometimes in B, without remaining attached to a privileged position as during the preceding stage. (p. 67)

However, Piaget points out that true object permanence remains incomplete because the child is unable to understand what he called "invisible displacements." Imagine the following example. You watch someone place a coin in a small box and then, with their back to you, they walk over to the dresser and open a drawer. When they return you discover that the box is empty. This is an invisible displacement of the object. Naturally, you would go to the dresser and look in the drawer. Well, as Piaget demonstrated, perhaps that is not so natural.

Observation 55. At 1;6 Jacqueline is sitting on a green rug and playing with a potato, which interests her very much (it is a new object for her). She . . . amuses herself by putting it into an empty box and taking it out again. I then take the potato and put it in the box while Jacqueline watches. Then I place the box under the rug and turn it upside down, thus leaving the object hidden by the rug without letting the child see my maneuver, and I bring out the empty box. I say to Jacqueline, who has not stopped looking at the rug and who realized that I was doing something under it: "Give Papa the potato." She searches for the object in the box, looks at me, again looks at the box minutely, looks at the rug, etc., but it does not occur to her to raise the rug in order to find the potato underneath. During the five subsequent attempts the reaction is uniformly negative. (p. 68)

STAGE 6. (18 to 24 months) Finally, as the child approaches the end of the sensori-motor period (refer back to Table 1), the concept of the permanent object becomes fully realized. Entry into this stage is determined by the child's ability to represent mentally objects that undergo invisible displacements.

Observation 66. At 1;7 Jacqueline reveals herself to be . . . capable of conceiving of the object under a series of superimposed or encasing screens. . . . I put the pencil in the box, put a piece of paper around it, wrap this in a handkerchief, then cover the whole thing with the beret and the coverlet. Jacqueline removes these last two screens, then unfolds the handkerchief. She does not find the box right away, but continues looking for it, evidently convinced of its presence; she then perceives the paper, recognizes it immediately, unfolds it, opens the box, and grasps the pencil. (p. 81)

Piaget considered this cognitive skill of object permanence to be the beginning of true thought: the ability to use insight and mental symbolism to solve problems. This, then, prepares the child to move into the next full stage of cognitive development: the preoperational period, during which thought separates from action, which allows the speed of mental operations to increase greatly. In other words, object permanence is the foundation for all subsequent advances in intellectual ability. As Piaget stated, "The conservation of the object is, among other things, a function of its localization; that is, the child simultaneously learns that the object does not cease to exist when it disappears and he learns where it does go. This fact shows from the outset that the formation of the schema of the permanent object is closely related to the whole spatio-temporal and causal organization of the practical universe" (Piaget and Inhelder, 1969).

DISCUSSION

This method of exercises and observation of behavior formed the basis of Piaget's work throughout his formulation of all four stages of cognitive development. Piaget contended that all of his stages applied universally to all children, regardless of cultural or family background. Additionally, he stressed several important aspects relating to the stages of development of the object concept during the sensori-motor period (see Ginzburg and Opper, 1979, for an elaboration of these points).

1. The ages associated with each stage are approximate. Since Piaget's early work only involved three children, it was difficult for him to predict age ranges with a great deal of confidence. For example, certain abilities he observed in Jacqueline at age 1;7 were present in Lucienne at 1;3. However, as research has continued over the years, the ages described by Piaget have proven to be, on average, quite accurate.
2. Piaget maintained, however, that the sequence of the stages was invariant. All children must pass through each stage before going on to the next, and no stage can ever be skipped.
3. Changes from one stage to the next occur gradually over time so that the errors being made at one stage slowly begin to decrease as new intellectual abilities mature. Piaget believed that it is quite common and normal for children to be between stages and exhibiting abilities from earlier and later stages at the same time.
4. As a child moves into the next higher stage, the behaviors associated with the lower stages do not necessarily disappear completely. It would not be unusual for a child in stage 6 to apply intellectual strategies used in stage 5. Then when these prove unsuccessful, the child will invoke new methods for solving the problem typical of stage 6 reasoning.

CRITICISMS OF PIAGET'S THEORY

Although Piaget's conceptualization of cognitive development has dominated the field of developmental psychology for the last 40 years, he has certainly not been without critics. Some of them have focused primarily on questioning Piaget's basic notion that cognitive development happens in discrete stages. Many learning theorists have disagreed with Piaget on this issue and contend that intellectual development is continuous, without any particular sequence built into the process. They believe that cognitive abilities, like all other behaviors, are a result of modeling and a person's learning and conditioning history.

Other critics of Piaget's ideas have claimed that the age ranges at which he claimed certain abilities appear are incorrect, and some even argue that certain abilities may not develop at all, but are already present at birth. Object permanence is one of those abilities that has been drawn into question. In a series of ingenious studies, using newly developed methodologies, Rene Baillargeon has demonstrated that infants as young as 3 months old appear to possess object permanence (Baillargeon, 1987). She and others assert that the methods used by Piaget were inadequate to accurately measure the abilities of small infants.

CONCLUSION

As new methods for studying infants' cognitive abilities have been developed, such as preference-looking and habituation-dishabituation techniques, some of Piaget's discoveries are being drawn into question (see Dworetzky, 1990, pp. 126–27, for a discussion of such research methods). In fact, there are numerous ongoing controversies surrounding his theory of cognitive development. This controversy is healthy in that it motivates research that will eventually lead to even greater improvements in our knowledge about our intellectual abilities.

Controversy notwithstanding, Piaget's theory remains the catalyst and foundation for all related research. His work continues to guide enlightened people's ideas about research with children, methods of education, and styles of parenting. Piaget's contribution was and is immeasurable.

BAILLARGEON, R. (1987) Object permanence in 3-and-a-half- and 4-and-a-half-month-old infants. *Developmental Psychology*, 23, 655–64.
DWORETZKY, J. (1990) *Introduction to child development*, 4th ed. New York: West.
GINZBURG, H., and OPPER, S. (1979) *Piaget's theory of intellectual development*. Englewood Cliffs, N.J.: Prentice Hall.
PIAGET, J., and INHELDER, B. (1969) *The psychology of the child*. New York: Basic Books.

BORN FIRST, BORN SMARTER?

Zajonc, Robert B., and Markus, Gregory B. (1975) Birth order and intellectual development. *Psychological Review*, 82, 74–88.

Do you have brothers or sisters? Where do you fall in your family's birth order? Are you first-born, last-born, or somewhere in the middle? You probably have heard many theories about how birth order has influenced your development in some way. In fact, bookstores carry many books that claim to account for your entire personality based on your birth position in your family. Clearly, this overstates the case for the effect of birth order on development, but several studies have determined that being the first-born child in a family is related to certain characteristics. First-born children tend to be more verbally articulate, less impulsive, more active, better performers in school, more likely to go to college, and tend to have a greater need to achieve (see Ernst and Angst, 1983, for a complete discussion of birth order effects). One frequently cited example points out that of the first 23 American astronauts, 21 were first-borns. It is important to keep in mind that these research findings are general trends and certainly do not apply to all members of all families.

One of the more consistent findings in this line of research has been the relationship between birth order and intelligence. In general, studies have found that earlier-born children tend to score higher on tests of intelligence and aptitude than those born into the family later. If it is true that first-born children have greater intellectual abilities than their later-born siblings, the question of greatest interest to social and behavioral scientists is, why? One possible answer is that something about our genetic composition changes with birth order due to biological factors such as the age of the mother or chemical alterations caused by previous births. Scientists, however, have rejected these "nature" explanations in favor of more environmentally based "nurture" theories. There is little question that the environment in which a child develops can exert strong influences over his or her intellectual capacities and abilities (refer to the readings on the research by Rosenzweig, et al., 1972 and Rosenthal and Jacobson, 1968).

One environmental factor present in the development of all children is birth order. To understand the potential power of this factor, consider the first-born child who enters a world consisting only of (usually) two adult parents. Now compare this environment with that of the second child, born into an environment of two adults and one, often small, child. Even if all other influences are equal, the second child's developmental conditions are significantly different simply because of the presence of the other child. These differences grow and compound as each subsequent child is born.

Based on this idea, Robert Zajonc (pronounced zy-ence, "rhymes with science"), one of the foremost researchers in the history of psychology, and his associate, Gregory Markus, developed an ingenious theory to explain the relationship between birth order and intelligence. Their article was and still is one of the landmark publications in the literature on birth order. Theirs was an unusual study in that the researchers never came in contact with any subjects, never observed any subjects, and never asked subjects to do anything. In fact, one might say that they did not even have subjects. Instead, they applied their theory to a set of data that had been gathered and published by other researchers; or perhaps more correctly, they applied the other researchers' data to their theory.

In the late 1960s and early 1970s, an extensive research project was carried out in the Netherlands. It was designed to study the effects of malnutrition on the intellectual abilities of children born at the end of World War II. As part of this research, an intelligence test (called the "Raven" test, similar to our I.Q. tests) was given to over 350,000 Dutch males when they became 19 years of age. Two of the researchers on that project later reported a discovery that was not anticipated. They found a strong relationship in their data between the birth order of the men and their scores on the Raven test (see Belmont and Marolla, 1973). The surprising findings were that scores decreased as family size increased and also declined with birth order. The data from the Netherlands study are graphically shown in Figure 1.

Zajonc writes, "Belmont and Marolla, with their large data set, were able to rule out socioeconomic status as a significant factor in birth order effects, but they did not suggest factors or processes that might have explained their interesting results" (p. 76). Such an explanation was what Zajonc and Markus offered in their article.

THEORETICAL PROPOSITIONS

The authors theorized that children will attain higher intellectual capacities if they grow up in environments that provide greater intellectual stimulation. This stimulation, they contended, stems in part from the combined intellectual influences among the parents and children (these mutual influences were termed "confluences"). The key to their theory was that a family's intellectual environment may be calculated by averaging the intellectual contributions of all the family members. Moreover, this average necessarily changes as children develop and whenever an additional child is born into the family. So, you might be thinking, the bigger the family, the higher the intellectual

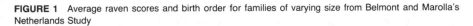

FIGURE 1 Average raven scores and birth order for families of varying size from Belmont and Marolla's Netherlands Study

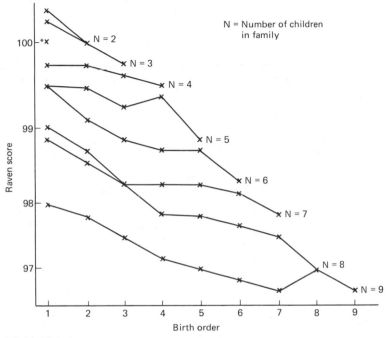

*Only-child average
(adapted from p. 75)

environment. This would predict that later-born children should possess greater intellectual skills. However, this was the opposite of the findings from the Netherlands study. To explain this, Zajonc and Markus proposed the theory that as family size increases, the average intellectual climate of the family *decreases*.

More specifically, their reasoning was as follows. When a couple have their first child, the intellectual climate consists of two adults and one infant. In order to find an actual confluence score for this family, intellectual values can be assigned to the family members. If each adult is assigned an intellectual value of 100, and the newborn infant receives a value of zero, the average intellectual level of the family is 67 (100 + 100 + 0 = 200 ÷ 3 = 67). Keep in mind, these are not I.Q. scores, but simple arbitrary values. Now, let's assume that a child's contribution to the intellectual climate of the family increases by 5 points each year. If this family has a second child two years after the first, the first child will now contribute 10 points, but the new average intellectual level for the family will drop to 52.5 (100 + 100 + 10 + 0 = 210 ÷ 4 = 52.5). If a third child is born in another two years, the family average will drop to 46 (100 + 100 + 20 + 10 + 0 = 230 ÷ 5 = 46). The authors contended that if this theory were to be applied to the data from the Belmont and Marolla study, it would explain their findings.

METHOD AND RESULTS

Table 1 summarizes how the intellectual climate of a large hypothetical family with 10 children would change over the years, according to the confluence model developed by Zajonc and Markus, assuming the children were spaced about two years apart.

As you can see by examining the third column in the table, the average intellectual climate drops steadily through the fifth child and then slowly begins to rise again. If you compare this to the data in Figure 1 you will see that in larger families there is somewhat of a leveling off or even an increase in scores for the extreme later-born children, with the exception of the last child, whose score dropped considerably. The authors contended that the data from Belmont and Marolla, for the most part, confirmed their theory.

However, Zajonc and Markus also noticed in the Netherlands research a surprising "only-child" effect. Based on the confluence theory, it would be logical to assume that children without siblings would grow up in the highest possible intellectual climate and consequently should have achieved the highest average Raven intelligence scores. Belmont and Marolla's findings indicated, however, that only children scored at the level of the first child in a family of four children (indicated with asterisk in Figure 1).

In their discussion, the authors addressed the possible reasons for these seemingly strange only-child and last-child effects, the improvement in later-born children in large families, and the implications of their findings in terms of intellectual development and family spacing.

DISCUSSION

The researchers concluded that their theoretical model explained the birth order and family size effects in the Belmont-Marolla data. The fundamental reason for this was that each successive child born into the family enters a lower average intellectual climate. This effect increases in strength if the time gaps between offspring are smaller. In Table 1, the gap between children is two years. If the gap were to be reduced to one year, the decrease in average intellectual level would drop much more sharply. In the extreme case, then, twins and triplets who are born with no gap should perform lower on tests of intelligence than non-twin

TABLE 1   Calculation of Intellectual Climate of a Large Family with Children Spaced Two Years Apart

NUMBER OF CHILDREN	INTELLECTUAL CLIMATE FORMULA	AVERAGE INTELLECTUAL CLIMATE
1	Mother (100) + Father (100) + Infant (0) Number in Family (3)	= 67.0
2	M (100) + F (100) + 2-year-old (10) + Infant (0) Number in Family (4)	= 52.5
3	230 ÷ 5	= 46.0
4	260 ÷ 6	= 43.3
5	300 ÷ 7	= 42.9
6	360 ÷ 8	= 45.0
7	480 ÷ 9	= 53.3
8	560 ÷ 10	= 56.0
9	650 ÷ 11	= 59.1
10	750 ÷ 12	= 62.5

Adults = 100 points
Children = 5 points per year of age

siblings. Several studies have found that twins and triplets do indeed score lower on such tests. As Zajonc and Markus point out, there could be many influences on the intellectual development of multiple birth children. However, they maintain that one reason for this difference may be that the average intellectual level for twins (in families with two children) is 50 (100 + 100 + 0 + 0 ÷ 4). For non-twin families with two children this average is 67 (100 + 100 + 0 = 200 ÷ 3) for the first child, and, assuming a three-year gap, 54 for the second (100 + 100 + 15 + 0 = 215 ÷ 4).

You will also notice in Table 1 that after the fifth child, the average begins to rise and continues to increase for each additional child (although it never reaches the level that the first child enjoyed). Zajonc and Markus claimed the reason for this is that the earlier-born children are old enough now to boost the intellectual climate of the family more than the newborn reduces it. In other words, children who are born late into very large families benefit from the intellectual contributions of their older brothers and sisters.

In addition, imagine a large family in which the gap between children is four years. Of course, the total family size would be smaller because the parents would run out of childbearing years, but the average intellectual climate for each child would decrease much less at first and begin to rise again after only two children. If you carry this logic to its extreme, consider a couple that has one child and then waits 15 years to have another (this is highly unusual, but not unheard of).

The second child would enter an intellectual climate that is *higher* than most first-borns. This is due to the fact that the first child is at an age that adds to the overall level rather than lowering it. As Zajonc and Markus point out, "large gaps help younger children surpass older children, and they may cause a reversal in the relationship between birth order and intellect" (p. 81).

There were two findings in the data from the Netherlands study that seemed to defy the logic and pattern of the model developed by Zajonc and Markus. One of these was that only children performed more poorly than first-borns in families with up to four children. Since the only child is also the first child, the intellectual climate is high (67) and therefore the child should, according to the theory, score among the highest. Obviously, however, this was not the case. The other odd finding was for last-born children, regardless of family size. If you refer back to Figure 1, you will notice a large drop in scores for the last-born following a leveling off or even an increase in the score of the second- and third-to-last children. In order for Zajonc and Markus to complete the application of their theory to the Netherlands data, they needed to explain these peculiar results.

To solve this dilemma, they looked for factors in the intellectual environment that might be similar for the only child and the last child. If you stop to think about this, it seems that there is virtually nothing similar; an only child's environment, in terms of intellectual confluence, appears to be completely different from that of the last child in a large family. However, the researchers uncovered one important difference: They never get to be "teachers." Zajonc and Markus explain it very clearly:

> If a child does not know how to solve a particular problem, he is not likely to ask the youngest; if he is missing a word, it is not the youngest who will supply it; if there is an ambiguity about the rules of a game, . . . it will not be resolved by the youngest. In short, the last born is not a "teacher" and neither is the only child. It would be quite surprising if the opportunity to perform such a "teaching" function did not have beneficial effects for intellectual development (p. 83).

So, what do these findings mean to prospective parents who want to use this research in deciding how best to plan a family? Well, the authors themselves acknowledge that they have presented a parents' dilemma. Obviously it would be best for the first-born child if a second child arrived after only a short gap, since this would reduce the time that the first child would suffer from the lack of teaching opportunity (the "last-child effect"). However, the second child would then enter an inferior intellectual environment. It would be better for the second child to arrive after the longest possible gap, but this increases the "last-child" handicap for the first child. For larger families, the researchers draw the conclusion that longer gaps are generally beneficial. However (and there is always a "however"), as the gaps get larger, siblings end up spending less time together because they share fewer interests, and the older children leave home earlier in the lives of their younger siblings.

Finally, it should be noted that Zajonc and Markus did not try to claim that family size and birth order are the only determinates of intellectual ability. Clearly other factors, such as genetic heritage, child-rearing practices, prenatal care, and so on, all contribute to intellectual development as well.

CRITICISMS AND SUBSEQUENT RESEARCH

Probably the most important criticism of Zajonc and Markus' model questions whether the differences in I.Q. scores between first-born and later-born are large enough to be significant. The average Raven score for the first-born in a two-child family is only about 5 points higher than that for the last-born in a family with nine children. This difference may mean very little in terms of a person's actual abilities in life.

Additionally, there are other prominent researchers who dispute the existence of a birth order effect on intelligence, and have carried out studies that support their dissenting views (Galbraith, 1982). In defense of Zajonc and Marcus, however, most studies involving large samples of subjects have generally supported their theory of "average intellectual climate."

Before you become depressed at being a later-born child or start to gloat about being the first-born, it is important to realize that there is a down side to being first and certain advantages to arriving later into the family. Although first-borns tend to excel in intellectual abilities, they also are prone to be more anxious and neurotic than later-born children. Furthermore, children born later have been found to be more sociable, affectionate, friendly, and comfortable in social situations. Consequently they are more popular with their peers and are more at ease when interacting with strangers. Finally, the youngest children in families generally demonstrate greater creativity and originality in their thinking (Ickes and Turner, 1983).

These criticisms and observations notwithstanding, the work of Zajonc and Markus continues to exert an influence on behavioral scientists' attempts to understand differences in intellectual abilities. For example, prior to 1980, this country saw a decline in high school students' average scores on the Scholastic Aptitude Test (SAT). After 1980 the scores began to rise. Zajonc, along with other researchers in the field, explained these trends based on the effects of birth order as follows. Prior to 1980, more later-born children were taking the test. During the 1980s the first-born children of the parents from the "baby-boom" generation reached high school age and began to take the SAT. The model developed by Zajonc and Markus predicts that SAT scores will continue to rise until approximately the year 2000 when they will level off and then begin to decline again as a greater number of later-borns are included in the average scores (Zajonc, 1986). If these predictions turn out to be correct (and thus far it appears that they will), this will further validate Zajonc and Markus' confluence model of intellectual development.

BELMONT, L., and MAROLLA, F. (1973) Birth order, family size, and intelligence. *Science*, 182, 1096–1101.
ERNST, C., and ANGST, J. (1983) *Birth order: Its influence on personality.* New York: Springer-Verlag.
ICKES, W., and TURNER, M. (1983) On the social advantage of having an older, opposite-sex sibling: Birth order influences in mixed-sex pairs. *Journal of Personality and Social Psychology*, 45, 210–22.
ZAJONC, R.B. (1986) The decline and rise of scholastic aptitude scores: A prediction derived from the confluence model. *American Psychologist*, 41, 862–67.

IN CONTROL AND GLAD OF IT!

Langer, Ellen J., and Rodin, Judith (1976) The effects of choice and enhanced personal responsibility for the aged: A field experiment in an institutional setting. *Journal of Personality and Social Psychology*, 34, 191–98.

Control. This seemingly small psychological concept may be the single most important influence on all of human behavior. What we are talking about here is not your ability to control the actions of others, but the personal power you possess over your own life and the events in it. Related to this ability are your feelings of competence and personal power, and the availability of choices in any given situation. Most of us feel that we have at least *some* control over our individual destinies. You have made choices in your life—some good ones, and maybe some poor ones—and they have brought you to where you are today. And while you may not consciously think about it, you will make many more choices in your life. Each day you make choices and decisions about your behavior. When your sense of control is threatened, you experience negative feelings (anger, outrage, indignation) and will rebel by behaving in ways that will restore your perception of personal freedom. It's the well-worn idea that if someone tells you that you have to do something, you very likely will either refuse or do exactly the opposite. Or, conversely, forbid someone to do something and they will find that activity more attractive than they did before it was forbidden (remember Romeo and Juliet?). This tendency to resist any attempt to limit our freedom is called "reactance."

Well, if our need to control our personal environment is as basic to human nature as it appears to be, what do you think would happen if that control were taken away from you and you were unable to get it back? You would very likely experience psychological distress that could take the form of anxiety, anger, outrage, depression, helplessness, and even physical illness. Studies have shown that when people are placed in stressful situations, the negative effects of the stress can be reduced if the subjects believe they have some control over the stressful event. For example, people in a crowded elevator perceive the elevator to be less crowded and feel less anxiety if they are standing next to the control panel in the elevator car; they believe they have a greater sense of control over their environment (Rodin, Solomon, and Metcalf, 1978). Another well-known study exposed subjects to loud bursts of noise and then had them perform problem-solving tasks. One group had no control over the noise. Another group was told that they could press a button and stop the noise at any time. However, they were asked not to press the button if they could avoid it. Subjects in the no-control group performed significantly worse on the tasks than the subjects who believed they could exert control over the noise. By the way, none of the subjects in this latter group actually pressed the button, so they were exposed to just as much noise as the group that had no perception of control.

What this all boils down to is that we are happier and more effective people when we have the power to *choose*. Unfortunately in our society, there comes a stage in many people's lives when they lose this power; when they are no longer allowed to make even the simplest of choices for themselves. This life stage is called old age. Many of us have heard about or experienced firsthand the tragic sudden decline in health and alertness of an elderly person when he or she is placed in a retirement home or nursing home. Many illnesses such as colitis, heart disease, and depression have been linked to feelings of helplessness and loss of control that occur prior to the illness. One of the most difficult transitions elderly people must go through when entering a "home" is the loss of the personal power to control their daily activities and influence their own destinies. Langer and Rodin, who had been studying these issues of power and control for some time prior to the study we are considering here, decided to put these ideas to the test in a real nursing home.

THEORETICAL PROPOSITIONS

If the loss of personal responsibility for one's life causes a person to be less happy and healthy, then *increasing* control and power should have the opposite effect. Langer and Rodin wanted to test this theoretical idea directly by enhancing personal responsibility and choice for a group of nursing home residents. Based on previous literature and their own earlier studies, they predicted that the patients who were to be given this control should demonstrate improvements in mental alertness, activity level, satisfaction with life, and other measures of behavior and attitude.

METHOD

Subjects

Langer and Rodin obtained the cooperation of a Connecticut nursing home called Arden House. This facility was rated by the state as one of the finest care units in the area, offering quality medical care, recreational facilities, and residential conditions. It was a large and modern home with four residential floors. The residents in the home were all of generally similar physical and psychological health and came from similar socioeconomic backgrounds. When a new resident entered the home, he or she was assigned to a room on the basis of availability. Consequently the characteristics of the residents on all floors were, on average, equivalent. Two floors were randomly selected for the two treatment conditions. Fourth-floor residents (eight men and 39 women) received the "increased-responsibility" treatment. The second floor, which was the comparison or control group, consisted of nine men and 35 women. These 91 subjects ranged in age from 65 to 90.

Procedure

The nursing home administrator agreed to work with the researchers in implementing the two experimental conditions. He was described as an outgoing and friendly 33-year-old who interacted with the residents daily. He called a meeting of the two floors and spoke with them in order to give them some new information about the home. The two messages informed the residents of the home's desire that their lives there be as comfortable and pleasant as possible and discussed several of the services that were available to them. However, within these messages there were some important differences for the two groups.

The "responsibility-induced group" (fourth floor) was told that they have the responsibility of caring for themselves and deciding how they should spend their time. He went on to explain the following:

> You should be deciding how you want your room arranged—whether you want it to be as it is or whether you want the staff to help you rearrange the furniture. . . . It's your responsibility to make your complaints known to us, to tell us what you would like to change, to tell us what you would like. Also, I wanted to take this opportunity to give each of you a present from Arden House. [A box of small plants was passed around and the patients were given two decisions to make: first, whether or not they wanted a plant at all, and second, to choose which one they wanted. All residents did select a plant.] The plants are yours to keep and take care of as you'd like.
>
> One last thing: I wanted to tell you that we're showing a movie two nights next week, Thursday and Friday. You should decide which night you'd like to go, if you choose to see it at all. (p. 194)

The comparison group (second floor) was told how much the home wanted to make their lives fuller and more interesting. He explained the following to them:

> We want your rooms to be as nice as they can be and we've tried to make them that way for you. We want you to be happy here. We feel that it's our responsibility to make this a home you can be proud of and happy in and we'll do all we can to help you. . . .
>
> Also, I wanted to take this opportunity to give you each a present from Arden House. [The nurse walked around with a box of plants and each patient was handed one.] The plants are yours to keep. The nurses will water and care for them for you.
>
> One last thing: I wanted to tell you that we're showing a movie next week on Thursday and Friday. We'll let you know later which day you're scheduled to see it (p. 194).

Three days later, the director went around to each resident's room and reiterated the same message.

It's not difficult to see what the important difference was between these two messages. The fourth-floor group was given the opportunity to make choices and exercise control over their lives in various ways. The second-floor group, while other factors were basically the same, was given the message that most of their decisions would be made for them. These policies were then followed on these two floors for the next three weeks. (It should be noted that the level of control given to the fourth-floor residents was always available to all residents at the home. For this experiment it was simply reiterated and made clearer to the experimental group.)

Measuring the Outcome

Several methods of measurement (dependent variables) were used in this study to determine if the different responsibility conditions would make a difference. There were two questionnaires administered one week before the director's talk and again three weeks after. One questionnaire was given to the residents; it asked questions about how much control they felt they had and how active and happy they were at the home. The other questionnaire was given to nurses on each floor (who were not aware of the research being conducted) asking them to rate patients on 10-point scales for how happy, alert, dependent, sociable, and active they were and about their sleeping and eating habits. There were also two measures of the residents' actual *behavior*. Records were kept of the attendance at the movie that was being shown the next week. Also, there was a contest held for patients to guess how many jelly beans there were in a large jar. If residents wished to enter the contest they simply wrote their guess and their name on a slip of paper and placed it in a box next to the jar.

RESULTS

Table 1 summarizes the results of the two questionnaires. As can be seen clearly, the differences between the groups were striking, and supported Langer and Rodin's predictions about the positive effects of choice and personal power. The residents in the increased-responsibility group reported that they felt happier and more active than those in the comparison group. Also the interviewer's rating of alertness was higher for the fourth-floor residents. All these differences were statistically significant. Even greater differences were seen on the nurses' ratings. Keep in mind that the nurses who rated the patients were "blind" (uninformed) as to the two treatment conditions to avoid any bias in their ratings. They determined that, overall, the increased-responsibility group's condition improved markedly over the three weeks of the study, while the comparison group in general was seen to decline. In fact, "93 percent of the experimental group (all but one subject) were considered improved, whereas only 21 percent of the comparison group (six subjects) showed this positive change" (p. 196). Fourth-floor residents took to visiting others more and spent considerably more time talking to various staff members. On the other hand, the increased-responsibility residents began to spend less time engaged in passive activities such as simply watching the staff.

The behavioral measures that were taken added further support to the positive effects of control. Significantly more subjects from the experimental group attended the movie. This difference in attendance

TABLE 1   Summary of Questionnaire Responses

QUESTIONNAIRE ITEM	DIFFERENCE BETWEEN FIRST AND SECOND ADMINISTRATION		
	INCREASED-RESPONSIBILITY GROUP	COMPARISON GROUP	SIGNIFICANT DIFFERENCE?
RESIDENT'S SELF-REPORT:			
● Happy	+0.28	−0.12	YES
● Active	+0.20	−1.28	YES
● Interviewer's rating of alertness	+0.29	−0.37	YES
NURSES' RATINGS:			
● General improvement	+3.97	−2.39	YES
● Time spent:			
—visiting other patients	+6.78	−3.30	YES
—visiting others	+2.14	−4.16	YES
—talking to staff	+8.21	+1.61	YES
—watching staff	−2.14	+4.64	YES

(adapted from p. 195)

was not found for a movie shown one month previously. While the jelly-bean guessing contest may have seemed a somewhat silly measurement for a scientific study, the results were quite interesting. Ten residents on the fourth-floor participated in the game, but only one second-floor patient did so.

DISCUSSION

Langer and Rodin pointed out that their study, combined with other previous research, demonstrated that when people who have been forced to give up their control and decision-making power are given a greater sense of personal responsibility, their lives and attitudes improve. As to the practical applications of this research, the authors are succinct and to the point:

> Mechanisms can and should be established for changing situational factors that reduce real or perceived responsibility in the elderly. Furthermore, this study adds to the body of literature suggesting that senility and diminished alertness are not an almost inevitable result of aging. In fact, it suggests that some of the negative consequences of aging may be retarded, reversed, or possibly prevented by returning to the aged the right to make decisions and a feeling of competence (p. 197).

SIGNIFICANCE OF FINDINGS
AND SUBSEQUENT RESEARCH

Probably the best example of the significance of the findings of this study were provided by the authors themselves in a subsequent study of the same residents in the same nursing home (Rodin and Langer, 1977). Eighteen months after their first study, Langer and Rodin returned to Arden House for a follow-up to see if the increased-responsibility conditions had any long-term effects. Only about half of the original subjects were still at the nursing home, since some had died, some had been transferred to other facilities, and some had been discharged. Approximately the same number had been discharged and transferred from the original experimental and control groups. For the patients still there, ratings were taken from doctors and nurses and a special talk on psychology and aging by one of the authors (J. Rodin) was given to the residents. The number of residents in each of the original conditions who attended the talk was recorded and the frequency and type of questions asked were noted.

Ratings from the nurses demonstrated continued superior condition of the increased-responsibility group. The average *total* ratings (derived by adding all their ratings together and averaging this total over all patients) for the experimental group was 352.33 vs. 262.00 for the comparison group (a highly significant statistical difference). The health ratings from doctors also indicated an increase in overall health status for the experimental group compared with a slight decline in health for the control residents. While there was no significant difference in the number of residents attending the lecture, most of the questions were asked by the increased-responsibility subjects and the content of the questions related to autonomy and independence. Probably the most important finding of all was that 30 percent of the subjects in the comparison group had died during the 18-month interval. For the experimental group, only 15 percent had died during that time. While there could be other reasons for this difference, both groups were equal on all other available characteristics other than the increased-responsibility treatment.

One important criticism of research such as this was pointed out by Langer and Rodin themselves. The consequences of intervention by researchers in any setting where the well-being of the participants is involved must be very carefully considered. For example, it could be dangerous and clearly unethical to provide the elderly with certain kinds of power and control only to have this responsibility taken away again when the research is completed. A study by Schulz (1976) allowed nursing home residents to have varying amounts of control over when they would be visited by local college students. Those having the most control over when and for how long the visits would take place showed significantly improved functioning just as Langer and Rodin found. However, when the study was completed and the students discontinued their visits, this (inadvertently on the part of the researchers) led to greater debilitation in health of the experimental group than of those residents who were never exposed to the increased-control situation. In Langer and Rodin's study this did not happen, since feelings of general control over normal day-to-day decision making were fostered among the residents. This, then, was a positive change that was able to be continued over time with sustained positive results.

CONCLUSION

As mentioned earlier in this chapter, personal power and control over one's life is a key factor in a happy and productive life. Old age is a time when the potential exists for this power to be lost. Langer and Rodin's studies and the ongoing work of Judith Rodin (see Rodin, 1986) have made it clear that the greater our sense of control, the healthier, happier, and smoother our process of aging. Awareness of this is growing even today as nursing homes, state nursing home certification boards, hospitals, and other institutional settings encourage and require increased choice, personal power, and control for the elderly.

RODIN, J. (1986) Aging and health: Effects of the sense of control. *Science*, 233, 1271–76.
RODIN, J., and LANGER, E.J. (1977) Long-term effects of a control relevant intervention with the institutionalized aged. *Journal of Personality and Social Psychology*, 35, 897–902.
RODIN, J., SOLOMON, S., and METCALF, J. (1979) Role of control in mediating perceptions of density. *Journal of Personality and Social Psychology*, 36, 988–99.
SCHULZ, R. (1976) Effects of control and predictability on the psychological well-being of the institutionalized aged. *Journal of Personality and Social Psychology*, 33, 563–73.

SIX

EMOTION
AND MOTIVATION

This section deals with our inner experiences of emotion and motivation. Many non-psychologists have trouble with the idea of the scientific exploration of these issues. There is a widespread belief that emotions and motivations just sort of happen, that we don't have much control over them, and that they are part of our "standard equipment" from birth. However, psychologists have always been fascinated with the issues of where your emotions come from and what *causes* you to act the way you do. Emotion and motivation are basic and powerful influences on behavior, and a great deal of research has been done to try to understand them better.

The first reading on emotion looks at a famous study that changed psychology's ideas about how a specific emotional experience evolves from a potentially emotional event. This study helps to explain why crying, for example, can be a sign of sadness or happiness. The second reading examines a fascinating study about facial expressions of emotions and demonstrates that the expressions for basic emotions are the same for everyone in all cultures throughout the world. The third reading in this section presents a study about how extreme emotions, or what we might call stress, can affect your health. The fourth reading allows you to experience the process of one of the most, if not the most, famous experiment in the area of motivation: the original demonstration of a psychological event called "cognitive dissonance."

EMOTIONS AND EMOTIONAL SITUATIONS . . .
Schachter, S., and Singer, J.E., (1962) Cognitive, social, and physiological determinants of emotional state. *Psychological Review,* 69, 379–99.

Research on emotion by psychologists began around the turn of the century when William James, considered to be one of the first psychologists, proposed a theory of emotion which flew directly in the face of popular belief and common sense. He suggested that our emotional experiences are based exclusively upon our bodily reactions. For example, suppose you are walking through the forest and stumble onto a large rattlesnake, coiled in your path and ready to strike. Your heart begins to race, your breathing increases, you perspire a lot, and you freeze. Slowly you back away, turn, and run away at top speed. James' theory says that you become aware of these bodily reactions (your heart, breathing, running, etc.) and from these determine that what you feel is *fear*. In other words, the body informs the mind and the mind then decides on the appropriate emotion. Later, this theory was called into question when it was found that various emotions were accompanied by nearly identical physiological reactions. That is, it was found that whether you are facing a rattlesnake or have just won $50,000, your bodily reactions are pretty much the same, but your emotional experiences are considerably different.

It wasn't until about 60 years after James' ideas that a new theory emerged to account for how we experience emotion. In the early 1960s Stanley Schachter was working on the notion that, as thinking beings, we are capable of analyzing a situation and making judgments regarding our emotions. He claimed that all of the theories explaining emotional reactions up to that time view the individual as a passive participant; someone to whom emotions simply happen. Schachter rejected this idea and reminded us that humans are intelligent beings; we are able to think and reason. So why shouldn't we also be able to *participate* in our own emotional responses to the situations we encounter in life? Schachter, in collaboration with Jerome Singer, proposed that it is not simply the physical arousal you feel that produces an emotional experience, but how you *interpret* the source of that arousal. If you see someone crying, how do you know if they are sad, happy, frustrated, or angry? Well, you can tell from the situation in which the emotional behavior is taking place. Is it a wedding? a funeral? a sporting event? This concept of participation in emotional responses was what Schachter and Singer set about testing experimentally.

THEORETICAL PROPOSITIONS

While he did not deny the importance of physical responses in emotions, Schachter proposed that other factors, such as the environment and our interpretation of the situation (cognitions), play a crucial role in the formation of the many and varied emotions we humans experience. In other words, we consider the context in which an emotion-producing event occurs and then label the emotion based on this context. In order to test this idea, Schachter and Singer carried out an ingenious study that changed the way behavioral scientists view human emotion.

METHOD

Subjects for their study were 185 undergraduate males at the University of Minnesota. These subjects were divided into three groups. (Historically, and still today, university undergraduates enrolled in lower division psychology courses commonly participate in studies as subjects to fulfill part of their course requirements. Their participation is voluntary, and alternate assignments are always offered for those who choose not to participate. Furthermore, no dangerous procedures are ever used and any subject may withdraw from any experiment at any time.)

Two of the three groups were given injections of epinephrine (synthetic adrenalin), which produces physiological reactions like those produced by intense emotional experiences. In order for the true intent of the experiment to be disguised, the subjects were all told that the injection was a vitamin compound and that the experimenters were interested in studying the vitamin's effect on vision. The third group was injected with a simple saline solution, a placebo. We will call that group "group C" for "control group."

One of the adrenalin groups was given *correct* information about the physical effects of the injection (i.e., "you will feel an increase in your heart rate and respiration, you'll feel warm and flushed, you will perspire more, and you'll feel generally physiologically aroused"). We will refer to this group as "group I" for "informed." The other group was given no information at all about the effects of the injection. We'll call them group "N." Then came the second and crucial part of the study.

Immediately after receiving the injection, each subject was placed in a room with a person who was supposedly another subject who had received the same injection. (In reality, this person was in on the experiment, a "confederate" playing a part.) Both were asked to fill out a questionnaire. With half the subjects in groups I, N, and C, the confederate behaved as if he was extremely happy and having a terrific time. He made paper airplanes, played with a hula hoop, laughed a lot, and engaged the subject in a game of wastebasket basketball. With the other half of the subjects in each group, the confederate acted as if he was angry about the questionnaire, became increasingly hostile, and finally stormed out of the room.

Remember, half of each group were exposed to a happy confederate, and half to an angry confederate. The only other difference between the groups was the information they had received about the injection. What Schachter and Singer were looking for were any differences among the groups in emotional responses.

RESULTS

The subjects were observed while interacting with the confederate, and the amount of anger or happiness they displayed was recorded. Subjects were also asked to rate how angry or happy they felt.

The results supported Schachter and Singer's theory. The *uninformed* subjects (group N) exposed to the happy confederate became happy and the *uninformed* subjects exposed to the angry confederate became angry. What about the group I subjects who were accurately informed about what the injection would do, and what about the control subjects? Well, they didn't become particularly happy or angry! Table 1 summarizes the results of the study. As you can see, only those subjects who experienced physiological arousal from the epinephrine *and* had no explanation for the arousal experienced the emotion portrayed by the confederate. A reasonable explanation for the arousal (the correct information about the drug's effects) or the lack of physiological arousal prevented subjects from absorbing the confederate's emotional state. So how did these findings support Schachter and Singer's theory?

TABLE 1   Reactions of Subjects to Emotional State of Experimental Confederate

	SUBJECT GROUPS		
	N. UNINFORMED OF DRUG EFFECT	I. INFORMED OF DRUG EFFECT	C. CONTROL SUBJECTS
Happy Confederate	Subjects became happy	No emotional experience	No emotional experience
Angry Confederate	Subjects became angry	No emotional experience	No emotional experience

DISCUSSION

You'll remember the authors' claim that people consider the circumstances surrounding an event that produces a physical reaction in order to label the emotional experience they are having. So, consider first those subjects who knew in advance that this injection would cause them to feel physiologically aroused. To them, the adrenalin-produced arousal they felt was easily explained as being due to the injection. They had no additional need to explain it based on the circumstances in the study (their contact with the confederate). Therefore, they did not have an emotional experience.

The subjects who were not informed about the true effects of the injection, on the other hand, were feeling the effects of the drug, but had no immediate explanation for their arousal. As Schachter predicted, they looked to the situation to find this explanation and they found it in the behavior of the confederate. They experienced an emotion based on the confederate's actions: either happy or angry.

Finally, the control subjects, while misinformed about the injection, failed to experience emotion based on the confederate's behavior because they had received a placebo and were, therefore, not physiologically aroused.

Based upon the results of this study, Schachter and Singer concluded that emotion is a two-stage process. In an emotionally charged situation, we first experience physiological arousal. We then draw information out of the situation and, based on this information, we *label* the emotion we are experiencing. This, of course, can happen very quickly. Does this make intuitive sense to you? Perhaps a typical example from everyday life will further clarify.

Imagine you have been waiting 45 minutes in a long line at the movie theater. Suddenly someone walks up and cuts right in front of you in the line with his back to you. Chances are, you will begin to have a physiological reaction to this and, based on the situation of someone rudely cutting the line, you will label your arousal as anger. You probably won't be aware of this mental labeling process because it will happen very quickly. Now consider the exact same situation, but you realize that the person cutting in front of you is an old friend you haven't seen in many months. Again, you will have the same increases in heart rate, respiration, muscle tension, etc., but, based on this very different situation, your emotional experience will be happiness!

Schachter and Singer called this the *two factor theory of emotion*. It is based on the principles of multiplication. That is, both arousal *and* situational cues are necessary for an emotion to develop; either one alone is insufficient. The model would be diagrammed as follows:

Physiological arousal × *Environmental cues* = *Emotional experience*

Since these components are *multiplied* rather than added, you can see that if either factor in the equation, either arousal or cognitive cues, equals zero, the product (emotion) will also be zero.

SIGNIFICANCE OF FINDINGS

This study and the more formal and complete theory that grew out of it became widely accepted as the best explanation of human emotional experience. It was (and is) used to explain the full range of human emotions, including anger, happiness, sadness, fear, disgust, surprise, and all the many intensities and combinations of these. Subsequent research tended to support most of Schachter and Singer's findings, and behavioral science's view of human emotion was forever changed. However, as with any new approach to anything, some modifications and criticisms were sure to arise.

CRITICISMS AND SUBSEQUENT RESEARCH

Schachter's theory of emotion rests on a consistent sequence of events; that is, arousal, followed by appraisal of the situation, followed by the emotional experience. Other researchers have argued that for some emotional experiences, the arousal and the appraisal happen so closely together that it is not possible to always be sure of this sequence. It is conceivable that sometimes we may interpret a situation first, then have a physiological reaction, and then label the emotion (see Lazarus, 1984).

   Another criticism has centered on Schachter's rejection of James' notion of identifying our emotions based on our perception of bodily reactions. There is evidence to show that the body's response to different emotional situations is *not* always the same. For example, rather clear differences have been found in the pattern of physiological reactions (heart rate, blood pressure, etc.) for fear, sadness, and anger (see Schwartz, Weinberger, and Singer, 1981). This would indicate that we may, after all, as William James proposed, be able to tell something about what emotion we are experiencing from subtle differences in physiological responses, without always having to consider the situation.

   Finally, a few recent studies have demonstrated that when people are injected with adrenalin without knowing what it is, and without any environmental clues, they tend to label the physical arousal in negative emotional terms, such as anger, stress, or general discomfort (see Maslach, 1979). Schachter's theory would predict that without environmental cues, no emotion should be experienced.

   Although criticisms and controversy continue to surround Schachter and Singer's work on emotion, their contributions still exert a strong influence on psychology's view of human emotion. Moreover, the research discussed in this chapter was of crucial importance in that it did and still does generate a great deal of research in this field of psychology.

LAZARUS, R. (1984) On the primacy of cognition. *American Psychologist*, 39, 124–29.
MASLACH, C. (1979) Negative emotional biasing of unexplained physiological arousal. *Journal of Personality and Social Psychology*, 37, 953–69.
SCHWARTZ, G., WEINBERGER, C., and SINGER, J. (1981) Cardiovascular differentiation of happiness, sadness, anger, and fear following imagery and exercise. *Psychosomatic Medicine*, 43, 343–64.

I CAN SEE IT ALL OVER YOUR FACE!
Ekman, Paul, and Friesen, Wallace V. (1971) Constants across cultures in the face and emotion. *Journal of Personality and Social Psychology*, 17, 124–29.

Think of something funny. What is the expression on your face? Now think of something in your past that made you sad. Did your face change? Chances are it did. Undoubtedly, you are aware that certain facial expressions coincide with specific emotions. And, most of the time, you can probably tell how someone is feeling emotionally from the expression on their face. Now, consider this: Could you be equally successful in determining someone's emotional state based on their facial expression if that person is from a different culture—say, Romania, Sumatra, or Mongolia? In other words, this question is asking if you believe facial expressions of emotion are universal. Most people believe that they are, until they stop and consider how radically different other cultures are from their own. Think of the multitude of cultural differences in gestures, personal space needs, rules of interpersonal behavior and etiquette, religious beliefs, attitudes, and so on. With all these differences influencing behavior, it would be rather amazing if there are *any* human characteristics, including the emotional expressions, that are identical across all cultures.

Paul Ekman is considered the leading researcher in the area of the facial expression of emotion. This early article details his and his associate Wallace Friesen's research, which was designed to demonstrate the universality of these expressions. While the authors acknowledged in their introduction that previous researchers had found some evidence of facial behaviors being determined by culturally variable learning, they argued that this evidence was weak and that expressions of basic emotions are equivalent in all cultures.

Several years prior to this study, Ekman and Friesen had conducted research in which they showed photographs of faces to college-educated people in Argentina, Brazil, Chile, Japan, and the United States. All the subjects from every country successfully identified the same facial expressions as corresponding to the same emotions. The researchers presented their findings as evidence of universality in these expressions. However, as Ekman and Friesen themselves pointed out, these findings were open to criticism, since members of the cultures studied had all been exposed to international mass media (movies, magazines, television), which is full of facial expressions. What was needed to prove the universality of emotional expression was a culture that had not been exposed to any of these things. Imagine how difficult (perhaps impossible!) it would be to find such a culture today. Well, even in 1971, it wasn't easy.

Ekman and Friesen traveled to the Southeast Highlands of New Guinea to find subjects for their study among the Fore people who still existed then, in essence, as an isolated Stone Age society. Many of the members of this group had experienced little or no contact with Western or Eastern modern cultures (see the discussion on research by Eleanor Rosch, who, also studied Papua-New Guinea natives for similar reasons). Therefore, they had not been exposed to emotional facial expressions other than those of their own people.

THEORETICAL PROPOSITIONS

The theory underlying Ekman and Friesen's study was that the specific facial expressions corresponding to basic emotions are universal. Ekman and Friesen stated it quite simply: "The purpose of this paper was to test the hypothesis that members of a preliterate culture who had been selected to ensure maximum visual isolation from literate cultures will identify the same emotion concepts with the same faces as do members of literate Western and Eastern cultures" (p. 125).

METHOD

The subgroup of the Fore who were the most isolated were among those referred to as the South Fore. The individuals selected to participate in the study had seen no movies, did not speak English or Pidgin, had never worked for a Westerner, and had never lived in any of the Western settlements in the area. There were 189 adults and 130 children chosen to participate out of a total South Fore population of about 11,000. For comparison, there were also 23 adults chosen who had experienced a great deal of contact with Western society through watching movies, living in the settlements, and attending missionary schools.

Through trial and error, the researchers found that the most effective method of asking the subjects to identify emotions was to present them with three photographs of different facial expressions and read a brief description of an emotion-producing scene or story that corresponded to one of the photographs. The subject could then simply point to the expression that best matched the story. The stories used were selected very carefully to be sure that each scene was related to only one emotion and that it was recognizable to the Fore people. Table 1 lists the six stories developed by Ekman and Friesen. The authors explained that the fear story had to be longer to prevent the subjects from confusing it with surprise or anger.

Forty photographs of 24 different people, including men, women, boys, and girls, were used as examples of the six emotional expressions. These photographs had been validated previously by showing them to members of various other cultures. Each photograph had been judged by at least 70 percent of observers in at least two literate Western or Eastern cultures to be representative of the emotion being expressed.

The actual experiment was conducted by teams consisting of one member of the research group and a member of the South Fore tribe who explained the task and translated the stories. Each adult subject was shown three photographs (one correct and two incorrect), was told the

TABLE 1   Ekman and Friesen's Stories Corresponding to Six Emotions

EMOTION	STORY
1. Happiness	His (her) friends have come and he (she) is happy.
2. Sadness	His (her) child (mother) has died and he (she) feels very sad.
3. Anger	He (she) is angry and about to fight.
4. Surprise	He (she) is just now looking at something new and unexpected.
5. Disgust	He (she) is looking at something he (she) dislikes; or he (she) is looking at something that smells bad.
6. Fear	He (she) is sitting in his (her) house all alone and there is no one else in the village. There is no knife, axe, or bow and arrow in the house. A wild pig is standing in the door of the house and the man (woman) is looking at the pig and is very afraid of it. The pig has been standing in the doorway for a few minutes, and the person is looking at it very afraid, and the pig won't move away from the door, and he (she) is afraid the pig will bite him (her).

(from p. 126)

story that corresponded to one of them, and was asked to choose the expression that best matched the story. The procedure was the same for the children, except that they only had to choose between two photographs, one correct and one incorrect. Each subject was presented with various sets of photographs so that no single photograph ever appeared twice in the comparison.

The translators were given careful training to ensure that they would not influence the subjects. They were told that there was no absolutely correct response and were asked to not prompt the subjects. Also, they were taught how to translate the stories exactly the same way each time and to resist the temptation to elaborate and embellish them. To avoid unintentional bias, the Western member of the research team avoided looking at the subject and simply recorded the answers given.

Remember that these were photographs of Western facial expressions of emotions. So, could the Fore people correctly identify the emotions in the photographs, even though they may never have seen a Western face before?

RESULTS

First, analyses were conducted to see if there were differences between males and females or between adults and children. The adult women were found to be more hesitant to participate and were considered to have had less contact with Westerners than the men. However, no significant differences in ability to correctly identify the emotions in the photographs were found between any of the groups.

Tables 2 and 3 summarize the percentage of correct responses for the six emotions by the least Westernized adults and the children respectively. Not all subjects were exposed to all emotions, and sometimes subjects were exposed to the same emotion more than once.

TABLE 2   Percent of Adults Correctly Identifying Story Emotions in Photographs

EMOTION IN STORY	NUMBER OF SUBJECTS	PERCENT CHOOSING CORRECT PHOTOGRAPH
Happiness	220	92.3
Anger	98	85.3
Sadness	191	79.0
Disgust	101	83.0
Surprise	62	68.0
Fear	184	80.5
Fear (with surprise)	153	42.7

(adapted from p. 127)

TABLE 3   Percent of Children Correctly Identifying Story Emotions in Photographs

EMOTION IN STORY	NUMBER OF SUBJECTS	PERCENT CHOOSING CORRECT PHOTOGRAPH
Happiness	135	92.8
Anger	69	85.3
Sadness	145	81.5
Disgust	46	86.5
Surprise	47	98.3
Fear	64	93.3

(adapted from p. 127)

Therefore, the number of subjects in the tables do not equal the overall total number of participants. All of the percentages were statistically significant except when subjects were asked to distinguish fear from surprise. When this situation existed many errors were made and, for one group, surprise was actually selected a significant 67 percent of the time when the story described fear.

Comparisons were made between the Westernized and non-Westernized adults. No significant differences were found between these two groups on the number who chose the correct photographs matching the emotion stories. There were also no differences found between younger and older children. As you can see in Table 3, the children appeared to perform better than the adults, but Ekman and Friesen attributed this to the fact that they only had to choose between two photographs instead of three.

DISCUSSION

Ekman and Friesen did not hesitate to draw a confident conclusion from their data: "The results for both adults and children clearly support our hypothesis that particular facial behaviors are universally associated with particular emotions" (p. 128). This conclusion was based on the fact that the South Fore had no opportunity to learn anything about Western expressions and, thus, had no way of identifying them unless the expressions were universal.

As a way of double-checking their findings, the researchers videotaped members of the isolated Fore culture portraying the same six facial expressions. Later, when these tapes were shown to college students in the United States, the students correctly identified the expressions corresponding to each of the emotions.

"The evidence from both studies contradicts the view that all facial behavior associated with emotion is culture-specific, and that posed facial behavior is a unique set of culture-bound conventions not understandable to members of another culture" (p. 128).

There was one exception to their consistent findings, that of the confusion subjects seemed to experience in distinguishing between expressions of fear and surprise. Ekman and Friesen explained this finding by acknowledging that there are certainly *some* cultural differences in emotional expression, but this did not detract from the preponderance of evidence that nearly all the other expressions were correctly interpreted across the cultures. They speculated that fear and surprise may have been confused "because in this culture fearful events are almost always also surprising; that is, the sudden appearance of a hostile member of another village, the unexpected meeting of a ghost or sorcerer, etc." (p. 129).

IMPLICATIONS AND SUBSEQUENT RESEARCH

So this study by Ekman and Friesen served to demonstrate scientifically what you already suspected: that facial expressions of emotions are universal. However, you might still be asking yourself, "What is the significance of this information?" Well, part of the answer to that question relates to the nature-nurture debate about which human behaviors are present at birth and which are acquired through learning. Since facial expressions for the six emotions used in this study appear to be influenced very little by cultural differences, it is possible to conclude that they must be innate; that is, biologically "hard-wired" in at birth.

It should be reiterated here that these six emotions (happiness, anger, sadness, surprise, disgust, and fear) are the only emotions that have been consistently found in numerous studies to be universal. Most researchers agree with Ekman that these are our most basic emotions. This is not to imply that these are the only emotions or emotional expressions humans experience. If you think about it for a minute you can probably name 20 or 30 different emotions that are either combinations or variations in intensity of the six basic ones. For example, the extreme of happiness is joy and the combination of surprise and sadness might produce shock.

Another reason the notion of universal emotional expressions is interesting to behavioral scientists is that it addresses issues about how humans evolved. In 1872, Darwin published a famous book called *The Expression of Emotion in Man and Animals*. He maintained that facial expressions were *adaptive mechanisms* that assisted animals in adapting to their environment and, therefore, increased their ability to survive. The idea behind this was that if certain messages could be communicated within and across species of animals through facial expressions, survival would be enhanced. For example, an expression of fear would provide a silent warning of imminent danger from predators; an expression of anger would warn less dominant members of the group to stay away from more powerful ones; and an expression of disgust would communicate a message of, "Yuck! Don't eat that, whatever you do," and prevent a potential poisoning. These expressions, however, would do the animals no good if they weren't universal among all the individuals making up the various species. Even though these expressions may now be less important to humans in terms of their survival-enhancement value, the fact that they are universal among us would indicate that they have been passed on to us from our evolutionary ancestors and have assisted us in reaching our present position on the evolutionary ladder.

A fascinating recent study demonstrated this "leftover" survival value of facial expressions in humans. The researchers (Hansen and Hansen, 1988) reasoned that if facial expressions could warn of impending danger, then humans should be able to recognize certain expressions, such as anger, more easily than other, less threatening expressions. To test this, they presented subjects with photographs of crowds of nine people with different facial expressions. In some of the photographs, all of the people's expressions were happy except for one that was angry. In other photographs all of the expressions were angry except one that was happy. The subjects' task was to pick out the face that was different. The amount of time it took the subjects to accomplish the task was recorded. When looking for a single happy face in a crowd of angry faces the average time was 1.45 seconds. However, when searching the crowd of happy faces for a single angry face it took only an average of 0.91 seconds, significantly less. Furthermore, as the size of the crowds in the photographs increased, the time for subjects to find the happy face also increased, but finding the angry face did not take significantly longer. This and other similar findings have indicated that humans may be *biologically* programmed to respond to the information provided by certain expressions better than others because they offered adaptive survival information.

CONCLUSION

During the two decades following the early cross-cultural research on emotional expressions, Ekman has continued his emotion research both individually and in collaboration with Friesen and several other researchers. Within this body of work, many fascinating discoveries have been made. One example of Ekman's more recent research involved what is called the "facial feedback theory" of emotional expressions. The theory states that the expression on your face actually feeds information back to your brain to assist you in interpreting the emotion you are experiencing. Ekman tested this idea by identifying the exact facial muscles involved in each of the six basic emotions. He then instructed subjects to tense these muscles into expressions resembling the various emotions. When they did this, Ekman was able to measure physiological responses in the subjects that corresponded to the appropriate emotion resulting from the facial expression alone, and not from the actual presence of the emotion itself (Ekman, Levensen, and Friesen, 1983).

Ekman has also extended his research into the area of deception and how the face and the body "leak" information to others about whether or not someone is telling the truth. In general, his findings have indicated that people are able to detect when others are lying at a slightly better than chance level when observing their facial expressions. However, when allowed to observe another's entire body, subjects were much more successful in detecting lies, indicating that the body may provide better clues to certain states of mind than the face alone (see Ekman, 1985, for a complete discussion of this issue).

Ekman and his associates have provided us with a large literature on the non-verbal communication provided by facial expressions. And research in this area continues. There is little doubt that the studies will continue until we are successful in accomplishing the goal that was the title of Ekman and Friesen's 1975 book, *Unmasking the Face*.

EKMAN, P. (1985) *Telling lies*. New York: Norton.
EKMAN, P., and FRIESEN, W. (1975) *Unmasking the face*. Englewood Cliffs, N.J.: Prentice Hall.
EKMAN, P., LEVENSEN, R., and FRIESEN, W. (1983) Autonomic nervous system activity distinguishes between emotions. *Science*, 164, 86–88.
HANSEN, C., and HANSEN, R. (1988) Finding the face in the crowd: An anger superiority effect. *Journal of Personality and Social Psychology*, 54, 917–24.

LIFE, CHANGE, AND STRESS

Holmes, Thomas H., and Rahe, Richard H. (1967) The social readjustment rating scale. *Journal of Psychosomatic Research*, 11, 213–18.

Everyone knows about stress. For most of you, most of the time, stress is an unpleasant, negative experience. Stress is not easy to define, but one way of looking at it is to think of stress as any emotion in its extreme form. In this sense, extreme fear, anger, sadness, or even happiness could produce stress. Think for a moment about the last time you were under a heavy amount of stress: the kind of stress that lasts more than a few hours or even a few days. Maybe you had to move to a new city, had a legal problem, had difficulties in a relationship with another person, had a job change, lost your job, experienced the death of someone close to you, were injured, or experienced some other major stressful change. You know the kind of stress I mean—it goes on for a while and you have to cope with it every day. What happened to you? How well did you cope? Did you find that your health deteriorated in some way?

The connection between stress and illness is the focus of this chapter and this famous article by Thomas Holmes and Richard Rahe. Take a moment to answer this question: Do you believe that there truly is a link between stress and illness? I bet you answered with a resounding "Yes!" But if I had asked this same question of people 20 or 30 years ago, only a few would have believed that such an association existed. Together, psychology and medicine over the past couple of decades have established with a high degree of certainty that this connection does indeed exist, and they have worked to understand it and intervene in it. For the behavioral sciences, those who are primarily concerned with this issue are called health psychologists. Notice that the journal in which the article appears deals with *psychosomatic* illness. Psychosomatic illness refers to health problems that are caused primarily by psychological factors rather than physical ones. Such illnesses are real; the discomfort, pain, and suffering exist medically. Victims of psychosomatic problems should not be confused with "hypochondriacs," who suffer from *imaginary* illnesses.

Many studies by health psychologists have established that when certain external changes occur in people's lives that require them to make major internal, psychological adjustments, there is a tendency for a higher incidence of illness. These changes have been termed "life stress." The amount of life stress you experience varies over time. There may have been some periods in your past (or present) when many changes were occurring, while at other times things were relatively stable. Life stress also varies greatly from person to person. The overall number of changes that occur in your life is different from the number in someone else's. So if I were to ask you how much life stress you have experienced over the past year, what would you say? A lot? Not much? A moderate amount? These kinds of vague judgments were not much use to scientists who wanted to study the relationship between life stress and illness. Therefore, the first question in this area of research that needed to be answered was this: How can life stress be measured?

Obviously, researchers could not bring people into a laboratory, expose them to stressful events for a short time, and then expect to see a sudden appearance of illness. First, this would be unethical, and second, it would not represent how stress works in real life. To tackle this problem, Holmes and Rahe decided to develop a written scale to measure life stress. They acknowledged in their article that previous attempts to examine a person's level of stress only determined the number and types of stressful events. They proposed to take this line of reasoning one step further and develop a way to measure the size or magnitude of various stressful life experiences. The idea behind this was that if such a measure could be developed, then it would be possible to obtain a person's score in terms of life stress and relate this to the status of the person's health.

METHOD

Holmes and Rahe compiled a list from their clinical experiences of 43 life events that people commonly feel are stressful, in that they require a person to make psychological adjustments in order to adapt to the event. This list was then presented to nearly 394 subjects, who were asked to rate each item on the list for the amount of stress produced by the event. The actual instructions that were given to the subjects read, in part:

> In scoring, use *all of your experience* in arriving at your answer. This means personal experience where it applies as well as what you have learned to be the case for others. Some persons accommodate to change more readily than others; some persons adjust with particular ease or difficulty to only certain events. Therefore, strive to give your opinion of the average degree of adjustment necessary for each event rather than the extreme. . . . "Marriage" has been given an arbitrary value of 500. As you complete each of the remaining events, think to yourself, "Is this event indicative of more or less readjustment than marriage? Would the readjustment take longer or shorter to accomplish?" (p. 213)

Subjects were then instructed to assign a point value to each event relative to the 500 value given to marriage. If they saw an event as requiring more readjustment than marriage, the point value would be higher, and vice versa. All the subjects' ratings for each item were averaged and then divided by 10 to arrive at a score for the individual items.

As you can see, this was a study with a rather simple and straightforward method. The importance and value of the research was in the results and the applications of the measuring device, which they called the "social readjustment rating scale" (SRRS).

RESULTS

Table 1 lists the 43 life events in order by rank, and the average point value assigned to each one by the subjects in the study. You can see that "death of a spouse" was rated the most stressful, whereas "minor violations of the law" was rated as the least stressful of the items included on the list. As you examine the list, you'll note that two of the items would need to be drastically updated today to reflect economic changes since 1967: "mortgage over $10,000" and "mortgage under $10,000." You might notice as well that not all the items are what you might consider to be negative. However, events such as Christmas, marriage, and, yes, even a vacation can be stressful in terms of Holmes and Rahe's definition of stress: need for psychological readjustment to the event.

In order to check for consistency in the ratings, the researchers divided the subjects into several subgroups and correlated their ratings of the items. Some of these subgroups compared were male vs. female, single vs. married, college-educated vs. no college, white vs. black, younger vs. older, higher socioeconomic vs. lower socioeconomic, religious vs. non-religious, etc. For all the subgroup comparisons, the correlations were very high, indicating a strong degree of agreement among the subjects. What this meant was that Holmes and Rahe could assume with a reasonable amount of confidence that this scale could be applied to all people with an approximately equal degree of accuracy.

DISCUSSION

Holmes and Rahe note in their discussion that there was a clear common theme to all the life events listed on their scale. Every time one of these stressful events occurs in someone's life, they explained, it requires some degree of adaptation, change, or coping. "The emphasis," they wrote, "is on *change* from the existing steady state and not on psychological meaning, emotion, or social desirability" (p. 217). This explains why some of the items may be interpreted as positive by some and negative by others, but either way, change is required and stress is produced.

Remember, this article explains the research behind the development of a method for *measuring* life stress. If you want to try it yourself, just look down the list and circle the life changes that have occurred in your life over the past 12 months. Each change has a certain number of points assigned to it, called "life change units" (LCUs). Calculate your LCU total. This gives you an estimate of your amount of life stress. Take a moment now to find your score. Now that you've done this, it probably feels as if something is missing, doesn't it? Well, what's

TABLE 1   The Social Readjustment Rating Scale

RANK	LIFE EVENT	MEAN VALUE
1	Death of spouse	100
2	Divorce	73
3	Marital separation	65
4	Jail term	63
5	Death of close family member	63
6	Personal injury or illness	53
7	Marriage	50
8	Fired at work	47
9	Marital reconciliation	45
10	Retirement	45
11	Change in health of family member	44
12	Pregnancy	40
13	Sex difficulties	39
14	Gain of new family member	39
15	Business readjustment	39
16	Change in financial state	38
17	Death of close friend	37
18	Change to different line of work	36
19	Change in number of arguments with spouse	35
20	Mortgage over $10,000	31
21	Foreclosure of mortgage or loan	30
22	Change in responsibilities at work	29
23	Son or daughter leaving home	29
24	Trouble with in-laws	29
25	Outstanding personal achievement	28
26	Wife begin or stop work	26
27	Begin or end school	26
28	Change in living conditions	25
29	Revision of personal habits	24
30	Trouble with boss	23
31	Change in work hours or conditions	20
32	Change in residence	20
33	Change in schools	20
34	Change in recreation	19
35	Change in church activities	19
36	Change in social activities	18
37	Mortgage or loan less than $10,000	17
38	Change in sleeping habits	16
39	Change in number of family get-togethers	15
40	Change in eating habits	15
41	Vacation	13
42	Christmas	12
43	Minor violations of the law	11

(from p. 216)

missing is what your score means about your health. This, after all, was the researchers' whole point in developing the scale to begin with.

Holmes and Rahe didn't stop with developing the SRRS, but went on together and separately to examine the relationship between their scale and the probability of illness.

SUBSEQUENT RESEARCH

In the late 1960s the SRRS began to be used in many studies as a tool for examining the stress-illness relationship. The value of the scale rested on its ability to predict illness based on people's total LCU scores.

Early studies asked several thousand people to fill out the SRRS and to report their histories of illness. Figure 1 graphically illustrates the overall findings of these studies (see Holmes and Masuda, 1974). In another study of 2,500 naval personnel, LCUs for the past six months were recorded using the SRRS just prior to shipboard tours of duty. During the six-month tour, those with fewer than 100 LCUs reported an average of 1.4 illnesses, those with between 300 and 400 averaged 1.9 illnesses, and those with between 500 and 600 suffered 2.1 illnesses (Rahe, Mahan, and Arthur, 1970). These and other studies over the years have generally supported Holmes and Rahe's contention that the SRRS can be helpful in predicting stress-related illness. The findings reported here will also give you an idea of what your score on the scale means.

Think of your score (especially if it's high) as an important indicator of how stressful your life is and what impact this stress could have on your health. However, before you become too worried, there have been several meaningful criticisms of the SRRS and its ability to predict illness that need to be discussed.

CRITICISMS OF THIS RESEARCH

Since Holmes and Rahe developed their SRRS, many researchers have expressed serious concerns about its accuracy and usefulness (see Taylor, 1991, pp. 214–16, for a complete review of these criticisms). One of the most widely expressed criticisms regards the inclusion of both positive and negative life events in the same scale, as well as both events that are in your control (events of choice, such as marriage) and events over which you have no control (such as the death of a friend). Research has demonstrated that certain events such as those that are sudden, negative, and out of your control are much more predictive of illness than are positive, controllable life changes.

FIGURE 1   Relationship between life change units and illness.

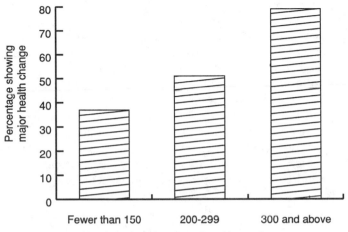

Number of LCUs accumulated in previous year

(adapted from Holmes and Masuda, 1974)

Also, others have maintained that the scale is flawed in that it does not take into account your *interpretation* of a particular event. For example, retirement for one person may mean an end of a career, being "forced out to pasture," while to another it is escape from drudgery into freedom. Related to this is the criticism that many of the items are vague, such as "personal injury or illness" (how serious? how incapacitating?) or "change in living conditions" (better? worse? which conditions?). It has been suggested that a more accurate scale would be one that allows a person to check an event and also rate it on some measure of severity (Cohen, 1983, has actually developed a scale designed to do this called the "perceived stress scale").

Finally, the way the research has related the SRRS to illness has been questioned. When carefully analyzed statistically, the predictive relationship between your LCU score and illness is a small one. In fact, it only accounts for about 10 percent of the total variation among people who become ill. In other words, if you examine 1,000 people to see who becomes sick over a six-month period, there will be a great variation in the individual factors leading to their illness or lack of illness. If you have them all complete an SRRS, you will find that out of all the possible reasons for health variation, their LCU scores explain only about 10 percent of it. This is a statistically significant correlation that confirms the ability of the SRRS to predict illness. However, it also says that it does not do so very well. Another way to look at it is that if you know someone's LCU score, your chances of predicting the future of that person's health are better than if you didn't have their score, but only a little better!

Finally, the studies using the SRRS have not taken into account the number of illnesses, the seriousness of the illnesses, or the length of the illnesses.

So, you might ask, if the SRRS has been so severely criticized, why is it so important and why is it in this book? Good question. Remember that some of the breakthroughs in the history of psychology were subsequently found to be lacking in some way, but that doesn't diminish the impact they had on our view of human behavior. As for this work of Holmes and Rahe, Shelly Taylor, a leading researcher in the field of health psychology expressed it best when she wrote, "The SRRS has been one of the methodological breakthroughs in studying stress; if its limitations are increasingly becoming evident, it is primarily because it has been a badly needed research tool that has enjoyed wide use" (Taylor, 1991, p. 216).

CONCLUSION

The relationship between stress and illness, while real, is complex. As can be seen from the discussion above, it is not a simple matter to study. Rahe himself has suggested that in addition to a simple LCU score several processes in a person must be considered to predict psychosomatic illness:

1. How much experience you have had in the past with stressful events.
2. Your coping skills; that is, your ability to psychologically defend yourself in times of life stress.
3. The strength of your physiological systems (such as your immune system) to defend you against the life stress that you are unable to cope with psychologically.
4. How you deal with illness when it does occur (such as practicing recuperative behaviors and seeking medical help).

Psychology and medicine, working together, are closing in on an understanding of the psychological component of illness. It has become clear to both fields that successful treatment of illness must involve the *entire* person: mind and body.

COHEN, S., KAMARCK, T., and MERMELSTEIN, R. (1983) A global measure of perceived stress. *Journal of Health and Social Behavior*, 24, 385–96.
HOLMES, T.H., and MASUDA, M. (1974) Life change and illness susceptibility. In B.S. DOHRENWEND and B.P. DOHRENWEND (eds.), *Stressful life events: Their nature and effects.* New York: Wiley.
RAHE, R.H., MAHAN, J., and ARTHUR, R. (1970) Prediction of near-future health change from subjects' preceding life changes. *Journal of Psychosomatic Research*, 14, 401–6.
TAYLOR, S. (1991) *Health psychology.* New York: McGraw-Hill.

THOUGHTS OUT OF TUNE

Festinger, Leon, and Carlsmith, James M. (1959) Cognitive
consequences of forced compliance. *Journal of Abnormal and
Social Psychology*, 58, 203–10.

Have you ever been in a position of having to do or say something that
was contrary to your attitudes or private opinions? Chance are you have;
everyone has at some time. When you behaved that way, what happened
to your true attitude or opinion? Nothing? Well, maybe nothing.
However, studies have shown that in some cases, when your behavior is
contrary to your attitude, your attitude will change in order to bring it
into alignment with your behavior. For example, if a person is *forced* (by
the demands of an experiment) to deliver a speech in support of a
viewpoint or position opposed to his or her own opinion, the speaker's
attitudes will shift toward those given in the speech.

In the early 1950s, various studies explained this opinion shift as a
result of (1) mentally rehearsing the speech, and (2) the process of
trying to think of arguments in favor of the forced position. In
performing those mental tasks, the early theories argued, subjects
convince themselves of the position they were about to take. In pursuing
this line of reasoning further, additional studies were conducted that
offered monetary rewards to subjects for giving convincing speeches
contrary to their own views. It was expected that the greater the reward,
the greater would be the resulting opinion change in the speaker (seems
logical, doesn't it?). However, as one of many examples of how common
sense is a poor predictor of human behavior, just the opposite was
found to be true. Larger rewards produced *less* attitude change than
smaller rewards. Based on the theories of learning that were popular at
the time (operant conditioning, reinforcement theory, etc.), such
findings were difficult for researchers to explain.

A few years later, Leon Festinger, a research psychologist at
Stanford University, proposed the highly influential and now famous
theory of cognitive dissonance, which could account for the seemingly
discrepant findings. The word *cognitive* refers to any mental processes,
such as thoughts, ideas, units of knowledge, attitudes, or beliefs;
dissonance simply means "out of tune." Therefore, Festinger suggested,
you will experience cognitive dissonance when you simultaneously hold
two or more cognitions which are psychologically inconsistent. When this
condition exists, it creates discomfort and stress to varying degrees,
depending on the importance of the dissonance to your life. This
discomfort then motivates you to change something in order to reduce
it. Since you cannot change your behavior (because you have already
done it, or because the situational pressures are too great), you change
your attitudes.

Festinger's theory grew out of reports of the rumors which spread throughout India following a 1934 earthquake there. In the areas outside the disaster zone, the rumors predicted that there would be additional earthquakes of even greater proportions and throughout an even greater portion of the country. These rumors were without any scientific foundation. Festinger wondered why people would spread such catastrophic and anxiety-increasing ideas. It occurred to him over time that perhaps the rumors were not anxiety-increasing, but anxiety-justifying. That is, these people were very frightened, even though they lived outside the danger area. This created cognitive dissonance: The cognition of fear was out of tune with the lack of any scientific basis for their fear. So, their spreading the rumors of greater disasters justified their fears and reduced their dissonance. *They made their view of the world fit with what they were feeling and how they were behaving.*

THEORETICAL PROPOSITIONS

Festinger theorized that normally in our society what you publicly state will be substantially the same as your private opinion or belief. Therefore, if you believe "X," but publicly state "not X," you will experience the discomfort of cognitive dissonance. However, if you know that the reasons for your statement of "not X" were clearly justified by pressures, promises of rewards, or threats of punishment, then dissonance will be reduced or eliminated. Therefore, the more you view your inconsistent behavior to be of your own choosing, the greater will be your dissonance.

One way for you to reduce this unpleasant dissonance is to alter your private opinion to bring it into agreement or consonance with your behavior (making the statement). Festinger contended that changes in attitudes and opinions will be greatest when dissonance is large. Think about it for a moment. Suppose someone offers you a great deal of money to publicly state views that are the opposite of your true views, and you agree to do so. Then suppose someone else makes the same request, but offers you just a little money, and even though it hardly seems worth it, you agree anyway. In which case will your dissonance be the greatest? Logically, you would experience more dissonance in the less-money situation, because of insufficient justification for your attitude-discrepant behavior. Therefore, according the Festinger's theory, your private opinion will shift more in the little-money condition. Let's see how Festinger (with the help of his associate James Carlsmith) set about testing this theory.

METHOD

Imagine you are a university student enrolled in an introductory psychology course. One of your course requirements is to participate for three hours during the semester as a subject in psychology experiments. You check the bulletin board that posts the various studies being carried out by professors and graduate students, and you sign up for one that lasts two hours and deals with "measures of performance." In this study by Festinger and Carlsmith, as in many psychology experiments, the true purpose of the study cannot be revealed to the subjects since this could seriously bias their responses and invalidate the results. The actual original group of subjects consisted of 71 male, lower-division psychology students.

You arrive at the laboratory at the appointed time (here, the laboratory is nothing more than a room). You are told that this experiment takes a little over an hour, so it had to be scheduled for two hours. Since there will be some time remaining, the experimenter informs you that some people from the psychology department are interviewing subjects about their experiences as subjects, and asks you to talk to them after participating. Then you are given your first task.

A tray containing 12 spools is placed in front of you and you are told to empty the tray onto the table, refill the tray with the spools, empty it again, refill it, and so on. You are to work with one hand and at your own speed. While the experimenter looks on with a stopwatch and takes notes, you do this over and over for 30 minutes. Then the tray is removed and you are given a board with 48 square pegs. Your task now is to turn each peg a quarter of a turn clockwise, and repeat this over and over for 30 minutes more! If this sounds incredibly boring to you, that was precisely the intention of the researchers. This part of the study was, in the authors' words, "intended to provide, for each subject uniformly, an experience about which he would have a somewhat negative opinion." Undoubtedly, you would agree that this objective was accomplished. Following completion of the tasks, the experiment really began.

The subjects were randomly assigned to one of three conditions. In the control condition, the subjects, after completing the tasks, were taken to another room where they were interviewed about their reactions to the experiment they had just "completed." The rest of the subjects were lured a little farther into the experimental manipulations. Following the tasks, the experimenter spoke to them as if to explain the purpose of the study. He told each of them that they were among the subjects in group A, who performed the tasks with no prior information, while subjects in group B always received descriptive information about the tasks prior to entering the lab. He went on to say that the information received by group B subjects was that the tasks were fun and interesting and that this message was delivered by an undergraduate student *posing* as a subject who had already completed the tasks. It is important to keep in mind here that none of this was true. It was a fabrication intended to make the next crucial part of the study realistic and believable. This was, in other words, the "cover story."

The experimenter then left the room for a few minutes. Upon returning he continued to speak, but now appeared somewhat confused and uncertain. He explained, a little embarrassed, that the undergraduate who usually gives the information to group B subjects had called in sick, there was a subject from group B waiting, and they were having trouble finding someone to fill in for him. He then very politely asked the subject if he would be willing to join in on the experiment and be the one to inform the waiting subject.

The experimenter offered some of the subjects a dollar each for their help, while others were offered $20. After a subject agreed, he was given a sheet of paper marked "FOR GROUP B" on which was written "IT WAS VERY ENJOYABLE, I HAD A LOT OF FUN, I ENJOYED MYSELF, IT WAS INTRIGUING, IT WAS EXCITING." The subject was then paid either $1 or $20 and taken into the waiting room to meet the incoming "subject." They were left alone in the waiting room for two minutes, after which time the experimenter returned, thanked the subject for his help, and led him to the interview room, where he was asked his opinions of the tasks exactly as had been asked of the subjects in the control condition.

If this whole procedure seems a bit complicated, it really is not. The bottom line is that there were three groups: one group who received $1 each to lie about the tasks, one group who were paid $20 each to lie about the tasks, and a control group who did not lie at all. The data from 11 of the subjects were not included in the final analysis because of procedural errors, so there were 20 subjects in each group.

RESULTS

The results of the study were reflected in how each of the subjects *actually* felt about the boring tasks in the final interview phase of the study. They were asked to rate the experiment as follows:

1. Were the tasks interesting and enjoyable? Measured on a scale of −5 (extremely dull and boring) to +5 (extremely interesting and enjoyable). The 0 point indicated the tasks were neutral, neither interesting nor uninteresting.
2. How much did you learn about your ability to perform such tasks? Measured on a 0 to 10 scale, where 0 means nothing learned and 10 means a great deal learned.

3. Do you believe the experiment and tasks were measuring anything important? Measured on a 0 to 10 scale, where 0 means no scientific value and 10 means great scientific value.
4. Would you have any desire to participate in another similar experiment? Measured on a scale of −5 (definitely dislike to participate) to +5 (definitely like to participate) with 0 indicating neutral feelings.

The averages of the answers to the interview questions arc presented in Table 1. Questions 1 and 4 were designed to address Festinger's theory of cognitive dissonance, and the differences indicated are clearly significant. Contrary to previous research interpretations in the field, and contrary to what most of us might expect using common sense, those subjects who were paid $1 for lying about the tasks were the ones who later reported liking the tasks more, compared with both those paid $20 to lie and those who did not lie. This finding is reflected both in the first direct question and also in the $1 group's greater willingness to participate in another similar experiment (question 4).

DISCUSSION

Let's examine how these findings support Festinger's theory. The theory states, in Festinger's words:

1. If a person is induced to do or say something that is contrary to his private opinion, there will be a tendency for him to change his opinion to bring it into correspondence with what he has said or done.
2. The larger the pressure used to elicit the overt behavior, the *weaker* will be the above-mentioned tendency.

In Festinger's study, subjects had to engage in extremely boring tasks and then make statements, contrary to their true opinions, that the

TABLE 1   Average Ratings on Interview Questions for Each Experimental Condition

QUESTION	CONTROL GROUP	$1 GROUP	$20 GROUP
1. How enjoyable tasks were (−5 to +5)*	−0.45	+1.35	−0.05
2. How much learned (0 to 10)	3.08	2.80	3.15
3. Scientific importance (0 to 10)	5.60	6.45	5.18
4. Participate in similar experiences (−5 to +5)*	−0.62	+1.20	−0.25

*Questions relevant to Festinger and Carlsmith's hypothesis.
(from p. 207)

tasks were fun and interesting. Following those statements, the subjects rated the tasks as more interesting (or, at least less boring) than control subjects who did not make such contrary statements (controls). Furthermore, those subjects who were paid $1 to lie reported finding the tasks much more interesting than those subjects paid $20 to lie. Festinger's explanation for this is that when people engage in *attitude-discrepant behavior* (the lie), but have strong justification for doing so ($20), they will experience only a small amount of dissonance and, therefore, not feel particularly motivated to make a change in their opinion. On the other hand, people who have *insufficient justification* ($1) for their attitude-discrepant behavior will experience greater levels of dissonance and, therefore, alter their opinions more radically in order to reduce the resultant discomfort. The theory may be presented graphically as follows:

$$\begin{matrix} & \textit{Sufficient} & & \textit{Attitude} \\ \textit{Attitude-discrepant} \rightarrow & \textit{justification for} \rightarrow & \textit{Dissonance} \rightarrow & \textit{change} \\ \textit{behavior} & \textit{behavior} & \textit{small} & \textit{small} \end{matrix}$$

$$\begin{matrix} & \textit{Insufficient} & & \textit{Attitude} \\ \textit{Attitude-discrepant} \rightarrow & \textit{justification for} \rightarrow & \textit{Dissonance} \rightarrow & \textit{change} \\ \textit{behavior} & \textit{behavior} & \textit{large} & \textit{large} \end{matrix}$$

QUESTIONS AND CRITICISMS

Festinger himself anticipated that previous researchers whose theories were threatened by this new idea would attempt to criticize the findings and offer alternate explanations for them (such as mental rehearsal and thinking up better arguments, as discussed at the beginning of this chapter). In order to counter these criticisms, the sessions in which the subject lied to the incoming "subject" were tape-recorded and rated by two independent raters who had no knowledge of which condition ($1 vs. $20) they were rating. Statistical analyses of these ratings showed no differences in the content or persuasiveness of the lies between the two groups. Therefore, the only apparent explanation remaining for the findings is what Festinger termed cognitive dissonance.

Over the years since cognitive dissonance was demonstrated by Festinger and Carlsmith, other researchers have refined—but not rejected—the theory. The various refinements were summarized by Cooper and Fazio (1984), who outlined four necessary steps for an attitude change to occur through cognitive dissonance. The first step is that the attitude-discrepant behavior must produce unwanted negative consequences. Festinger and Carlsmith's subjects had to lie to fellow students and convince them to participate in a very boring experiment. This produced the required negative consequences. This also explains why when you compliment someone on their clothes even though you can't stand them, your attitude toward the clothes doesn't change.

The second step is that personal responsibility must be taken for the negative consequences. This usually involves a choice. If you *choose* to behave in an attitude-discrepant way resulting in negative consequences, you will experience dissonance. However, if someone forces you to behave in that way, you will not feel personally responsible and no cognitive dissonance will result. Although Festinger and Carlsmith's article uses the phrase "forced compliance" in the title, the subjects actually believed that their actions were voluntary.

It has also been demonstrated that physiological arousal (step three) is a necessary component of the process of cognitive dissonance. Festinger felt that dissonance is an uncomfortable state of tension that motivates us to change our attitudes. Studies have shown that, indeed, when subjects freely behave in attitude-discrepant ways, they experience physiological arousal. Festinger and Carlsmith did not measure this with their subjects, but it is safe to assume that physiological arousal was present.

Finally, the fourth step is that the person must be aware that the arousal experienced is being caused by the attitude-discrepant behavior. The discomfort the subjects must have felt in Festinger and Carlsmith's study would have been easily and clearly attributed to the fact that they were lying about the experiment to a fellow student.

Festinger and Carlsmith's theory of cognitive dissonance has become a widely accepted and well-documented psychological event. Most psychologists agree that there are two fundamental processes by which our opinions and attitudes change. One is persuasion—when other people actively work to convince you to change your views—and the other is cognitive dissonance.

COOPER, J., and FAZIO, R. (1984) A new look at dissonance theory. In L. BERKOWITZ (ed.), *Advances in experimental social psychology*. New York: Academic Press.

SEVEN

PERSONALITY

If you ask yourself the question, "Who am I?," you are asking the same question posed by personality psychologists. Research on personality seeks to reveal those human characteristics that make each person unique and to determine where those characteristics came from. When behavioral scientists speak of personality, they are usually referring to qualities that are relatively stable across situations and consistent over time. Who you are does not change each day, each week, or, usually, even each year. Instead, there are certain things about you that are constant and predictable. It is this predictability that is of greatest interest to those who study personality. Hundreds of personality traits have been theorized by psychologists over the years. Most of these have been debated and argued so much that it is not clear whether they truly measure differences among individuals. However, a few characteristics have been repeatedly shown to predict specific *meaningful* behaviors. These are the focus of this section.

The first chapter discusses research that found differences in how people view the location of power in their lives. Some believe that their lives are controlled by external factors, such as fate, while others feel the control is internal; in their own hands. This quality of externality vs. internality has been shown to be a consistent and important factor in who you are. Next is a very famous body of research that attempted to explain how moral character develops and why some people appear to behave at a higher moral level than others. The third study is an experiment with dogs that demonstrated a phenomenon called "learned helplessness." This relates to personality in that it led to a theory explaining a possible source of depression in humans. Finally, you'll read about the highly influential study that first identified the personality characteristic of "Type A" and "Type B" behavior patterns and how Type A individuals are more prone to coronary heart disease.

ARE YOU THE MASTER OF YOUR FATE?

Rotter, Julian B. (1966) Generalized expectancies for internal vs. external control of reinforcement. *Psychological Monographs*, 80, 1–28.

Are the consequences of your behavior under your personal control or determined by forces outside of yourself? Think about it for a moment: When something good happens to you, do you take credit for it or do you think how lucky you were? When something negative occurs, is it usually your responsibility or do you just chalk it up to fate? The same question may be posed in more formal psychological language: Do you believe that there is a *causal* relationship between your behavior and its consequences?

Julian Rotter, one of the most influential behaviorists in psychology's history, proposed that individuals differ a great deal in where they place the responsibility for what happens to them. When people interpret the consequences of their behavior to be in the control of luck, fate, or powerful others, this indicates a belief in what Rotter called an "external locus of control" (locus simply means location). Conversely, he maintained that if people interpret their own behavior and personality characteristics as responsible for behavioral consequences, they have a belief in an "internal locus of control." In his frequently cited 1966 article that is the basis for this chapter, Rotter explained that a person's tendency to view events from an internal vs. an external locus of control can be explained from a *social learning theory* perspective.

In this view, as a person develops from infancy through childhood, behaviors are learned because they are followed by some form of reinforcement. This reinforcement increases the child's *expectancy* that a particular behavior will produce the desired reinforcement. Once this expectancy is established, the removal of reinforcement will cause the expectancy of such a relationship between behavior and reinforcement to fade. Therefore, reinforcement sometimes is seen as contingent upon behavior, and sometimes it is not (see the discussion of contingencies in the reading on work of B.F. Skinner). As children grow, some will have frequent experiences in which their behavior directly influences reinforcement, while for others, reinforcement will appear to result from actions outside of themselves. Rotter claimed that the totality of your specific learning experiences creates in you a *generalized expectancy* about whether reinforcement is internally or externally controlled.

"These generalized expectancies," Rotter wrote, "will result in characteristic differences in behavior in a situation culturally categorized as chance-determined vs. skill-determined, and may act to produce individual differences within a specific condition" (p. 2). In other words, you have developed an internal or external interpretation of the consequences for your behavior that will influence your future behavior in almost all situations. Rotter believed that your locus of control, whether internal or external, is an important part of who you are; a part of your personality.

So, look back at the questions posed at the beginning of this chapter. Which do you think you are, internal or external? Rotter wanted to study differences among people on this dimension and, rather than simply ask them, he developed a test that measures a person's locus of control. Once he was able to measure this characteristic in people, he could then study how it influenced their behavior.

THEORETICAL PROPOSITIONS

Rotter proposed to demonstrate two main points in his research. First, he predicted that a test could be developed to measure reliably the extent to which individuals possess an internal or an external locus of control orientation toward life. Second, he hypothesized that people will display stable individual differences in their interpretations of the causes of reinforcement in the same situations. He proposed to demonstrate his hypothesis by presenting research comparing behavior of "internals" with that of "externals" in various contexts.

METHOD

Rotter designed a scale containing a series of many pairs of statements. Each pair consisted of one statement reflecting an internal locus of control and one reflecting an external locus of control. Those taking the test were instructed to select "the one statement of each pair (and only one) which you more strongly believe to be the case as far as you're concerned. Be sure to select the one you actually *believe* to be more true rather than the one you think you should choose or the one you would like to be true. This is a measure of personal belief: Obviously there are no right or wrong answers" (p. 26). The test was designed so that subjects were forced to choose one statement for each pair and could not designate "neither" or "both."

Rotter's measuring device endured many revisions and alterations. In its earliest form, it contained 60 pairs of statements, but by using various tests for reliability and validity, it was eventually refined and streamlined down to 23 items. Added to these were six "filler items," which were designed to disguise the true purpose of the test. Such filler items are often used in tests such as this because if subjects were able to guess what the test is trying to measure, they might alter their answers in some way in an attempt to "perform better."

Rotter called his test the "I-E Scale," which is the name it is known by today. Table 1 includes examples of typical items from the I-E Scale, plus samples of the filler items. If you examine the items, you can see quite clearly which statements reflect an internal or external orientation. Rotter contended that his test was a measure of the extent to which a person possesses the personality characteristic of internal or external locus of control.

Rotter's next step was to demonstrate that this characteristic could actually be used to predict people's behavior in specific situations. To do this he reported on several studies (by Rotter and others) in which scores on the I-E Scale (in various forms) were examined in relation to individuals' interactions with various events in their lives. These studies found significant correlations between I-E scores and situations such as those involving gambling, hospitalization, political activism, persuasion, smoking, achievement motivation, and conformity.

RESULTS

Following is a brief summary of the findings reported by Rotter of research in the areas mentioned in the previous paragraph (see pp. 19–24 in the original study for complete discussion and citation of specific references).

Gambling

Rotter reported on studies that looked at betting behavior in relation to locus of control. These found that individuals identified as internals by the I-E scale tended to prefer betting on "sure things" and

TABLE 1   Sample Items and Filler Items from Rotter's I-E Scale

ITEM #	STATEMENTS
2a.	Many of the unhappy things in people's lives are partly due to bad luck.
b.	People's misfortunes result from the mistakes they make.
11a.	Becoming a success is a matter of hard work; luck has little or nothing to do with it.
b.	Getting a good job depends mainly on being in the right place at the right time.
18a.	Most people don't realize the extent to which their lives are controlled by accidental happenings.
b.	There is really no such thing as "luck."
23a.	Sometimes I can't understand how teachers arrive at the grades I get.
b.	There is a direct connection between how hard I study and the grades I get.

FILLER ITEMS

1a.	Children get into trouble because their parents punish them too much.
b.	The trouble with most children nowadays is that their parents are too easy with them.
14a.	There are certain people who are just no good.
b.	There is some good in everybody.

(from pp. 13–14)

liked intermediate odds over the long shots. Externals, on the other hand would wager more money on risky bets. In addition, externals would tend to engage in more unusual shifts in betting called the "gambler's fallacy" (such as betting more on a number that has not come up for a while on the basis that it is "due").

Hospitalization

Rotter believed that the more external someone is, the greater is their sense of powerlessness. A study cited to illustrate this gave the I-E Scale to patients in a tuberculosis hospital. Forty-three patients who were found to have an internal locus of control were compared with the same number of patients with an external orientation. Subjects in the two groups were equivalent, on average, on other factors such as income, education, and health status. It was found that the internals were more aware of their physical condition, discussed and questioned the doctors and nurses more, and were less satisfied with the amount of feedback they received from the hospital staff about their condition. The relationship between locus of control and health will be discussed in more detail shortly.

Political Activism

Rotter and others questioned African-American students in the 1960s at colleges in the southern United States about their activities related to the civil rights movement. Findings indicated that those who participated in marches and joined civil rights groups were significantly more oriented toward an internal locus of control.

Persuasion

An interesting study cited by Rotter used the I-E scale to select two groups of students, one highly internal and the other highly external. Both groups shared similar attitudes, on average, about the fraternity and sorority system on the campus. Both groups were asked to try to persuade other students to change their attitudes about these organizations. The internals were found to be significantly more successful than externals in altering the attitudes of others. Conversely, other studies demonstrated that internals were more resistant to manipulation of their attitudes by others.

Smoking

An internal locus of control appeared to relate to self-control as well. Two studies discussed by Rotter found that (1) smokers tended to be significantly more external than non-smokers, and (2) individuals who quit smoking after the original Surgeon General's warning appeared on cigarette packs were more internally oriented, even though both internals and externals believed the warning was true.

Achievement Motivation

If you believe your own actions are responsible for your successes, it is logical to assume that you should be more motivated to achieve success than someone who believes success is more a matter of fate. Rotter pointed to a study of 1,000 high school students that found a positive relationship between an internal score on the I-E Scale and 15 out of 17 indicators of this achievement motivation. These included plans to attend college, amount of time spent on homework, and how interested the parents were in the students' school work. Each of these achievement-oriented factors were more likely to be found for students with an internal locus of control.

Conformity

One study was cited that exposed subjects to the conformity test developed by Solomon Asch, in which a subject's willingness to agree with a majority's incorrect judgment was evidence for conforming behavior (see the reading on Asch's conformity study). Asch's method was altered slightly to allow subjects to bet (with money provided by the experimenters) on the correctness of their judgments. Under this betting condition, those found to be internals conformed significantly *less* to the majority and bet more money on themselves when making judgments contrary to the majority than did the externals.

DISCUSSION

As part of his discussion, Rotter posed possible sources for the individual differences he found on the dimension of internal-external locus of control. He referred to several studies that addressed the issue of possible causes. Three potential sources for the development of an internal or external orientation were suggested: cultural differences, socioeconomic differences, and variations in styles of parenting.

One study cited found differences in locus of control among various cultures. In an isolated community in the United States, three distinct groups could be compared: Ute Indians, Mexican-Americans, and whites. It was found that those individuals of Ute Indian heritage were, on average, the most external, while the whites were the most internal. The Mexican-Americans scored between the other two groups on the I-E Scale. These findings appeared to be independent of socioeconomic level and suggested ethnic differences in locus of control.

Rotter also referred to some early and tentative findings indicating that socioeconomic level even within a particular culture may relate to locus of control findings. These findings suggested that a lower socioeconomic position predicts greater externality.

Styles of parenting were implicated by Rotter as an obvious source for learning to be internal or external. While he did not offer supportive research evidence at the time, he suggested that parents who administer rewards and punishments to their children in ways that are unpredictable and inconsistent would likely encourage the development of an external locus of control. (Later research to be discussed shortly addressed this issue in greater detail.)

Rotter summarized his findings by pointing out that the consistency of the results leads to the conclusion that locus of control is a definable characteristic of individuals that operates fairly consistently across various situations. Furthermore, the influences on behavior produced by the internal-external dimension are such that it will influence different people to behave differently when faced with the same situation. In addition, Rotter contended that locus of control can be measured, and that the I-E Scale is an effective tool for doing so.

Finally, based on the research reported, Rotter hypothesized that those with an internal locus of control (that is, those who have a strong belief that they can control their own destiny) are more likely than externals to: (1) gain information from the situations in their life in order to improve future behavior in those situations or similar ones, (2) take the initiative to change and improve their condition in life, (3) place greater value on inner skill and achievement of goals, and (4) be more able to resist manipulation by others.

SUBSEQUENT RESEARCH

There have been hundreds of studies since Rotter developed his I-E Scale that have examined the relationship between locus of control and various behaviors. Following is a brief sampling of a few of those as they relate to rather diverse human behaviors.

In his 1966 article, Rotter touched on how locus of control might relate to health behaviors. Since then, other studies have examined the same relationship. In a review of locus of control research, Strickland (1978) found that individuals with an internal focus generally take more responsibility for their own health. They are more likely to engage in more healthy behaviors (such as not smoking and better nutritional habits) and practice greater care in avoiding accidents. Additionally, studies have found that internals generally have lower levels of stress and are less likely to suffer from stress-related illnesses.

Rotter's hypotheses regarding the relationship between parenting styles and locus of control have been at least partially confirmed. Research has shown that parents of children who are internals tend to be more affectionate, more consistent with discipline, and more concerned with teaching children to take responsibility for their actions. Parents of externally oriented children have been found to be more authoritarian and restrictive, and do not allow their children much opportunity for personal control (see Davis and Phares, 1969, for a discussion of those findings).

A fascinating study demonstrated how the concept of locus of control may have sociological and even catastrophic implications. Sims and Baumann (1972) applied Rotter's theory to explain why more people die in tornados in Alabama than in Illinois. These researchers noticed that the death rate from tornados was five times greater in the South than in the Midwest, and they set out to determine why. One by one they eliminated all of the explanations related to the physical locations, such as storm strength and severity (the storms are actually stronger in Illinois), time of day of the storms (an equal number occur at night in both regions), type of business and residence construction (masonry is as dangerous as wood-frame, but for different reasons), and the quality of warning systems (even before warning systems existed, Alabama had the same higher death rate).

With all the obvious environmental reasons ruled out, Sims and Baumann suggested that the difference might be due to psychological variables, and proposed the locus-of-control concept as a likely possibility. Questionnaires containing a modified version of Rotter's I-E Scale were administered to residents of four counties in Illinois and Alabama that had experienced a similar incidence of tornados and tornado-caused deaths. They found that the respondents from Alabama demonstrated a significantly more external locus of control than did those from Illinois. From this finding, as well as from responses to other items on the questionnaire relating to tornado behavior, the researchers concluded that an internal orientation promotes behaviors that are more likely to save lives in the event of a hurricane (such as paying attention to the news media or alerting others). This stems directly from the internals' belief that their behavior will be effective in changing the outcome of the event. In this study, Alabamians were seen as "less confident in themselves as causal agents, less convinced of their ability to engage in effective action. . . . The data . . . constitute a suggestive illustration of how man's personality is active in determining the quality of his interaction with nature" (Sims and Baumann, 1972, p. 1391).

CONCLUSION

The dimension of internal-external locus of control has been generally accepted as a relatively stable aspect of human personality that has meaningful implications for predicting behavior across a wide variety of situations. The phrase "relatively stable" is used because a person's locus of control can change under certain circumstances. Those who are externally oriented often will become more internal when their profession places them in positions of greater authority and responsibility. People who are highly internally oriented may shift toward a more external focus during times of extreme stress and uncertainty. Moreover, it is possible for individuals to *learn* to be more internal, if given the opportunity.

Implicit in Rotter's concept of locus of control is the assumption that internals are better adjusted and more effective in life. Although most of the research confirms this assumption, Rotter, in his later writings, sounded a note of caution (see Rotter, 1975). Everyone, especially internals, must be attentive to the environment around them. If a person sets out to change a situation that is not changeable, frustration, disappointment, and depression are the potential outcomes. When forces outside of the individual are actually in control of behavioral consequences, the most realistic and healthy approach to take is probably one of an external orientation.

DAVIS, W., and PHARES, E. (1969) Parental antecedents of internal-external control of reinforcement. *Psychological Reports*, 24, 427–36.

ROTTER, J. (1975) Some problems and misconceptions related to the construct of internal vs. external reinforcement. *Journal of Consulting and Clinical Psychology*, 43, 56–67.
SIMS, J., and BAUMANN, D. (1972) The tornado threat: Coping styles in the North and South. *Science*, 176, 1386–92.
STRICKLAND, B. (1977) Internal-external control of reinforcement. In T. BLASS (ed.), *Personality variables in social behavior*. Hillsdale, N.J.: Erlbaum.

HOW MORAL ARE YOU?
Kohlberg, Lawrence (1963) The development of children's orientations toward a moral order: Sequence in the development of moral thought. *Vita Humana*, 6, 11–33.

Have you ever really thought about your personal morality? What are the moral principles guiding your decisions in life? If you stop to think about it, experience tells you that people vary a great deal in terms of the morality of their thought and actions. Morals are generally defined by psychologists as attitudes and beliefs that children and adults hold that help them decide what is right and wrong. Your concept of morality is determined by the rules and norms of conduct that are set forth by the culture in which you have been raised and that have been *internalized* by you. Morality is not part of your "standard equipment" at birth: You were born without morals. Then, as you developed through childhood into adolescence and adulthood, you also developed your ideas about right and wrong. Every normal adult has a conception of morality. But where did this conception originate? What was the process by which it went from being a set of cultural rules to being part of who you are?

Probably the two most famous and influential figures in the history of research on the formation of morality were Jean Piaget (see the reading on Piaget's work) and Lawrence Kohlberg. Following Piaget's work and before Kohlberg's there had been a period of 20 to 30 years during which child psychologists paid little attention to morality. Kohlberg's research at the University of Chicago incorporated and expanded upon many of Piaget's ideas about intellectual development and sparked renewed interest in this area of study. As others had done in the past, Kohlberg was addressing this question: "How does the amoral infant become capable of morality?"

Using the work of Piaget as a starting point, Kohlberg theorized that the uniquely human ability to make moral judgments develops in a predictable way during childhood. Moreover, he believed that there are specific, identifiable "stages" of moral development, related and similar in concept to Piaget's stages of intellectual development. As Kohlberg explained, "The child can internalize the moral values of his parents and culture and make them his own only as he comes to relate these values to a comprehended social order and to his own goals as a social self" (Kohlberg, 1964). In other words, a child must reach a certain stage of intellectual ability in order to develop a certain level of morality.

With these ideas in mind, Kohlberg set about formulating a method for studying children's abilities to make moral judgments. From that research came his widely recognized theory of moral development.

THEORETICAL PROPOSITIONS

When Kohlberg asserted that morality is acquired in developmental stages, he was using the concept of *stage* in a precise and formal way. It is easy to think of nearly any ability as occurring in stages, but psychologists draw a clear distinction between changes that develop gradually over time (such as a person's height) and those that develop in distinct and separate stages. So when Kohlberg referred to "structural moral stages in childhood and adolescence," he meant that (1) each stage is a uniquely different kind of moral thinking and not just an increased understanding of an adult concept of morality; (2) the stages always occur in the same step-by-step sequence so that no stage is ever skipped and there is never backward progression; and (3) the stages are prepotent, meaning that children comprehend all stages below their own and perhaps have some understanding of no more than one stage above. Children are incapable of understanding higher stages, regardless of encouragement, teaching, or practice. Furthermore, they prefer to function at the highest moral stage they have reached. Also implied in this stage formulation of moral development is the notion that the stages are universal and they occur in the same order, regardless of individual differences in experience and culture.

Kohlberg believed that his theory of the formation of morality could be explored by giving children at various ages the opportunity to make moral judgments. If the reasoning they used to make moral decisions could be found to progress predictably at increasing ages, this would be evidence that his stage theory was essentially correct.

METHOD

Kohlberg's research methodology was really quite simple. He presented children of varying ages with 10 hypothetical moral dilemmas. Each child was interviewed for two hours and asked questions about the moral issues presented in the dilemmas. The interviews were tape recorded for later analysis of the moral reasoning used. Two of Kohlberg's most widely cited moral dilemmas were as follows.

The Brother's Dilemma. Joe's father promised he could go to camp if he earned the $50 for it, and then changed his mind and asked Joe to give him the money he had earned. Joe lied and said he had only earned $10 and went to camp using the other $40 he had made. Before he went, he told his younger brother, Alex, about the money and about lying to their father. Should Alex tell their father? (p. 12)

The Heinz Dilemma. In Europe, a woman was near death from a special kind of cancer. There was one drug that the doctors thought might save her. It was a form of radium that a druggist in the same town had recently discovered. The drug was expensive to make, but the druggist was charging 10 times what the drug cost him to make. He paid $200 for the radium and charged $2,000 for a small dose of the drug. The sick woman's husband, Heinz, went to everyone he knew to borrow the money, but he could only get together about $1,000, which is half of what it cost. He told the druggist that his wife was dying and asked him to sell it cheaper or let him pay later. But the druggist said: "No, I discovered the drug and I'm going to make money from it." So Heinz got desperate and broke into the man's store to steal the drug for his wife. Should the husband have done this? (p. 17)

The subjects in Kohlberg's original study were 72 boys living in the Chicago suburbs. The boys were in three different age groups, 10, 13, and 16 years. Half of each group were from lower-middle socioeconomic brackets and the other half were from the upper-middle brackets. During the course of the two-hour interviews, the children expressed between 50 and 150 moral ideas or statements.

Following are four examples quoted by Kohlberg of responses made by children of different ages to these dilemmas.

Danny, age 10, The Brother's Dilemma. "In one way it would be right to tell on his brother, or [else] his father might get mad at him and spank him. In another way it would be right to keep quiet, or [else] his brother might beat him up" (p. 12).

Don, age 13, The Heinz Dilemma. "It really was the druggist's fault, he was unfair, trying to overcharge and letting someone die. Heinz loved his wife and wanted to save her. I think anyone would. I don't think they would put him in jail. The judge would look at all sides and see the druggist was charging too much" (p. 19).

Andy, age 13, The Brother's Dilemma. "If my father finds out later, he won't trust me. My brother wouldn't either, but I wouldn't [feel so bad] if he (the brother) didn't" (p. 20).

George, age 16, The Heinz Dilemma. "I don't think so, since it says the druggist had a right to set the price. I can't say he'd actually be right; I suppose anyone would do it for a wife, though. He'd prefer to go to jail than have his wife die. In my eyes he'd have just cause to do it, but in the law's eyes he'd be wrong. I can't say more than that as to whether it was right or wrong" (p. 21).

Based on such statements, Kohlberg and his associates defined six stages of moral development and assigned the statements to one of the six stages. Additionally, there were six types of motives the subjects used to justify their reasoning, which corresponded to the six stages. It should be noted that each of the six stages of moral reasoning delineated by Kohlberg was intended to apply universally to any situation the child might encounter. The stages do not predict a specific action a child might take when faced with a real dilemma, but rather the reasoning the child would use in determining a course of action.

RESULTS

Kohlberg grouped the six stages he had found into three "moral levels," outlined in Table 1.

The early stages of morality, which Kohlberg called the "pre-moral" level, are characterized by egocentrism and personal interests. In stage 1, the child fails to recognize the interests of others and behaves morally out of fear of punishment for "bad" behavior. In

TABLE 1   Kohlberg's Six Stages of Moral Development

LEVEL 1. PRE-MORAL LEVEL

Stage 1.	Punishment and obedience orientation (consequences for actions determine right and wrong)
Stage 2.	Naive instrumental hedonism (satisfaction of one's own needs defines what is good)

LEVEL 2. MORALITY OF CONVENTIONAL ROLE–CONFORMITY

Stage 3.	"Good boy–nice girl" orientation (what pleases others is good)
Stage 4.	Authority maintaining morality (maintaining law and order, doing one's duty is good)

LEVEL 3. MORALITY OF SELF-ACCEPTED MORAL PRINCIPLES

Stage 5.	Morality of agreements and democratically determined law (society's values and individual rights determine right and wrong.)
Stage 6.	Morality of individual principles of conscience (right and wrong are a matter of individual philosophy according to universal principles)

(adapted from p. 13)

stage 2, the child begins to recognize the interests and needs of others, but behaves morally in order to get moral behavior back. Good behavior is, in essence, a manipulation of a situation to meet the child's own needs.

In level 2, conventional morality that is a part of a recognition of one's role in interpersonal relationships comes into play. In stage 3, the child behaves morally in order to live up to the expectations of others and maintain relationships that contain trust and loyalty. It is during this stage, according to Kohlberg, that "Golden Rule" thinking begins and the child becomes concerned about the feelings of others. Stage 4 begins the child's recognition of and respect for "law and order." Here a person takes the viewpoint of the larger social system and sees good behavior in terms of being a law-abiding citizen. There is no questioning of the established social order, but rather the belief that whatever upholds the law is good.

When a person enters level 3, judgments about morality begin to transcend formal societal laws. In stage 5, a recognition takes place that some laws are better than others. Sometimes what is moral may not be legal, and vice versa. The individual still believes that laws should be obeyed to maintain social harmony, but may seek to change laws through due process. At this stage, Kohlberg maintained, a person will experience conflict in attempting to integrate morality with legality. Finally, if a person reaches stage 6, his or her moral judgments will be based upon the belief that there are universal ethical principles. When laws violate these principles, the person behaves according to his or her ethical principles, regardless of the law. Morality is determined by the individual's own conscience. Kohlberg was to find in this and later studies that very few individuals actually reach stage 6. He eventually ascribed this level of reasoning to great leaders of conscience such as Gandhi, Thoreau, and Martin Luther King.

Kohlberg claimed that

> "a motivational aspect of morality was defined by the motive mentioned by the subject in justifying moral action. Six levels of motive were isolated, each congruent with one of the developmental types. They were as follows: 1. punishment by another; 2. manipulation of goods or rewards by another; 3. disapproval by others; 4. censure by legitimate authorities followed by feelings of guilt; 5. community respect and disrespect; 6. self-condemnation" (p. 13).

Finally, it was crucial to Kohlberg's stage theory that the different levels of moral reasoning advance with the age of the person. To test this, he analyzed the various stages corresponding to the children's answers according to the ages of the children. Figure 1 summarizes these findings. It is obvious from the data that as the age of the subjects

FIGURE 1 Stages of moral reasoning by age.

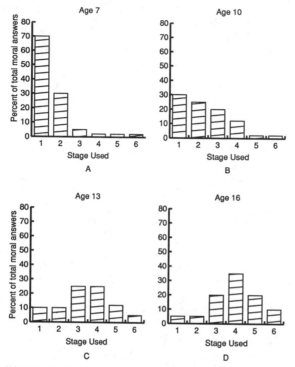

*Kohlberg notes that the data for this age group were acquired from an additional group of 12 7-year-old boys.
(figures adapted from data on p. 15 of original study)

increased, the children used increasingly higher stages of moral reasoning to respond to the dilemmas. Other statistical analyses demonstrated that the ability to use each stage appeared to be a prerequisite to moving to the next higher level.

DISCUSSION

In Kohlberg's discussion of the implications of his findings, he pointed out that this new conceptualization clarified how children actively organize the morality of the world around them in a series of predictable, sequential stages. For the child, this was not seen simply as an assimilation and internalization of adult moral teachings through verbal explanation and punishment, but as an *emergence* of cognitive moral structures that developed as a result of the child's interaction with the social and cultural environment. In this view, children do not simply learn morality, they *construct* it. What this means is that a child is literally incapable of understanding or using stage 3 moral reasoning before passing through stages 1 and 2. And a person would not apply the moral concepts of basic human rights found in stage 5 to solve a dilemma unless that person had already experienced and constructed the patterns of morality inherent in the first four stages. Further implications of this and later work of Kohlberg will be discussed shortly.

CRITICISMS AND SUBSEQUENT RESEARCH

As Kohlberg expanded and revised his stage theory of moral development over the nearly 30 years following this original study, it has received criticism from several perspectives. One of the most often cited of those is that even if Kohlberg was correct in his ideas about moral reasoning, this does not mean they can be applied to moral behavior. In other words, what a person *says* is moral may not be reflected in the person's moral *actions*. Several studies have demonstrated a lack of correspondence between moral reasoning and moral behavior, while others have found evidence that such a relationship does exist. One interesting line of research related to this criticism focused on the importance of situational factors, inadequately addressed by Kohlberg, in determining whether someone will act according to his or her stage of moral reasoning (see Kurtines, 1986). While there appears to be some validity in this criticism, Kohlberg acknowledged that his theory was intended to apply to moral *reasoning*. The fact that situational forces may sometimes alter moral behavior does not imply that moral reasoning does not progress through the stages he described.

Another criticism of Kohlberg's work has focused on his claim that the six stages of moral reasoning are universal. These critics claim that Kohlberg's stages represent an interpretation of morality that is uniquely found in Western democratic societies and, therefore, would not apply to the non-Western cultures that make up most of the world's population. As one of these critics has pointed out: "The definition of the stages and the assumptions underlying them, including the view that the scheme is universally applicable, are ethnocentric and culturally biased" (Simpson, 1974, p. 82). In defense of the universality of Kohlberg's ideas, recent research examined 45 studies that have been conducted in 27 different cultures (see Snarey, 1987). In each study, researchers found that their subjects all passed through the stages in the same sequence, without reversals, and that stages 1 through 5 were present in all the cultures studied. Interestingly, however, in a few of the cultures (Taiwan, Papua–New Guinea, and Israel), some of the moral judgments did not fit into any of Kohlberg's six stages. These were judgments based on the welfare of the entire community. Such reasoning was not found in the judgments made by American male subjects.

Finally, a third area of criticism deals with the belief that Kohlberg's stages of moral development may not apply equally to males and females. The researcher leading this line of questioning is Carol Gilligan (see Gilligan, 1982). She has maintained that women and men do not think about morality in the same way. In her own research she found that in making moral decisions, women talked more than men about interpersonal relationships, responsibility for others, avoiding hurting others, and the importance of the connections among people. She called this foundation upon which women's morality rests a "care orientation." Based on this gender difference, Gilligan has argued that women will score lower on Kohlberg's scale because the lower stages deal more with these relationship issues (such as stage 3, which is based primarily on building trust and loyalty in relationships). Men, on the other hand, Gilligan says, make moral decisions based on issues of justice, which fit more easily into Kohlberg's highest stages. She contends that neither of these approaches to morality is superior, and that if women are judged to be at a lower moral level than men it is because of an unintentional gender bias built into the theory.

Researchers, for the most part, have failed to find support for Gilligan's assertion. Several studies have found no significant gender differences in moral reasoning using Kohlberg's methods. Gilligan has responded to those negative findings by acknowledging that although women are capable of using all levels of moral reasoning, in their real lives they choose not to. Instead, women focus on the human relationship aspects discussed in the preceding paragraph. This has been demonstrated by research (not employing Kohlberg's methods specifically) showing how girls are willing to make a greater effort to help another person in need and tend to score higher on tests of emotional empathy (see Hoffman, 1977, for a complete discussion of these gender issues).

CONCLUSION

Dialog and debate on Kohlberg's work within the behavioral sciences has continued to the present and shows every sign of continuing vigorously into the future. Its ultimate validity and importance remain to be clearly defined. However, few new conceptualizations of human development have produced the amount of research, speculation, and debate that surrounds Kohlberg's theory of moral development. And its usefulness to society, in one sense, was predicted by Kohlberg in this statement from 1964:

> While any conception of moral education must recognize that the parent cannot escape the direct imposition of behavior demands and moral judgments upon the child, it may be possible to define moral education

primarily as a matter of stimulating the development of the child's *own* moral judgment and its control of action. . . .The writer [Kohlberg] has found teachers telling 13-year-olds not to cheat 'because the person you copied from might have it wrong and so it won't do you any good.' Most of these children were capable of advancing much more mature reasons for not cheating. . . . Children are almost as likely to reject moral reasoning beneath their level as to fail to assimilate reasoning too far above their level (Kohlberg, 1964, p. 425).

GILLIGAN, C. (1982) *In a different voice: Psychological theory and women's development.* Cambridge: Harvard University Press.

HOFFMAN, M.L. (1977) Sex differences in empathy and related behavior. *Psychological Bulletin*, 84, 712–22.

KOHLBERG, L. (1964) Development of moral character and moral ideology. In H. HOFFMAN and L. HOFFMAN (eds.), *Review of Child Development Research* (Vol. 1). New York: Russell Sage.

KURTINES, W. (1986) Moral behavior as rule-governed behavior: Person and situation effect on moral decision making. *Journal of Personality and Social Psychology*, 50, 784–91.

SIMPSON, E. (1974) Moral development research: A case of scientific cultural bias. *Human Development*, 17, 81–106.

SNAREY, J. (1987) A question of morality. *Psychological Bulletin*, 97, 202–32.

LEARNING TO BE DEPRESSED

Seligman, Martin E.P., and Maier, Steven F. (1967) Failure to escape traumatic shock. *Journal of Experimental Psychology*, 74, 1–9.

If you are like most people, you expect that your actions will produce certain consequences. Your expectations cause you both to behave in ways that will produce desirable consequences and to avoid behaviors that will lead to undesirable consequences. In other words, your actions are determined, at least in part, by your belief that they will bring about a certain result; they are *contingent* upon a certain consequence (see the readings on B.F. Skinner and J. Rotter for discussions on behavioral contingencies).

Let's assume for a moment that you are unhappy in your present job, so you begin the process of making a change. You make contacts with others in your field, read publications that advertise positions in which you are interested, begin training in the evening to acquire new skills, and so on. All of those actions are motivated by your belief that your effort will eventually lead to the outcome of a better job and a happier life. The same is true of interpersonal relationships. If you are in a relationship that is wrong for you because it is abusive or it otherwise makes you unhappy, you will take the necessary actions to change it or end it because you *expect* to succeed in making the desired changes.

All of these are issues of power and control. Most people believe they are personally powerful and able to control what happens to them, at least part of the time, because they have exerted control in the past and have been successful. They believe they are able to help themselves achieve their goals. If this perception of power and control is lacking, all that is left is helplessness. If you feel you are stuck in an unsatisfying job and you are unable to find another job or learn new skills to improve your professional life, you will be unlikely to make the effort needed to change. If you are too dependent on the person with whom you have a damaging relationship and you feel powerless to fix it or end it, you may simply remain in the relationship and endure the pain.

Perceptions of power and control are crucial for psychological and physical health (refer to the discussion on the research by Langer and Rodin on issues of control for the elderly in nursing homes). Imagine how you would feel if you suddenly found that you no longer had the power or control to make changes in your life; that what happened to you was *independent* of your actions. You would probably feel helpless and hopeless, and you would give up trying altogether. In other words, you would become depressed.

Martin Seligman, a well-known and influential behavioral psychologist, maintains that our perceptions of power and control are learned from experience. He believes that when a person's efforts at controlling certain life events fail repeatedly, the person may stop attempting to exercise control altogether. If these failures happen often enough, the person may generalize the perception of lack of control to all situations, even when control may actually be possible. This person then begins to feel like a "pawn of fate" and becomes helpless and depressed. Seligman termed this cause of depression *learned helplessness*. He developed his theory at the University of Pennsylvania, in a series of now classic experiments that used dogs as subjects. The research discussed here that Seligman conducted with Steven Maier is considered to be the definitive original demonstration of his theory.

THEORETICAL PROPOSITIONS

Seligman had found in an earlier experiment on learning that when dogs were exposed to electrical shocks they could neither control nor escape from, they later failed to learn to escape from shocks when such escape was easily available. You have to imagine how odd this looked to a behaviorist. In the laboratory, dogs had experienced shocks that were designed to be punishing, but not harmful. Later, they were placed in a "shuttle box," which is a large box with two halves divided by a partition. An electrical current could be activated in the floor on either side of the box. When a dog was on one side and felt the electricity, it simply had to jump over the partition to the other side to escape the shock. Normally, dogs and other animals learn this escape behavior very quickly (it's not difficult to see why!). In fact, if a signal (such as a flashing light or a buzzer) warns the dog of the impending electrical current, the animal will learn to jump over the partition before the shock and thus avoid it completely. However, in Seligman's experiment, when the dogs that had already experienced electrical shocks from which they could not escape were placed into the shuttle box, they did not learn this escape-avoidance behavior.

Seligman theorized that there was something in what the animals had learned about their ability to *control* the unpleasant stimulus that determined the later learning. In other words, these dogs had learned from previous experience with electrical shocks that their actions were ineffective in changing the consequence of the shocks. Then, when they were in a new situation where they *did* have the power to escape—to exercise control—they just gave up. They had learned to be helpless.

To test this theory, Seligman and Maier proposed to study the effect of controllable vs. uncontrollable shock on later ability to learn to avoid shock.

METHOD

This is one of several classic studies in this book that used animals as subjects. However, this one, probably more than any of the others, raises questions about the ethics of animal research. Dogs received electrical shocks that were designed to be painful (though not physically harmful) in order to test a psychological theory. Whether such treatment was (or is) ethically justifiable is an issue that must be faced by every researcher and student of psychology. (This issue will be addressed again after a discussion of the results of Seligman's research.)

Subjects for this experiment were 24 "mongrel dogs, 15 to 19 inches high at the shoulder and weighing between 25 and 29 pounds" (p. 2). They were divided into three groups of eight. One group was the "escape group," another the "no-escape group," and the third was the no-harness control group.

The dogs in the escape and no-escape groups were placed individually in a harness similar to that developed by Pavlov (see page 68 for a description of Pavlov's methods); they were restrained, but not completely unable to move. On either side of the dog's head was a panel to keep the head facing forward. A subject could press the panel on either side by moving its head. When an electrical shock was delivered to a dog in the escape group, it could terminate the shock by pressing either panel with its head. For the no-escape group, each dog was paired with a dog in the escape group (this is an experimental procedure called "yoking"). Identical shocks were delivered to each pair of dogs at the same time, but the no-escape group had no control over the shock. No matter what those dogs did, the shock continued until it was terminated by the panel press of the dog in the escape group. This ensured that both groups of dogs received exactly the same duration and intensity of shock, the only difference being that one group had the power to stop it and the other did not. The eight dogs in the no-harness control group received no shocks at this stage of the experiment.

The subjects in the escape and no-escape groups received 64 shocks at about 90-second intervals. The escape group quickly learned to press the side panels and terminate the shocks (for themselves and for the no-escape group). Then, 24 hours later, all the dogs were tested in a shuttle box similar to the one described above. There were lights on either side of the box. When the lights were turned off on one side, an electrical current would pass through the floor of the box 10 seconds later. If a dog jumped the barrier within those 10 seconds, it escaped the shock completely. If not, it would continue to feel the shock until it jumped over the barrier or until 60 seconds of shock passed, at which time the shock was discontinued. Each dog was given 10 trials in the shuttle box.

Learning was measured by the following: (1) how much time it took, on average, from the time the light in the box went out until the dog jumped the barrier, and (2) the percentage of dogs in each group that failed entirely to learn to escape the shocks. Also, the dogs in the no-escape group received 10 additional trials in the shuttle box seven days later to assess the lasting effects of the experimental treatment.

RESULTS

In the escape group, the time it took for the dogs to press the panel and stop the shock quickly decreased over the 64 shocks. In the no-escape group, panel pressing completely stopped after 30 trials.

Figure 1 shows the average time to escape for the three groups of subjects over all the trials in the shuttle box. Remember, this was the time between when the lights were turned off and when the animal jumped over the barrier. The difference between the no-escape group and the other two groups was statistically significant, but the small difference between the escape group and the no-harness group was insignificant. Figure 2 illustrates the percentage of subjects from each

FIGURE 1   Average time to escape in shuttle box.

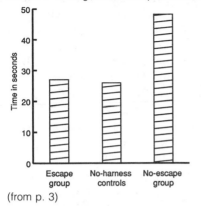

(from p. 3)

group that failed to jump over the barrier and escape the shock in the shuttle box in at least nine of the 10 trials. This difference between the escape and no-escape groups was also highly significant. Six of the subjects in the no-escape group failed entirely to escape on either nine or all 10 of the trials. Those six dogs were tested again in the shuttle box seven days later. In this delayed test, five of the six failed to escape on every trial.

DISCUSSION

Since the only difference between the escape and the no-escape groups was the dogs' ability to actively terminate the shock, Seligman and Maier concluded that it must have been this control factor that accounted for the clear difference in the two groups' later learning to escape the shock in the shuttle box. In other words, the reason the escape group subjects

FIGURE 2   Percent of subjects failing to learn to escape shock in shuttle box.

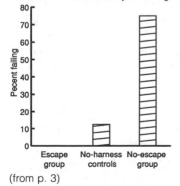

(from p. 3)

performed normally in the shuttle box was that they had learned in the harness phase that their behavior was correlated with the termination of the shock. Therefore, they were motivated to jump the barrier and escape from the shock. For the no-escape group, the termination of shock in the harness was independent of their behavior. Thus, since they had no expectation that their behavior in the shuttle box would terminate the shock, they had no incentive to attempt to escape. They had, as Seligman and Maier had predicted, *learned* to be *helpless*.

Occasionally, a dog from the no-escape group made a successful escape in the shuttle box. Following this, however, it reverted to helplessness on the next trial. Seligman and Maier interpreted this to mean that the animals' previous ineffective behavior in the harness prevented the formation of a new behavior (jumping the barrier) to terminate shock in a new situation (the shuttle box), even after a successful experience.

In their article, Seligman and Maier reported the results of a subsequent experiment that offered some interesting additional findings. In this second study, dogs were first placed in the harness-escape condition where the panel press would terminate the shock. They were then switched to the no-escape harness condition before receiving 10 trials in the shuttle box. These subjects continued to attempt to panel press throughout all the trials in the no-escape harness and did not give up as quickly as did those in the first study. Moreover, they all successfully learned to escape and avoid shock in the shuttle box. This indicated that once the animals had learned that their behavior could be effective, subsequent experiences with failure were not adequate to extinguish their motivation to change their fate.

SUBSEQUENT RESEARCH

Of course, Seligman wanted to do what you are probably already doing: apply these findings to humans. In later research, he asserted that the development of depression in humans involves processes similar to those of learned helplessness in animals. In both situations there is passivity, giving up and "just sitting there," lack of aggression, slowness to learn that a certain behavior is successful, weight loss, and social withdrawal. Both the helpless dog and the depressed human patient have learned from specific past experiences that their actions are useless. The dog was unable to escape the shocks, no matter what it did, while the human had no control over events such as the death of a loved one, an abusive parent, the loss of a job, or a serious illness (see Seligman, 1975).

The learned helplessness that leads to depression in humans can have serious consequences beyond the depression itself. Research has demonstrated that the elderly who, for various reasons such as nursing-home living, are forced to relinquish control over their daily activities have poorer health and a greater chance of dying sooner than those who are able to maintain a sense of personal power (for a discussion of related research by Langer and Rodin see the reading on the study). In addition, several studies have demonstrated that uncontrollable stressful events can play a role in serious diseases such as cancer. One such study found an increased risk of cancer in individuals who in previous years had suffered the loss of a spouse, the loss of a profession, or the loss of prestige (Horne and Picard, 1979). In hospitals, patients are expected by the doctors and staff to be cooperative, quiet, and willing to place their fates in the hands of the medical authorities. Patients believe that they must follow doctors' and nurses' instructions without question in order to recover as quickly as possible. A prominent health psychologist has suggested that being a "good hospital patient" implies that one must be passive and give up all expectations of control. This actually may create a condition of learned helplessness in the patients whereby they fail to exert control later when control is both possible and desirable for continued recovery (Taylor, 1979).

As further evidence of the learned helplessness effect, consider the following remarkable study by Finkelstein and Ramey (1977). Groups of human infants had rotating mobiles mounted over their cribs. One group of infants had special pressure-sensitive pillows so that by moving their heads, they could control the rotation of the mobile. Another group of infants had the same mobiles, but these were programmed to turn randomly without any control by the infants. After a two-week exposure to the mobiles for 10 minutes each day, the control-pillow group had become very skilled at moving their heads to make the mobiles turn. However, the most important finding came when the no-control group of infants was later given the same control pillows and an even greater amount of learning time than the first group. The infants failed entirely to learn to control the rotation of the mobiles. Their experience in the first situation had taught them that their behavior was ineffective, and this knowledge transferred to the new situation where control was possible. In terms of moving mobiles, the infants had learned to be helpless.

CONCLUSION

In conclusion, it is important to return to the issue of experimental ethics. For most of us, it is difficult to read about animals, especially dogs, being subjected to painful shocks in a psychology laboratory. Over the years, standards have been developed to ensure that laboratory animals are treated humanely (see the discussion of this issue in the preface of this book). However, there are many, both within and outside the scientific professions, who believe these standards to be inadequate. Some advocate the complete elimination of animal research in psychology, medicine, and all the sciences. Whatever your personal stand on this issue, the question you should be asking is this: Do the findings from the research extend our knowledge, reduce human suffering, and improve the quality of life sufficiently to justify the methods used to carry out the study?

Ask yourself that question about this study by Seligman and Maier. What they found were the beginnings of a theory to explain why some people become helpless, hopeless, and depressed. Seligman went on to develop a widely accepted model of the origins of and treatments for depression. Over the years his theory has been refined and detailed so that it applies more accurately to types of depression that occur under well-defined conditions. For example, individuals are most likely to become depressed if they have learned to attribute their lack of control to causes that are (1) permanent rather than temporary, (2) related to factors within their own personality (instead of situational factors), and (3) pervasive across many areas of their life (see Abramson, Seligman, and Teasdale, 1978). By understanding this, therapists and counselors have become better able to understand, intervene in, and treat serious depression.

Does this knowledge justify the methods used in the early research on learned helplessness? You decide.

ABRAMSON, L., SELIGMAN, M., and TEASDALE, J. (1978) Learned helplessness in humans: Critique and reformulation. *Journal of Abnormal Psychology*, 87, 49–74.

FINKELSTEIN, N., and RAMEY, C. (1977) Learning to control the environment in infancy. *Child Development*, 48, 806–19.

HORN, R., and PICARD, R. (1979) Psychosocial risk factors for lung cancer. *Psychosomatic Medicine*, 41, 503–14.

SELIGMAN, M. (1975) *Helplessness: On depression, development, and death.* San Francisco: Freeman.

TAYLOR, S. (1979) Hospital patient behavior: Reactance, helplessness, or control? *Journal of Social Issues*, 35, 156–84.

RACING AGAINST YOUR HEART

Friedman, Meyer, and Rosenman, Ray H. (1959) Association of specific overt behavior pattern with blood and cardiovascular findings. *Journal of the American Medical Association*, 169, 1286–96.

Who are you? If someone were to ask you that question, you would probably respond by describing some of your more obvious or dominant characteristics. Such characteristics, often referred to as traits, are important in making you the unique person that you are. Traits are assumed to be consistent across situations and over time. The psychologists who have supported the trait theory of personality (and not all have) have proposed various groups of traits that exist in all of us, but in different amounts. An example of a trait that appears to influence a great deal of our behavior is that of introversion-extroversion. Introverts tend to be reserved, withdrawn, and more focused on ideas than social relations. Extroverts are more sociable and friendly, and are more involved in events outside the self. You probably have a sense of which you are (most of the time), and you can also place family and friends in one category or the other. This trait, which is only one of many, allows us to predict something about a person's behavior in a given situation. The predictive ability of personality traits is what makes them interesting to most psychologists. Therefore, it is easy to imagine how dramatically this interest would increase if certain personality characteristics were found to predict how healthy you will be or even predict your chances of dying from a heart attack.

Well, most of you are probably aware of one group of characteristics related to health, popularly known as the "Type A personality." This name is somewhat inaccurate however, because in the scientific research, Type A refers to a specific pattern of behavior rather than the overall personality of an individual. This behavior pattern was first reported in the late 1950s by two cardiologists, Meyer Friedman and Ray Rosenman, and it has had a huge influence in how we view the causes of certain illnesses.

The story of where these doctors obtained the idea for their research demonstrates how careful observation of small details can sometimes lead to major scientific breakthroughs. Dr. Friedman was having the furniture in his office waiting room reupholstered. The upholsterer pointed out that the material on the couches and chairs had not worn out in a normal way. Instead, the front edges of the seat cushions had worn away faster than the rest had. It was as if Dr. Friedman's cardiac patients were literally sitting on the edge of their seats. This observation prompted him to wonder if there was something different about the overall behavior of his patients (people with heart disease), compared with that of healthy people.

Through surveys of executives and physicians, Friedman and Rosenman found that there was a common belief that people exposed over long periods of time to chronic stress from excessive drive, pressure to meet deadlines, competitive situations, and economic frustration are more likely to develop heart disease. They decided to put these ideas to a scientific test.

THEORETICAL PROPOSITIONS

Using their earlier research and clinical observations, the two cardiologists developed a model or set of characteristics for a specific overt (observable) behavior pattern that they believed was related to increased levels of cholesterol and consequently to coronary heart disease (CHD). This pattern, labeled pattern A, consisted of the following characteristics (see p. 1286 of the original study): (1) an intense, sustained drive to achieve one's personal goals; (2) a profound tendency and eagerness to compete in all situations; (3) a persistent desire for recognition and advancement; (4) continuous involvement in multiple activities that are constantly subject to deadlines; (5) habitual tendency to rush to finish activities; and (6) extraordinary mental and physical alertness.

The researchers then developed a second set of overt behaviors, labeled pattern B. Pattern B was described as essentially the opposite of pattern A, and was characterized by a relative absence of the following: drive, ambition, sense of time urgency, desire to compete, or involvement in deadlines.

A third set of behaviors, pattern C, was also formulated for this study. It involved a similar pattern to B, but also included a chronic state of anxiety or insecurity. The researchers chose 46 unemployed blind men for this group. Because this group differed from the other two groups of subjects (to be discussed momentarily) in many ways, and because the important and meaningful findings of the study focused on patterns A and B, the portions of the research dealing with pattern C will be omitted from the discussion here.

Friedman and Rosenman next needed to find subjects for their research who fit the descriptions of patterns A and B. To do this they contacted managers and supervisors of various large companies and corporations. They explained the behavior patterns and asked the managers to select from among their associates those who most closely fit the particular patterns. The groups that were finally selected consisted of various levels of executives and non-executives, all males. There were 83 men in each group, with an average age in group A of 45; in group B, 43. All subjects were given several tests relating to the goals of the study.

The Personal Interview

The interviews were designed to assess the history of CHD in the subjects' parents; the subjects' own history of heart trouble; the number of hours of work, sleep, and exercise each week; and smoking, alcohol, and dietary habits. Also during these interviews, the researchers determined if a subject had a fully or only partially developed behavior pattern in his group (either A or B), based on body movements; tone of conversation; teeth clenching; gesturing; general air of impatience; and the subjects' own admission of drive, competitiveness, and time urgency. It was determined that 69 of the 83 men in group A exhibited this *fully* developed pattern, while 58 of the 83 subjects in group B were judged to be of the *fully* developed Type B.

Diet and Alcohol Survey

All subjects were asked to keep a diary of everything they ate or drank over one week's time. Code numbers were assigned to the subjects so that they would not feel reluctant to report alcohol consumption honestly. The diets of the subjects were then broken down and analyzed by a hospital dietitian who was not aware of the subjects' identities or to which group they belonged.

Blood and Cardiovascular Tests

Blood was taken from all subjects to measure cholesterol levels and clotting time. Instances of coronary heart disease were determined through careful questioning of the subjects about past coronary health and through standard electrocardiogram readings. These readings were interpreted by Rosenman and by an independent cardiologist not involved in the study. With one exception, their interpretations agreed for all subjects.

The number of subjects with *arcus senilis* was determined through illuminated inspection of the subjects' eyes. *Arcus senilis* refers to the formation of an opaque ring around the cornea of the eye caused by the breakdown of fatty deposits in the bloodstream.

Now let's try to boil down all of Friedman and Rosenman's data and see what they found.

RESULTS

From the interviews, it appeared that the men chosen for each group fit the profile developed by the researchers. Group A subjects were found to be chronically harassed by commitments, ambitions, and drives. Also, they were clearly eager to *compete* in all of their activities, both professional and recreational. In addition, they also admitted a strong desire to *win*. The men in group B were found to be strikingly different from those in group A, especially in their lack of the sense of time urgency. The men in group B appeared to be satisfied with their present positions in life and avoided pursuing multiple goals and competitive situations. They were much less concerned about advancement and typically spent more time with their families and in non-competitive recreational activities.

Table 1 is a summary of the most relevant comparisons for the two groups on the characteristics from the tests and surveys. Table 2 summarizes the outcome measurements relating to blood levels and illnesses. As can be seen in Table 1, the two groups were similar on nearly all of the measured characteristics. Although the men in group A tended to be a little higher on most of the measurements, the only differences that were *statistically* significant were the number of cigarettes smoked each day and the percentage of men whose parents had a history of coronary heart disease.

However, if you take a look at the cholesterol and illness levels in Table 2, some very convincing differences emerge. First, though, considering the overall results in the table, it appears that no meaningful difference in blood clotting time was found for the two groups. The speed at which your blood coagulates relates to your potential for heart disease and other vascular illness. The *slower* your clotting time, the less your risk. In order to examine this statistic more closely, Friedman and Rosenman compared the clotting times for those subjects who exhibited a "fully developed" Type A pattern (6.8 minutes) with those judged as "fully developed" Type Bs (7.2 minutes). This difference in clotting time was statistically significant.

There is little doubt about the other findings in Table 2. Cholesterol levels were clearly and significantly higher for group A subjects. This difference was even greater if the subjects with the fully developed patterns were compared. The incidence of *arcus senilis* was three times greater for group A and five times greater in the fully developed comparison groups.

Finally, the key finding of the entire study, and the one that secured its place in history, was the striking difference in the incidence of clinical coronary heart disease found in the two groups. In group A, 23 of the subjects (28 percent) exhibited clear evidence of CHD,

TABLE 1 Comparison of Characteristics for Group A and Group B (Averages)

	WEIGHT	WORK HOURS/WEEK	EXERCISE HOURS/WEEK	NUMBER OF SMOKERS	CIGARETTES/DAY	ALCOHOL CALORIES/DAY	TOTAL CALORIES	FAT CALORIES	PARENTS WITH CHILDREN
Group A	176	51	10	67	23	194	2,049	944	36
Group B	172	45	7	56	15	149	2,134	978	27

(compiled from data on 1289–93)

TABLE 2 Comparisons of Blood and Illness for Group A and Group B

	AVERAGE CLOTTING TIME (MINUTES)	AVERAGE SERUM CHOLESTEROL	ARCUS SENILIS (PERCENT)	CORONARY DISEASE (PERCENT)
Group A	6.9	253	38	28
Group B	7.0	215	11	4

(compiled from data on p. 1293)

compared with three men (4 percent) in group B. When the researchers examined these findings in terms of the fully developed subgroups, the evidence became even stronger. All 23 of the CHD cases in group A came from those men with the fully developed Type A pattern. For group B, all three of the cases were from those subjects exhibiting the *incomplete* Type B pattern.

DISCUSSION OF FINDINGS

The conclusion implied by the authors was that the Type A behavior pattern was a major cause of CHD and related blood abnormalities. However, if you carefully examine the data in the tables, you will notice a couple of possible alternative explanations for those results. One was that group A men reported a greater incidence of CHD in their parents. Therefore, maybe it was something genetic rather than the behavior pattern that accounted for the differences found. The other rather glaring difference was the greater number of cigarettes smoked per day by group A subjects. Today we know that smoking contributes to CHD. So, perhaps it was not the Type A behavior pattern that produced the results, but rather the heavier smoking.

Friedman and Rosenman responded to both of those potential criticisms in their discussion of the findings. First, they found that within group A, an equal number of light smokers (10 cigarettes or fewer per day) had CHD as did heavy smokers (more than 10 cigarettes per day). Second, in group B there were 46 men who smoked heavily, yet only two exhibited CHD. These findings led the authors to suggest that cigarette smoking may have been a characteristic of the Type A behavior pattern, but not a direct cause of the CHD that was found. It is important to remember that this study was done over 30 years ago, before the link between smoking and CHD was as firmly established as it is today.

As for the possibility of parental history creating the differences, "the data also revealed that of the 30 group A men having a positive parental history, only eight (27 percent) had heart disease and of 53 men without a parental history, 15 (28 percent) had heart disease. None of the 23 group B men with a positive parental history exhibited clinical heart disease" (p. 1293). Again, more recent research that controlled carefully for this factor has demonstrated a family link in CHD. However, it is not clear whether it is a tendency toward heart disease or toward a certain behavior pattern (such as Type A) that is inherited.

SIGNIFICANCE OF THE RESEARCH
AND SUBSEQUENT FINDINGS

This study by Friedman and Rosenman was of crucial importance to the history of psychological research for three basic reasons. First, this was one of the earliest systematic studies to establish clearly that specific behavior patterns characteristic of some individuals can contribute in dramatic ways to serious illness. This sent a message to physicians that to consider only the physiological aspects of illnesses may be wholly inadequate for successful prognosis, treatment, intervention, and prevention. Second, this study began a new line of scientific inquiry into the relationship between behavior and CHD that has produced scores of research articles. The concept of the Type A behavior pattern and its connection to CHD has been refined to the point that it may be possible to prevent heart attacks in high-risk individuals before the first one occurs.

The third long-range outcome of Friedman and Rosenman's research is that it has played an important role in the creation and growth of a relatively new branch of the behavioral sciences called health psychology. Health psychologists study all aspects of health and medicine in terms of the psychological influences that exist in health promotion and maintenance, the prevention and treatment of illness, the causes of illness, and the health care system.

One subsequent study is especially important to report here. In 1976, Rosenman and Friedman published the results of a major eight-year study of over 3,000 men who were diagnosed at the beginning of the study as being free of heart disease and who fit the Type A behavior pattern. Compared with the subjects with Type B behavior pattern, these men were twice as likely to develop CHD, suffered significantly more fatal heart attacks, and reported five times more coronary problems. What was perhaps even more important, however, was that the Type A pattern predicted *who* would develop CHD independently of other predictors such as age, cholesterol level, blood pressure, or smoking habits (Rosenman et al., 1976).

One question you might be asking yourself by now is, Why? What is it about this Type A pattern that causes CHD? The most widely accepted theory answers that Type As respond to stressful events by becoming excessively physiologically aroused. This extreme arousal causes the body to produce more hormones such as epinephrine (adrenalin) and also increases heart rate and blood pressure. Over time these exaggerated reactions to stress damage the arteries which, in turn, leads to heart disease (Matthews, 1982).

CONCLUSION

Do you have a Type A pattern of behavior? How would you know? As with your level of introversion or extroversion, mentioned at the beginning of this chapter, your "Type A-ness" vs. your "Type B-ness" is a part of who you are. Tests have been developed to assess people's Type A or Type B behavior patterns. You can get a rough idea by examining the list of Type A characteristics below to see how many apply to you.

1. Frequently doing more than one thing at a time.
2. Urging others to hurry up and finish what they are saying.
3. Becoming very irritated when traffic is blocked or when you are waiting in line.
4. Gesturing a lot while talking.
5. Having a hard time sitting with nothing to do.
6. Speaking explosively and using obscenities often.
7. Playing to win all the time, even with children.
8. Becoming impatient when watching others carry out a task.

If you suspect that you are a Type A, you may want to consider a more careful evaluation by a trained physician or a psychologist. Several successful programs to intervene in the connection between Type A behavior and serious illness have been developed, largely in response to the work of Friedman and Rosenman.

MATTHEWS, K.A. (1982) Psychological perspectives on the Type A behavior pattern. *Psychological Bulletin*, 91, 293–323.
ROSENMAN, R.H., BROND, R., SHOLTZ, R., and FRIEDMAN, M. (1976) Multivariate prediction of CHD during 8.5-year follow-up in the Western Collaborative group study. *American Journal of Cardiology*, 37, 903–10.

EIGHT

PSYCHOPATHOLOGY

Most people, unless they have studied a little psychology, have the impression that it is primarily or only concerned with the area called psychopathology or *mental illness* (the subfield that studies mental illness is called *abnormal psychology*). However, as you may have noticed, nearly all of the research up to this point has focused on *normal* behavior. Overall, psychologists are more interested in normal behavior than in abnormal behavior because the vast majority of human behavior is normal. Consequently, we would not know very much about human nature if we only studied the small percentage of it that is abnormal. Having said that, the study of mental illness is to many people one of the most fascinating in all of psychology. A wide variety of studies with crucial historical importance are included here.

First is a study that has kept the mental health profession talking for nearly 20 years. In this study, people posing as mental patients entered psychiatric hospitals to see if the doctors and staff could distinguish them from those who were actually mentally ill. Second, no book about the history of psychological research would be complete without reference to Sigmund Freud. Therefore, a discussion of his theory of the "ego defense mechanisms," through the writings of his daughter, Anna Freud, is included in this section since it relates to his work with psychological disorders. Next comes the famous Rorschach inkblot test that has been used, among other purposes, to diagnose psychopathology. And finally in this section is an intriguing and well-known experiment involving overcrowded rats and their resultant deviant behavior, which may have important implications for humans.

WHO'S CRAZY HERE, ANYWAY?

Rosenhan, D.L. (1973) On being sane in insane places. *Science,* 179, 250–58.

The question of how to discriminate between normal and abnormal behavior is fundamental in psychology. The definition of abnormality plays a key role in determining whether or not someone is diagnosed as mentally ill, and the diagnosis largely determines the treatment received by a patient. The line that divides normal from abnormal is certainly not clear. Rather, all behavior can be seen to lie on a continuum with normal, or what might be called "effective psychological functioning," at one end and abnormal, or "personality disorganization," indicating mental illness, at the other:

Normal <<-->>*Abnormal*

　　(Effective　　　　　　　　　　　　　　　　　　　　　　(Mental
　　functioning)　　　　　　　　　　　　　　　　　　　　　illness)

It is up to mental health professionals to determine where on this continuum a particular person's general behavior lies. In order to make this determination, clinical psychologists, psychiatrists, and other psychotherapists may use one or more of the following criteria.

Bizarreness of the Behavior

This is a subjective judgment, but you know that some behaviors are clearly bizarre in a given situation. For example, there is nothing bizarre about standing outside watering your lawn, unless you are doing it during a rainstorm! So, a judgment about bizarreness must carefully consider the context in which a behavior or behavior pattern occurs.

Persistence of Behavior

We all have, to varying degrees, our crazy moments. It is possible for a person to exhibit abnormal behavior on occasion without necessarily demonstrating the presence of mental illness. For instance, you might have just received some great news and, as you are walking along a busy downtown sidewalk, you dance for half a block or so. This behavior, while abnormal, would not indicate mental illness unless you began to dance down that sidewalk on, say, a weekly or daily basis. Therefore, this criterion for mental illness requires that a bizarre, antisocial, or disruptive behavior pattern persist over time.

Social Deviance

When a person's behavior violates expected assumptions and norms so that it does disturb others, the behavior is considered to be socially deviant. When this deviant behavior is extreme and persistent, such as auditory or visual hallucinations, it is evidence of psychological problems.

Subjective Distress

Frequently, as intelligent beings, we are aware of our own psychological difficulties and the suffering they are causing us. When a person is so afraid of enclosed spaces that he or she cannot ride in an elevator, or when someone finds it impossible to form meaningful relationships with others, they do not need a professional to tell them they are in psychological pain. This subjective distress is often a great help to mental health professionals in making a psychological diagnosis.

Psychological Handicap

When a person finds it impossible to be satisfied with life due to psychological problems, this is considered to be a psychological handicap. A person who fears success, for example, and therefore sabotages in some way each new endeavor in life is suffering from a psychological handicap.

Effect on Functioning

This could be considered the bottom line in psychological diagnosis: the extent to which the behaviors in question interfere with a person's ability to live the life that he or she desires and that society will accept. A behavior could be bizarre and persistent, but if it does not impair your ability to function in life, true pathology may not be indicated. For example, suppose you have an uncontrollable need to stand on your bed and sing the national anthem every night before going to sleep. This is certainly bizarre and persistent, but unless you are waking up the neighbors or disturbing other household members, your behavior may have little effect on your general functioning; therefore, it may not be a clinical problem.

These definitions and characteristics of mental illness all require judgments on the part of psychologists, psychiatrists, and other mental health professionals. Therefore, the foregoing guidelines notwithstanding, two questions remain: Are mental health professionals truly able to distinguish between the mentally ill and the mentally healthy? And what are the consequences of mistakes? These are the questions addressed by David Rosenhan in his famous study of mental hospitals.

THEORETICAL PROPOSITIONS

Rosenhan questioned whether the characteristics that lead to psychological diagnoses reside in the patients themselves or in the situations and contexts in which the observers (those who do the diagnosing) find the patients. He reasoned that if the established criteria and the training mental health professionals have received for diagnosing mental illness are adequate, then those professionals should be able to distinguish between the insane and the sane. (Please note that technically the words *sane* and *insane* are legal terms, and are not usually used in psychological contexts. They are used here because Rosenhan incorporated them into his research.) Rosenhan proposed that one way to test mental health professionals' ability to correctly categorize would be to have normal people seek admittance to psychiatric facilities to see if they would be discovered to be, in reality, psychologically healthy. If these "pseudopatients" behaved in the hospital as they would on the outside, and if they were not discovered to be normal, this would be evidence that diagnoses of the mentally ill are tied more to the situation than to the patient.

METHOD

Rosenhan recruited eight subjects (including himself) to serve as pseudopatients. The eight participants (three women and five men) consisted of one graduate student, three psychologists, one pediatrician, one psychiatrist, one painter, and one homemaker. The subjects' mission was to present themselves for admission to 12 psychological hospitals, in five states on both the east and west coasts of the United States.

All of the pseudopatients followed the same instructions: They called the hospital and made an appointment. Upon arrival at the hospital they complained of hearing voices that said "empty," "hollow," and "thud." Other than this single symptom, all subjects acted completely normal and gave totally truthful information to the interviewer (except that they changed their names and occupations). *All the subjects were admitted to the various hospitals, and all but one was admitted with a diagnosis of "schizophrenia."*

Once inside the hospital, the pseudopatients displayed no symptoms whatsoever and behaved normally. The subjects had no idea of when they would be released. It was up to each of them to be released by convincing the hospital staff that they were healthy enough to be discharged. All of the subjects took notes of their experiences. At first they tried to conceal this activity, but soon it was clear to all that this secrecy was unnecessary, since "notetaking behavior" was seen as just another symptom of their illness. They all desired to be released as soon as possible, so they behaved as model patients, cooperating with the staff and accepting all medications (which were not swallowed, but flushed down the toilet).

RESULTS

The length of hospital stay for the pseudopatients ranged from seven days to 52 days, with an average stay of 19 days. The key finding in this study was that *not one of the pseudopatients was detected by anyone on the hospital staff*. When they were released, their mental health status was recorded in their files as "schizophrenia in remission." There were other interesting findings and observations.

While the hospital's staff of doctors, nurses, and attendants failed to detect the subjects, the other patients could not be so easily fooled. In three of the pseudopatients' hospitalizations, 35 out of 118 real patients voiced suspicions that the subjects were not actually mentally ill. They would make comments such as, "You're not crazy! You're a journalist or a reporter. You're checking up on the hospital!"

Contacts between the patients (whether subjects or not) and the staff were minimal and often bizarre. One of the tests made by the pseudopatients in the study was to approach various staff members and attempt to make verbal contact by asking common, normal questions (e.g., "When will I be allowed grounds privileges?" or "When am I likely to be discharged?"). Table 1 summarizes the responses they received.

TABLE 1   Responses by Doctors and Staff to Questions Posed by Pseudopatients

RESPONSE	PSYCHIATRISTS	NURSES AND ATTENDANTS
Moves on, head averted	71%	88%
Makes eye contact	23	10
Pauses and chats	2	2
Stops and talks	4	0.5

(from p. 255)

When there was a response it frequently took the following form:

PSEUDOPATIENT: "Pardon me, Dr. ———. Could you tell me when I am eligible for grounds privileges?"

PSYCHIATRIST: "Good morning, Dave. How are you today?"

The doctor would then move on without waiting for a response.

In contrast to the severe lack of personal contact in the hospitals studied, there was no shortage of drugs. The eight pseudopatients in this study were given a total of 2,100 pills which, as mentioned above, were not swallowed. The subjects noted that many of the real patients also secretly disposed of their pills down the toilet.

Another anecdote from one of the pseudopatients tells of a nurse who unbuttoned her uniform to adjust her bra in front of a dayroom full of male patients. It was not her intention to be provocative, according to the subject's report, she simply did not consider the patients to be real people.

DISCUSSION

Rosenhan's study demonstrated rather strongly that normal "patients" cannot be distinguished from the mentally ill in a hospital setting. According to Rosenhan, this is because of the disproportionate strength of the psychiatric setting over the individual's behavior. Once patients are admitted to such a facility, there is a strong tendency for them to be viewed in ways that remove all individuality. The attitude that ensues is one of: "If they are here, they must be crazy." More importantly, is what Rosenhan refers to as the "stickiness of the diagnostic label." That is, when a patient is labeled as "schizophrenic," it becomes his or her central characteristic or personality trait (see the discussion of Asch's 1946 study, "Forming Impressions of Personality"). From the moment the label is given and the staff knows it, they perceive all of the patient's behavior as stemming from that label; thus, the lack of concern or suspicion over the pseudopatients' notetaking, which became just another behavioral manifestation of the psychological label.

The hospital staff tended to ignore the situational pressures on patients and saw only the behavior relevant to the pathological traits assigned to the patients. This was demonstrated by the following observation of one of the subjects:

> One psychiatrist pointed to a group of patients who were sitting outside the cafeteria entrance half an hour before lunchtime. To a group of young resident psychiatrists he indicated that such behavior was characteristic of the 'oral-acquisitive' nature of the syndrome. It seemed not to occur to him that there were simply very few things to do in a psychiatric hospital besides eating. (p. 253)

Beyond this, the sticky diagnostic label even colored how a pseudopatient's history would be interpreted. Remember that all the subjects gave honest accounts of their pasts and families. Here is an example from Rosenhan's research of a pseudopatient's stated history, followed by its interpretation by the staff doctor in a report after the subject was discharged. The subject's true account was as follows:

> The pseudopatient had a close relationship with his mother, but was rather remote with his father during his early childhood. During adolescence and beyond, however, his father became a very close friend while his relationship with his mother cooled. His present relationship with his wife was characteristically close and warm. Apart from occasional angry exchanges, friction was minimal. The children had rarely been spanked. (p. 253)

The director's interpretation of this rather normal and innocuous history was as follows:

> This white 39-year-old male . . . manifests a long history of considerable ambivalence in close relationships which begins in early childhood. A warm relationship with his mother cools during his adolescence. A distant relationship with his father is described as becoming very intense. Affective stability is absent. His attempts to control emotionality with his wife and children are punctuated by angry outbursts and, in the case of the children, spankings. And while he says he has several good friends, one senses considerable ambivalence embedded in those relationships also. (p. 253)

It should be pointed out that there was no indication that any of the staff's distortions were done intentionally. They believed in the diagnosis (in this case, schizophrenia) and *interpreted* a patient's history and behavior in ways that were consistent with that diagnosis.

SIGNIFICANCE OF FINDINGS

Rosenhan's study shook the mental health professional community. The results pointed out two crucial factors. First, it appeared that the "sane" could not be distinguished from the "insane" in mental hospital settings. As Rosenhan himself stated in his article, "The hospital itself imposes a special environment in which the meaning of behavior can be easily misunderstood. The consequences to patients hospitalized in such an environment . . . seem undoubtedly countertherapeutic" (p. 257). Second, Rosenhan demonstrated the danger of diagnostic labels. Once a person is labeled as having a certain psychological "condition" (such as schizophrenia, manic-depressive illness, etc.), that label eclipses any and all of his or her other characteristics. All behavior and personality characteristics are seen as stemming from the labeled disorder. The worst part of this sort of treatment is that it can become self-confirming. That is, if a person is treated in a certain way consistently over time, he or she may begin to *behave* that way.

Out of Rosenhan's work grew greater care in diagnostic procedures and increased awareness of the dangers of applying labels to patients. Additionally, the problems addressed by his study began to decline with the decrease in patients confined to mental hospitals. This decrease in hospital populations was brought about by the discovery and widespread use of antipsychotic medications, which have the power to reduce symptoms in most patients enough for them to live outside a hospital and in many cases lead relatively normal lives. Concurrent to this was the growth of community mental health facilities, crisis intervention centers, and behavior therapies that focus on specific problems and behaviors and tend to avoid labels altogether.

This does not imply by any means that the mental health profession has eliminated labels. However, largely because of Rosenhan's research and other research in the same vein, psychiatric labels are now used carefully and treated with the respect their power demands.

QUESTIONS AND CRITICISMS

There was one research and teaching hospital whose staff had heard about Rosenhan's findings before they were published and doubted that such mistakes in diagnosis could be made in their hospital. To test this,

Rosenhan informed the hospital staff that during the next three months one or more pseudopatients would try to be admitted to their psychiatric unit. Each staff member was asked to rate each presenting patient on a 10-point scale as to the likelihood that he or she was a pseudopatient. At the end of three months, 193 patients had been admitted. Of those, 41 were considered with high confidence to be pseudopatients by at least one staff member. Twenty-three were suspected by at least one psychiatrist, and 19 were identified as pseudopatients by one psychiatrist and one other staff member. Rosenhan (the tricky devil) *had not sent any pseudopatients to the hospital* during the three-month period! "The experiment is instructive," states Rosenhan. "It indicates that the tendency to designate sane people as insane can be reversed when the stakes (in this case prestige and diagnostic ability) are high. But one thing is certain: Any diagnostic process that lends itself so readily to massive errors of this sort cannot be a very reliable one" (p. 252).

Rosenhan replicated this study several times in 12 hospitals between 1973 and 1975. Each time he found similar results (see Greenberg, 1981, and Rosenhan, 1975). In fairness, however, other researchers dispute the conclusions Rosenhan drew from this research. Spitzer (1976) has argued that while the methods used by Rosenhan appeared to invalidate psychological diagnostic systems, in reality they did not. For example, it should not be difficult for pseudopatients to lie their way into a mental hospital, since many such admissions are based on verbal reports (and who would ever suspect someone of using trickery to get *into* such a place?). The reasoning here is that you could walk into a medical emergency room complaining of severe intestinal pain and you might get yourself admitted to the hospital with a diagnosis of gastritis. Even though the doctor was tricked, the diagnostic methods were not invalid. Additionally, Spitzer has pointed out that just because the pseudopatients behaved normally once admitted to the hospital, this does not mean that the staff was incompetent. Many psychological diagnoses are based on past as well as present symptoms, and it is not uncommon for the symptoms to vary.

The controversy over the validity of psychological diagnosis which began with Rosenhan's 1973 article continues. Regardless of the eventual outcome, there is little question that Rosenhan's study remains one of the most influential in the history of psychology.

GREENBERG, J. (1981, June/July) An interview with David Rosenhan. *APA Monitor*, 4–5.
ROSENHAN, D.L. (1975) The contextual nature of psychiatric diagnosis. *Journal of Abnormal Psychology*, 84, 442–52.
SPITZER, R.L. (1976) More on pseudoscience in science and the case of the psychiatric diagnosis: A critique of D.L. Rosenhan's "On being sane in insane places" and "The contextual nature of psychiatric diagnosis." *Archives of General Psychiatry*, 33, 459–70.

YOU'RE GETTING DEFENSIVE AGAIN!
Freud, Anna (1946) *The ego and the mechanisms of defense.*
New York: International Universities Press.

In a book about the history of research that changed psychology, there is one imposing figure who would be extremely difficult to omit: Sigmund Freud (1856–1939). It is very unlikely that psychology would exist today as it does, in spite of its varied and complex forms, without Freud's contributions. It was he who was largely responsible for elevating our interpretations of human behavior (especially abnormal behavior) from superstitions of demonic possession and evil spirits to the rational ideas of reason and science. So without an examination of his work, this book would be incomplete. Now you may be asking yourself, If Sigmund Freud is so important, why is this chapter about a book written by his daughter, Anna Freud? Well, there is a very good reason for the choice of material in this chapter, which will be explained momentarily.

Although Sigmund Freud was integral to psychology's history and, therefore, a necessary part of this book, the task of including his research here along with all the other researchers was a difficult one. The reason for this difficulty was that Freud did not reach his discoveries through a clearly defined scientific methodology. It was not possible to choose a single study or series of experiments to represent his work, as has been done for other researchers in this book. Freud's theories grew out of careful observations of his patients over decades of clinical analysis. Consequently, his writings were abundant, to say the least. The English translation of his collected writings, *The Standard Edition of the Complete Psychological Works of Sigmund Freud* (London: Hogarth Press, 1953 to 1974), totals 24 volumes! Obviously, only a very small piece of his work could be discussed in this short chapter.

In choosing what to include here, consideration was given to the portions of Freud's theories that have stood the test of time relatively unscathed. Over the past century a great deal of criticism has been focused on Freud's ideas and, in the last 40 years especially, his work has been drawn into serious question from a scientific perspective. Critics have argued that many of his theories either cannot be tested scientifically; or if they are tested, they prove to be generally unreliable. Therefore, while few would doubt the historical importance of Freud, many of his theories about the structure of personality, the development of personality through the psychosexual stages, and the sources of people's psychological problems have been rejected by most psychologists today. However, some aspects of his work have received more positive "reviews" through the years and now enjoy relatively wide acceptance.

One of these is his concept of the "defense mechanisms." These are weapons that your ego uses to protect you from your own self-created anxiety. This element from his work has been selected to represent Freud in this book.

The reference given at the top of this chapter is for Anna rather than Sigmund Freud because his discovery of these defense mechanisms occurred gradually over 30 or more years as his experiences in dealing with psychological problems grew. A cohesive, self-contained discussion of this topic does not appear anywhere in Sigmund Freud's many volumes. In fact, he passed that job on to his daughter, who was an important psychoanalyst in her own right, specializing in children. Freud acknowledged this fact in 1936 just before Anna's book, *The Ego and the Mechanisms of Defense*, was originally published in German: "There are an extremely large number of methods (or mechanisms, as we say) used by the ego in the discharge of its defensive functions. My daughter, the child analyst, is writing a book about them" (S. Freud, 1936). Since it was Anna Freud who synthesized her father's theories regarding the defense mechanisms into a single work, her book has been chosen for our discussion of the work of Sigmund Freud.

THEORETICAL PROPOSITIONS

In order to examine Freud's notion of defense mechanisms, it is necessary to explain briefly his theory of the structure of personality. Freud proposed that personality consists of three components: the id, the ego, and the superego.

The id consists of basic biological urges such as hunger, thirst, and sexual impulses. Whenever these needs are not met, the id generates strong motivation for the person to find a way to satisfy them, and do so immediately! The id operates on what Freud called the "pleasure principle" and demands instantaneous gratification of all desires, regardless of reason, logic, safety, or morality. Freud believed that there are dark, antisocial, and dangerous instinctual urges (especially sexual ones) present in everyone's id that constantly seek expression. You are not usually aware of these because the id operates on the unconscious level. However, if you were lacking the other parts of your personality and only had an id, your behavior would be amoral, shockingly deviant, and even fatal to you and others.

The reason you do not behave in these dangerous and deviant ways is that your ego and superego develop to place limits and controls on the impulses of your id. According to Freud, the ego operates on the "reality principle," which means it is alert to the real world and the consequences of behavior. The ego is conscious and its job is to satisfy your id's urges, but to do so using means that are rational, socially acceptable, and reasonably safe.

However, the ego also has limits placed upon it by the superego. Your superego, in essence, requires that the solutions the ego finds to the id's needs are moral and ethical, according to your own internalized set of rules about what is good or bad. These rules were instilled in you by your parents, and if you behave in ways that violate them your superego will punish you with its own very effective weapon: guilt. Do you recognize this? It is commonly referred to as your conscience. Freud believed that your superego operates on both conscious and unconscious levels.

So, Freud's conceptualization of your personality was a dynamic one in which the ego is constantly trying to balance the needs and urges of the id with the moral requirements of the superego in determining your behavior. Here is an example of how this might work. Imagine a 16-year-old boy strolling down the street in a small town. It is 10 p.m. and he is on his way home. Suddenly he realizes he is hungry. He passes a grocery store and sees food on the other side of the large windows, but the store is closed. His id might say, "Look! Food! Jump through the glass and get some!" (Remember, the id wants immediate satisfaction, regardless of the consequences.) He would probably not be aware of the id's suggestion because it would be at a level below his consciousness. The ego would "hear" it, though, and since its job is to protect the boy from danger, it might respond, "No, that would be dangerous. Let's go around back, break into the store, and steal some food!" At this, the superego would remark indignantly, "You can't do that! It's immoral, and if you do it I will punish you!" So his ego reconsiders and makes a new suggestion that is acceptable to both the id and the superego! "You know, there's an all-night fast-food place four blocks over. Let's go there and buy some food." This solution, assuming that the boy is psychologically healthy, is the one that makes it to his consciousness and is reflected in his behavior.

According to Freud, most people do not behave in antisocial or deviant ways because of this system of checks and balances among the three parts of the personality. But what would happen if the system malfunctioned—if this balance were lost? One way this could happen would be if the demands of the id became too strong to be controlled adequately by the ego. What if the unacceptable urges of the id edged their way into your consciousness (into what Freud called the "preconscious") and began to overpower the ego? Freud contended that if this happens, you will experience a very unpleasant condition called *anxiety*. Specifically, he called it "free-floating" anxiety, because although you feel anxious and afraid, you are not sure why you feel this way, since the causes are still not fully conscious.

When this state of anxiety exists, it is uncomfortable and we are motivated to change it. To do this the ego will bring on its "big guns," called the *defense mechanisms*. The purpose of the defense mechanisms is to prevent the id's forbidden impulse from entering consciousness. If this is successful, the discomfort of the anxiety associated with the impulse is relieved. You might be asking, How do the defense mechanisms ward off anxiety? Well, they do it through self-deception and the distortion of reality so that the id's urges will not have to be acknowledged.

METHOD

As mentioned earlier, Freud gradually discovered the defense mechanisms over many years of clinical interactions with his patients. These were compiled and more fully explained in Anna Freud's book. It should be noted that in the years since Sigmund Freud's death and since the publication of Anna Freud's book, many refinements have been made in the interpretation of the defense mechanisms. The next section summarizes a selection of only those mechanisms identified by Sigmund Freud and elaborated on by his daughter.

RESULTS AND DISCUSSION

Anna Freud identified 10 defense mechanisms that had been described by her father (see p. 44 of her book). Five of the original mechanisms that are most commonly used and recognized today will be discussed here: repression, regression, projection, reaction formation, and sublimation. Keep in mind that the primary function of the defense mechanisms is to alter reality in order to protect against anxiety.

Repression

Repression is the most basic and commonly used mechanism of defense. In his early writings, Freud used the terms *repression* and *defense* interchangeably and interpreted repression to be virtually the only defense mechanism. Later, however, he acknowledged that repression was only one of many psychological processes available to protect a person from anxiety (p. 43). Repression does this by forcing disturbing impulses out of consciousness. If this is accomplished successfully, the anxiety associated with the impulses is avoided. This is often referred to as "motivated forgetting." In Freud's view, repression is often employed to defend against the anxiety that would be produced by unacceptable sexual desires. For example, a woman who has sexual feelings about her father would probably experience intense anxiety if these impulses were to become conscious. To avoid that anxiety, she might repress her unacceptable desires, forcing them fully into her unconscious. This would not mean that her urges are gone, but since they are repressed, they cannot produce anxiety.

You might be wondering how these urges are ever discovered if they remain in the unconscious. According to Freud, these hidden impulses may be revealed through slips of the tongue, through dreams, or by the various techniques used in psychoanalysis, such as free association. Furthermore, repressed desires can create psychological problems that are expressed in the form of neuroses. For instance, consider again the woman who has repressed sexual desires for her father. She might express these impulses by becoming involved in successive failed relationships with men in an unconscious attempt to resolve her conflicts about her father.

Regression

Regression is a defense used by the ego to guard against anxiety by causing the person to retreat to the behavior of an earlier stage of development that was less demanding and safer. Often when a second child is born into a family, the older sibling will regress to using earlier speech patterns, wanting a bottle, and even bed-wetting. Adults can use regression as well. Consider a man experiencing a "mid-life crisis" who is afraid of growing old and dying. To avoid the anxiety associated with these unconscious fears, he might regress to an adolescent stage by becoming irresponsible, cruising around in a sports car, trying to date younger women, and even eating the foods associated with his teenage years. Another example of regression is the married adult who "goes home to mother" whenever there is a problem in the marriage.

Projection

Imagine for a moment that your ego is being attacked by your id. You're not sure why, but you are experiencing a lot of anxiety. If your ego uses the defense mechanism of projection to eliminate the anxiety, you will begin to see your unconscious urges in other people's behavior. That is, you will *project* your impulses onto others. This externalizes the anxiety-provoking feelings and reduces the anxiety. You will not be aware that you're doing this, and the people onto whom you project will probably not be guilty of your accusations. An example of this offered by Anna Freud involves a husband who is experiencing impulses to be unfaithful to his wife (p. 120). He may not even be conscious of these urges, but they are creeping up from his id and creating anxiety. To ward off the anxiety, he projects his desires onto his wife, becomes intensely jealous, and accuses her of having affairs, even though there is no evidence to support his claims. Another example is the woman who is afraid of aging and begins to point out how old her friends and acquaintances are looking. The individuals in these examples are not acting or lying, but truly believe their projections. If they did not, the defense against anxiety would fail.

Reaction Formation

The defense identified by Freud as a reaction formation is exemplified by a line from Shakespeare's *Hamlet*, when Hamlet's mother, after watching a scene in a play, remarks to Hamlet, "The lady doth protest too much, me thinks." When a person is experiencing unacceptable, unconscious "evil" impulses, anxiety over them might be avoided by engaging in behaviors that are the exact opposite of the id's real urges. Anna Freud pointed out that these behaviors are usually exaggerated or even obsessive (p. 9). By adopting attitudes and behaviors that demonstrate outwardly a complete rejection of the id's true desires, anxiety is blocked. Reaction formations tend to appear rapidly and usually become a permanent part of an individual's personality unless the id-ego conflict is somehow resolved. As an example of this, reconsider the husband who unconsciously desires other women. If he employs reaction formation rather than projection to prevent his anxiety, he may become overly devoted to his wife and shower her with gifts and pronouncements of his unwavering love. Another example comes from recent disturbing news reports of the violent crime referred to as "gay bashing." In a Freudian interpretation, men who have unconscious homosexual tendencies might engage in this extreme opposite behavior of attacking and beating gay men to avoid their true desires and the anxiety associated with them.

Sublimation

Both Sigmund and Anna Freud considered most of the defense mechanisms, including the four described above, as indicating problems in psychological adjustment (neuroses). Conversely, the defense of sublimation was seen as not only normal, but desirable (p. 44). When people invoke sublimation, they are finding socially acceptable ways of discharging energy that is the result of unconscious forbidden desires. Freud maintained that since everyone's id contains these desires, sublimation is a necessary part of a productive and healthy life. Furthermore he believed that most strong desires can be sublimated in various ways. Someone who has intense aggressive impulses might sublimate them by engaging in contact sports or becoming a surgeon. A teenage girl's passion for horseback riding might be interpreted as sublimated unacceptable sexual desires. A man who has an erotic fixation on the human body might sublimate his feelings by becoming a painter or sculptor of nudes.

Interestingly, Freud believed that all of what we call civilization has been possible through the mechanism of sublimation. In his view, humans have been able to sublimate their primitive biological urges and impulses allowing them to build civilized societies. Sometimes, Freud suggested, our true unconscious forces overpower our "collective" ego and these primitive behaviors burst out in uncivilized expressions such as war. Overall, however, it is only through sublimation that civilization can exist at all (S. Freud, 1930).

IMPLICATIONS OF FREUD'S THEORIES OF DEFENSE MECHANISMS

Although Anna Freud made it clear in her book that the use of defense mechanisms (with the exception of sublimation) is often associated with neurotic behavior, it should be pointed out that this is not always the case. Nearly everyone uses various defense mechanisms occasionally in their lives, especially to help them deal with periods of increased stress. They help us reduce our anxiety and maintain a positive self-image. Nevertheless, defense mechanisms involve self-deception and distortions of reality that can produce negative consequences if they are overused. For example, a person who uses regression every time life's problems become overwhelming might never develop the strategies necessary to deal with the problems and solve them. Consequently the person's life will not become as effective as it could be. Moreover, Freud and many other psychologists have contended that when anxiety over specific conflicts is repressed, it is sometimes manifested in other ways, such as phobias, anxiety attacks, or obsessive-compulsive disorders.

CONCLUSION

Freud's theories have always been extremely controversial. Do the defense mechanisms really exist? Do they actually function unconsciously to block the anxiety created by the forbidden impulses of the id trying to enter the conscious? Probably the most often cited criticism of all of Freud's work is that to test it scientifically is difficult at best, impossible at worst. Many studies have tried to demonstrate clearly the existence of various Freudian concepts. The results have been mixed. Some of his ideas have found scientific support, while others have been disproven and still others simply cannot be studied (see Fisher and Greenberg, 1977, for a complete discussion of this issue).

Nevertheless, the idea that people use defense mechanisms has received wide support, even though not everyone agrees on the psychological basis for them. Probably the most meaningful interpretation is that through an awareness and understanding of the defense mechanisms, it is possible to obtain important insights into the causes of people's actions. This understanding can show you that a person's behavior may be motivated by forces other than those readily observable. You will find that if you keep a mental list of the defense mechanisms, you may begin to notice them in others or even in yourself. By the way, if you think someone is using a defense mechanism, remember that he or she is doing so to avoid anxiety. Therefore, it would probably *not* be a good idea to bring it to his or her attention. Knowledge of the defense mechanisms can be a powerful tool in your interactions with others, but it must be used carefully and responsibly.

FISHER, S., and GREENBERG, R. (1977) The scientific credibility of Freud's theories and therapy. New York: Basic Books.

FREUD, S. (1936) *A disturbance of memory on the Acropolis*. London: Hogarth Press (original publication in German, 1936).

FREUD, S. (1961) *Civilisation and its discontents*. London: Hogarth Press (original publication in German, 1930).

PROJECTIONS OF WHO YOU ARE
Rorschach, Hermann (1942) *Psychodiagnostics: A diagnostic test based on perception.* New York: Grune and Stratton.

Picture yourself and a friend relaxing in a grassy meadow on a warm summer's day. The blue sky above is broken only by a few white puffy clouds. Pointing to one of the clouds, you say to your friend, "Look! That cloud looks like a woman in a wedding dress with a long veil." To this your friend replies, "Where? I don't see that. To me, that cloud is shaped like a volcano with a plume of smoke rising from the top." As you try to convince each other of your differing perceptions of the same shape, the air currents change and transform the cloud into something entirely different. But why such a difference in what the two of you saw? You were looking at the same shape, and yet interpreting it as two entirely unrelated objects.

Since everyone's perceptions are often influenced by psychological factors, perhaps the different objects found in the cloud formations revealed something about the personalities of the observers. In other words, you and your friend were *projecting* something about yourselves onto the shapes in the sky. This is the concept underlying Rorschach's development of his "form interpretation test," better known as "the inkblot test." This was one of the earliest versions of a type of psychological tool known as the *projective technique*.

The two most widely known and used projective tests are the Rorschach inkblot and the "thematic apperception test" (TAT). Both of these instruments are pivotal in the history of clinical psychology. Since Rorschach's test, first described in 1922, involves direct comparisons among various groups of mental illnesses and is often associated with the diagnosis of psychological disorders, it will be covered here in the section on psychopathology. The TAT will be discussed in the next section on psychotherapy because it is more commonly used by therapists as a part of their interviews with and treatment of their clients.

A projective test presents a person with some ambiguous stimulus and assumes that the person will project his or her unconscious processes onto it. In the case of Rorschach's test the stimulus is nothing more than a symmetrical inkblot that can be perceived to be any number of objects. Rorschach suggested that what a person sees in the inkblot often reveals a great deal about his or her true psychological nature. He called this "the interpretation of accidental forms." There is an often-told story about Rorschach's inkblots that tells of a psychotherapist who is administering the test to a client. With the first inkblot card the therapist asks, "What does this suggest to you?" The client replies, "Sex." The same question is asked of the second card, to which the client again replies, "Sex." When the same one-word answer is given to the first five cards, the therapist remarks, "Well, you certainly seem to be preoccupied with sex!" To this the surprised client responds, "Me? Doctor, *you're* the one showing all the dirty pictures!" Of course, this story oversimplifies Rorschach's test and, although the inkblots themselves are selected to be vaguely suggestive of objects in order to encourage active interpretation, a sexual orientation should, on average, be no more likely than any other.

Rorschach believed that his projective technique could serve two main purposes. One was that it could be used as a research tool to reveal unconscious aspects of personality. The other purpose, claimed somewhat later by Rorschach, was that the test could be used to diagnose various types of psychopathology.

THEORETICAL PROPOSITIONS

The theory underlying Rorschach's technique was that in the course of interpreting a random inkblot, attention would be drawn away from the subject so that the person's usual psychological defenses would be weakened. This, in turn, would allow normally hidden aspects of the psyche to be revealed. When the stimulus being perceived is ambiguous (that is, having few clues as to what it really is), the interpretation of the stimulus has to come from inside the person doing the perceiving (for a related discussion of this concept see the reading on Murray's Thematic Apperception Test). In Rorschach's conceptualization, inkblots were about as ambiguous as you can get and, therefore, would allow for the greatest amount of projection from a person's unconscious.

METHOD

An examination of Rorschach's formulation of his inkblot test can be divided into two broad sections: the process he used to develop the original forms, and the methods suggested for interpreting and scoring the responses made by subjects or clients.

Development of the Test

Rorschach's explanation of how the forms are made sounded very much like instructions for a fun children's art project: "The production of such accidental forms is very simple: A few large inkblots are thrown on a piece of paper, the paper folded, and the ink spread between the two halves of the sheet" (p. 15). However, the simplicity stopped there. Rorschach went on to explain that only those designs that met certain conditions could be used. For example, the forms should be relatively simple, or else subjects' interpretations might be too complex to be analyzed. In addition, a figure should be suggestive enough so that a subject will be unlikely to interpret it simply as a blot of ink. He also suggested that the forms should be symmetrical, because asymmetrical inkblots are often rejected by subjects as impossible to interpret. After a great deal of testing, Rorschach finally arrived at a set of 10 forms that made up his original test. Of these, five were black on white, two used black and red, and three were multicolored. Figure 1 contains three figures of the type used by Rorschach.

Administration and Scoring

Rorschach's form interpretation test is administered simply by handing a subject each figure, one at a time, and asking, "What might this be?" Subjects are free to turn the card in any direction and to hold it as close to or as far from their eyes as they wish. The researcher or therapist administering the test notes down all the responses for each figure without suggestion to the subjects. There is no imposed time limit.

FIGURE 1   Examples of accidental forms of the type used in Rorschach's Form Interpretation test.

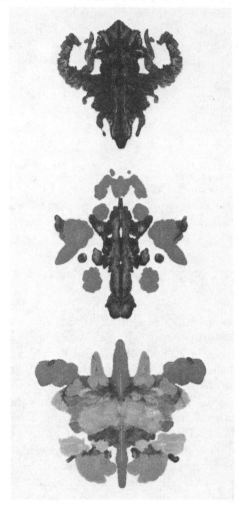

(Charles G. Morris, PSYCHOLOGY 7/E, © 1990, p. 479. Reprinted by permission of Prentice Hall, Englewood Cliffs, New Jersey.)

Rorschach pointed out that subjects almost always think the test is designed to study imagination. However, he is very careful to explain that it is not a test of imagination, and the creativity of a person's imagination does not significantly alter the result. It is, Rorschach claimed, a test of perception involving the processes of sensation, memory, and unconscious and conscious associations between the stimulus forms and other psychological forces within the individual.

Rorschach listed the following guidelines for scoring the subjects' responses to the 10 inkblots (see p. 19 of the original study):

1. How many responses were made? What was the reaction time; that is, how long did the subject look at the figure before responding? How often did the subject refuse to interpret a figure?
2. Was the subject's interpretation only determined by the shape of the figure, or were color or movement included in the perception?
3. Was the figure seen as a whole or in separate parts? Which parts were separated, and how were they interpreted?
4. What did the subject see?

It is interesting to note that Rorschach considered the content of the subject's interpretation the least important factor in the responses given to the inkblots. The following section summarizes Rorschach's observations, related to these four guidelines, of numerous subjects with a variety of psychological symptoms.

RESULTS

To discover how various groups of people might perform differently on the inkblot test, Rorschach and his associates administered it to subjects from several psychological groups. These included, but were not limited to, normal individuals with varying amounts of education, schizophrenic patients, and individuals diagnosed as manic-depressive.

Table 1 presents typical responses reported by Rorschach for the 10 inkblot figures. These, of course, vary from person to person and among different psychological groups, but the answers given in the table serve as examples.

TABLE 1   Typical Responses to Inkblot Figures for an Average Normal Subject

FIGURE NUMBER	RESPONSE
I.	Two santa clauses with brooms under their arms
II.	A butterfly
III.	Two marionette figures
IV.	An ornament on a piece of furniture
V.	A bat
VI.	A moth or a tree
VII.	Two human heads or two animal heads
VIII.	Two bears
IX.	Two clowns or darting flames
X.	A rabbit's head, two caterpillars, or two spiders

(from pp. 126–27)

Rorschach found that subjects generally gave between 15 and 30 total responses to the 10 figures. Depressed subjects generally gave fewer answers; happy subjects gave more; and among schizophrenics the number of answers varied a great deal from person to person. As for reaction time, the entire test usually took between 20 and 30 minutes to complete, with schizophrenics taking much less time on average. Normal subjects almost never failed to respond to all the figures, but schizophrenics would frequently refuse to answer.

Rorschach believed that the portion of the form interpreted by the subject, whether movement was part of the interpretation, and to what degree color entered into the response were all very important in analyzing the subject's performance on the test. His suggestions for scoring those factors were quite complex and required training and experience to analyze a person's responses properly. However, a useful and brief overall summary has been provided by Gleitman (1991):

> Using the entire inkblot is said to indicate integrative, conceptual thinking, whereas the use of a high proportion of small details suggests compulsive rigidity. A relatively frequent use of white space is supposed to be a sign of rebelliousness and negativism. Responses that describe humans in movement are said to indicate imagination and a rich inner life; responses that are dominated by color suggest emotionality and impulsivity (Gleitman, 1991, p. 684).

Finally, Rorschach addressed the final guideline for analyzing responses: what the subject actually sees in the inkblot. The most common category of responses involved animals and insects. The percentage of animal responses ranged from 25 to 50 percent. Interestingly, depressed subjects were among those giving the greatest percentage of animal answers, while artists were reported as giving the fewest.

Another category proposed by Rorschach was that of "original responses." These were answers that occurred fewer than once in 100 tests. Original responses were found most often among subjects who were diagnosed as schizophrenic and least often among normal subjects of average intelligence.

DISCUSSION

In his discussion of his form interpretation test, Rorschach pointed out that originally it had been designed to study theoretical questions about the unconscious workings of the human mind and psyche. The discovery that the test had the potential to serve as a diagnostic tool was made accidentally. Rorschach claimed that his test was often able to indicate schizophrenic tendencies, hidden neuroses, potential for depression, characteristics of introversion vs. extroversion, and intelligence. He did *not*, however, propose that the inkblot test should substitute for the usual practices of clinical diagnosis, but rather could aid in this process. Rorschach also warned that while the test can indicate certain unconscious tendencies, it cannot be used to probe the contents of the unconscious in detail. He allowed that the other common practices at the time, such as dream interpretation and free association, were superior methods for such purposes.

CRITICISMS AND SUBSEQUENT RESEARCH

Numerous studies over the decades since Rorschach developed his test have drawn many of his conclusions into question. One of the most important criticisms relates to the validity of the test—whether it actually measures what Rorschach claimed it measured; that is, underlying personality characteristics. Research has demonstrated that many of the response differences attributed by Rorschach to personality factors can be more easily explained by such things as verbal ability, age of the subject, intellectual level, amount of education, and even the characteristics of the person administering the test (see Anastasi, 1982, for a detailed discussion of these criticisms).

Several of Rorschach's specific findings have not been supported by scientific investigation. For example, in scoring the test, many responses involving movement of humans in the figures was said to indicate an advanced level of creativity. However, a study by Zubin, Eron, and Shumer (1965) compared Rorschach test results for a group of average people and a group of accomplished artists and found no significant differences in human movement responses.

Taken as a whole, the scientific research on Rorschach's test does not provide an optimistic view of its reliability or validity as a personality test or diagnostic tool. Nevertheless, the test remains in common use among clinical psychologists and psychotherapists. This apparent contradiction may be explained by the fact that in actual use, Rorschach's inkblot technique is not used as a formal test, but rather as a means of increasing a therapist's understanding of individual clients. It is, in essence, an extension of the verbal interaction that normally occurs between a therapist and a client. In this less rigid interpretation of the responses on the test, it appears to offer helpful insights for effective psychotherapy.

One interesting and more recent application of the Rorschach test has been to present the figures for interpretation by more than one person, such as couples, families, co-workers, gang members, and so on.

Participants are asked to reach a consensus about what the figures represent. This use of the test has shown promise as a method for studying and improving human interaction (Aronow and Reznikoff, 1976).

ANASTASI, A. (1982) *Psychological testing*, (5th ed.). New York: Macmillan.
ARONOW, E., and REZNIKOFF, M. (1976) *Rorschach content interpretation*. New York: Grune and Stratton.
GLEITMAN, H. (1991) *Psychology* (3rd ed.). New York: Norton.
ZUBIN, J., ERON, L., and SHUMER, F. (1965) *An experimental approach to projective techniques*. New York: Wiley.

CROWDING INTO THE BEHAVIORAL SINK
Calhoun, J.B. (1962) Population density and social pathology. *Scientific American*, 206, 139–48.

The effects of crowding on our behavior is something that has interested psychologists for decades. You have probably noticed how your emotions and behavior change when you are in a situation that you perceive as very crowded. You may withdraw into yourself and try to become invisible; you might look for an escape; or you may find yourself becoming irritable and aggressive. How you react to crowding depends on many factors.

You will notice that the title of the article of discussion in this chapter uses the phrase "population density" rather than "crowding." While these may seem very similar, psychologists draw a clear distinction between them. *Density* refers to the number of individuals in a given amount of space. If 20 people occupy a 12-by-12-foot room, the room would probably be seen as densely populated. *Crowding*, however, refers to the subjective psychological experience created by density. That is, if you are trying to concentrate on a difficult task in that room with 20 people, you may experience extreme crowding. Conversely, if you are at a party with 20 friends in that same room, you might not feel crowded at all.

One way behavioral scientists can study the effects of density and crowding on people is to observe places where crowding already exists, such as Manhattan, Mexico City, some housing projects, prisons, and so on. The problem with this method of research is that in all these places, there are many factors that can influence behavior. For example, if we find high crime rates in a crowded inner-city neighborhood, there's no way to know for sure that crowding is the cause of the crime. Maybe it's the fact that people there are poor, or that there's a higher rate of drug abuse, or perhaps all these factors combine with crowded conditions to produce the high crime rates.

Another way to study crowding is to put human subjects into high-density conditions for relatively short periods of time and study their reactions. While this method offers more control and allows us to isolate crowding as a cause of behavior, it is not very realistic in terms of real-life crowded environments, since they usually exist over extended periods of time. It should be pointed out, however, that both of these methods have yielded some interesting findings about crowding that will be discussed later in this chapter.

Since it would be ethically impossible (because of the stress and other potential damaging effects) to place humans in crowded conditions over long periods of time simply to do research on them, there is a third way of addressing the effects of density: do research using animal subjects (see the preface to this book for a discussion of ethics in animal research). One of the earliest and most classic series of studies of this type was conducted by John B. Calhoun in 1962. Calhoun allowed groups of white rats to increase in population to twice the number that would normally be found in a space the size of a 10-by-14-foot room and observed their "social" behavior for 16 months.

THEORETICAL PROPOSITIONS

Calhoun especially wanted to explore the effects of high density on social behavior. It may seem strange to you to think of rats as social animals, but they do socialize in various ways in their natural environment.

To appreciate what led Calhoun to the study being discussed in this chapter, it is necessary to back up several years to an earlier project he conducted. Calhoun had confined a population of rats to a quarter-acre of enclosed, protected outdoor space. Plenty of food was available; there were ideal protected nesting areas; there were no predators; and all disease was kept to a minimum. In other words, this was a rat's paradise. The point of Calhoun's early study was simply to study the population growth rate of the rats in a setting free from the usual natural controls on overpopulation (predators, disease, etc). After 27 months, the population consisted of only 150 adult rats. This was very surprising since with the low mortality rate of adult rats in this ideal setting, and considering the usual rate of reproduction, there should have been 5,000 adults in this period of time! The reason for this small population was an extremely high infant mortality rate. Apparently, reproductive and maternal behavior had been severely altered by the stress of social interaction among the 150 rats, and very few young rats survived to reach adulthood. Even though this number of rats (150 in a quarter-acre) does not seem to be particularly dense, it was obviously crowded enough to produce extreme behavioral changes.

These findings prompted Calhoun to design a more controlled and observable situation inside the lab in order to study more closely what sorts of changes occur in the rats when they are faced with high population density. In other words, he had observed what happened, and now he wanted to find out why.

METHOD

In a series of three studies, either 32 or 56 rats were placed in a 10-by-14-foot laboratory room that was divided into four sections or pens (see Figure 1). There were ramps that allowed the rats to cross from pen 1 to pen 2, from pen 2 to pen 3, and from pen 3 to pen 4. It was not possible for the rats to cross directly between pen 1 and pen 4. Therefore, these were end-pens. If a rat wanted to go from 1 to 4, it would have to go through 2 and 3. The partitions dividing the pens were electrified, so the rats quickly learned that they could not climb over them.

These pens consisted of feeders and waterers and enclosures for nests. The rats were supplied with plenty of food, water, and materials for building nests. In order to observe and record the rats' behavior there was a viewing window in the ceiling of the room.

From his years of studying rats, Calhoun was aware that this particular strain normally is found in colonies of 12 adults. Therefore, the observation room was of a size to accommodate 12 rats per pen, or a total of 48. After the groups were placed in the room, they were allowed to multiply until this normal density was nearly doubled to 80. Once the population level of 80 was reached, young rats that survived past weaning were removed so that the number of rats remained constant.

With this arrangement in place, all that was left was to observe these "crowded" animals for an extended period of time and record their behavior. These observations went on for 16 months.

RESULTS

It is important to keep in mind that the density of the rats was not extreme; in fact, it was quite moderate. If the rats wanted to spread out, there would only have to be 20 or so per pen. But this is not what

FIGURE 1 Diagram of laboratory room as arranged by Calhoun's study of crowding.

om pp. 140–45)

happened. When the male rats reached maturity, they began to fight with each other for social status as they do naturally. These fights took place in all the pens, but the outcome was not the same for all of them. If you think about the arrangement of the room, the two end-pens only had one way in and out. So when a rat won a battle for dominance in one of these pens, he could hold his position and territory (the whole pen) simply by guarding the entrance and attacking any other male that ventured over the ramp. So as it turned out only one male rat ended up in charge of each of the end-pens. However, he was not alone. The female rats distributed themselves more or less equally over all four pens. Therefore, the masters of pens 1 and 4 each had a harem of 8 to 12 females all to themselves. And they didn't take any chances. In order to prevent infiltration, the males took to sleeping directly at the foot of the ramp and were always on guard.

On occasion, there were a few other male rats in the end-pens, but they were extremely submissive. They spent most of their time in the nesting burrows with the females and only came out to feed. They did not attempt to mate with the females. The females in these pens functioned well as mothers. They built comfortable nests and nurtured and protected their offspring. In other words, life for most of the rats in these end-pens was relatively normal and reproductive behavior was successful. About half of the infant rats in those pens survived to adulthood.

The rest of the 60 or so rats crowded into the middle two pens. Since these two pens each had central feeding and watering devices, there were many opportunities for the rats to come in contact with each other. The kinds of behaviors observed among the rats in pens 2 and 3 demonstrates a phenomenon that Calhoun termed the "behavioral sink." A behavioral sink is "the outcome of any behavioral process that collects animals together in unusually great numbers. The unhealthy connotations of the term are not accidental: A behavioral sink does act to aggravate all forms of pathology that can be found within a group" (p. 144). Let's examine some of the extreme and pathological behaviors he observed.

1. *Aggression*. Normally in the wild, male rats will fight other male rats for dominant positions in the social hierarchy. These fights were observed among the more aggressive rats in this study as well. The difference was that here, unlike in their natural environments, top-ranking males were required to fight frequently in order to maintain their positions and often the fights involved several rats in a general brawl. Nevertheless, the strongest males were observed to be the most normal within the center pens. However, even those animals would sometimes exhibit "signs of pathology; going berserk; attacking females, juveniles, and less active males; and showing a particular

predilection—which rats do not normally display—for biting other rats on the tail" (p. 146).

2. *Submissiveness.* Contrary to this extreme aggression, there were other groups of male rats who ignored and avoided battles for dominance. One of these groups consisted of the most healthy-looking rats in the pens. They were fat and their fur was full, without the usual bare spots from fighting. However, these rats were complete social misfits. They moved through the pens as if asleep, ignoring all others, and were, in turn, ignored by the rest. They were completely uninterested in sexual activity and made no advances, even toward females in heat.

Another group of rats engaged in extreme activity and were always on the prowl for receptive females. Calhoun termed them "probers." Often, they were attacked by the more dominant males, but were never interested in fighting for status. They were hypersexual and many of them even became cannibalistic!

3. *Sexual deviance.* These probers also refused to participate in the natural rituals of mating. Normally, a male rat will pursue a female in heat until she escapes into her burrow. Then, the male will wait patiently and even perform a courtship dance directly outside her "door." Finally, she emerges from the burrow and the mating takes place. In Calhoun's study, this ritual was adhered to by most of the sexually active males except the probers. They completely refused to wait and followed the female right into her burrow. Sometimes the nests inside the burrow contained young that had failed to survive and it was here that late in the study the probers turned cannibalistic.

Another group of male rats was termed "the pansexuals" because they attempted to mate with any and all other rats indiscriminately. They sexually approached other males, juveniles, and females that were not in heat. This was a submissive group that was often attacked by the more dominant male rats, but did not fight for dominance.

4. *Reproductive abnormalities.* Rats have a natural instinct for nest building. In this study, small strips of paper were provided in unlimited quantities as nest material. The females are normally extremely active in the process of building nests as the time for giving birth approaches. They gather the material and pile it up so that it forms a cushion. Then they arrange the nest so that it has a small indentation in the middle to hold the young. However, the females in the behavioral sink gradually lost their ability (or inclination) to build adequate nests. At first they failed to form the indentation in the middle. Then, as time went on, they collected fewer and fewer strips of paper so that eventually the infants were born directly on the sawdust that covered the pen's floor.

The mother rats also lost their maternal ability to transport their young from one place to another if they felt the presence of danger. They would move some of the litter and forget the rest, or simply drop them onto the floor as they were moving them. Usually these infants were abandoned and died where they were dropped. They were then eaten by the adults. The infant mortality rate in the middle pens was extremely high, ranging from 80 to 96 percent.

In addition to these maternal deficits, the female rats in the middle pens, when in heat, were chased by large groups of males until they were finally unable to escape. These females experienced high rates of complications in pregnancy and delivery. By the end of the study, almost half of them had died.

DISCUSSION

You might expect that a logical extension of these findings would be to apply them to humans in high-density environments. However, for reasons to be discussed shortly, Calhoun did not draw any such conclusions. In fact, he discussed his findings very little—probably assuming, and logically so, that his results spoke volumes for themselves. He did comment on one clear result: that the natural social and survival behaviors of the rats were severely altered by the stresses associated with living in a high-population-density environment. In addition, he noted that through additional research, with improved methods and refined interpretation of the findings, his studies and others like them *may* contribute to our understanding of similar issues facing human beings.

SIGNIFICANCE OF FINDINGS

As with many of the studies in this book, one of the most important aspects of Calhoun's studies was that they sparked a great deal of related research—in this case, on the effects on humans of high-density living. It would be impossible to examine this large body of research in detail here, but perhaps a few examples should be mentioned.

One environment where the equivalent of a behavioral sink might exist for humans is in extremely overcrowded prisons. A study funded by the National Institute of Justice examined prisons where inmates averaged only 50 square feet each (or an area about 7 by 7 feet), compared with less crowded prisons. It was found that in the crowded prisons there were significantly higher rates of mortality, homicide, suicide, illness, and disciplinary problems (McCain, Cox, and Paulus, 1980). Again, however, remember that there could be other factors besides crowding influencing these behaviors.

Another interesting finding has been that crowding produces negative effects on problem-solving abilities. One study placed people in small, extremely crowded rooms (only 3 square feet per person) or in larger, less crowded rooms. The subjects were asked to complete rather complex tasks, such as placing various shapes into various categories while listening to a story on which they were to be tested later. Those in the crowded conditions performed significantly worse than those who were not crowded (Evans, 1979).

Finally, what do you suppose happens to you *physiologically* in crowded circumstances? Research has determined that your blood pressure and heart rate increase. Along with those effects, you tend to feel that other people are more hostile and that time seems to pass more slowly as density increases (Evans, 1979).

CRITICISMS

Calhoun's results with animals have been supported by later animal research (see Marsden, 1972). However, as has been mentioned before in this book, we must always be careful in applying animal research to humans. Just as substances that may be shown to cause illness in rats may not have the same effect on human physical health, environmental factors influencing rats' social behaviors may not be directly applicable to people. At best, animals can only *represent* certain aspects of humans. Sometimes animal research can be very useful and revealing and lead the way for more definitive research with people. At other times it can be a dead end.

In 1975, a study was undertaken in New York City that attempted to replicate with people some of Calhoun's findings (Freedman, Heshka, Levy, 1975). Data were collected for areas of varying population density on death rates, fertility rates (birth rates), aggressive behavior (court records), psychopathology (admissions to mental hospitals), and so on. When all the data were analyzed, no significant relationships were found between population density and any form of social pathology.

Nevertheless, Calhoun's work in the early 1960s focused a great deal of attention on the psychological and behavioral effects of crowding. This line of research, as it relates to humans, continues today.

EVANS, G.W. (1979) Behavioral and psychological consequences of crowding in humans. *Journal of Applied Social Psychology*, 9, 27–46.

FREEDMAN, J.L., HESHKA, S., and LEVY, A. (1975) Population density and social pathology: Is there a relationship? *Journal of Experimental Social Psychology*, 11, 539–52.

MARSDEN, H.M. (1972) Crowding and animal behavior. In J.F. WOHLHILL and D.H. CARSON (eds.), *Environment and the social sciences*. Washington, D.C.: American Psychological Association.

MCCAIN, G., COX, V.C., and PAULUS, P.B. (1976) The relationship between illness, complaints, and degree of crowding in a prison environment. *Environment and Behavior*, 8, 283–90.

NINE

PSYCHOTHERAPY

Psychotherapy simply means therapy for psychological problems. It involves what is usually a close and caring relationship between a therapist and a client. The history of psychotherapy consists primarily of a long series of hundreds of therapeutic techniques, each considered to be the best by those who developed them. The research demonstrating the effectiveness of all those methods has been generally weak and not very scientific. The subfield of psychology that focuses on treating psychological problems is clinical psychology, and much of the research is anecdotal in nature. However, there have been some important treatment breakthroughs in psychology's attempt to help people.

One question often raised about psychotherapy is, "Which method is best?" The first study in this section addressed this question by demonstrating that, in an overall analysis, various forms of therapy are equally effective. Another line of research discussed in the second study, however, suggested one exception to this. If you have a phobia (an intense and irrational fear of something), a form of therapy called "systematic desensitization" has been shown to be a superior method of treatment. The study included here was done by the person who invented the method. The third study involved the development of a therapeutic tool commonly used by therapists to help their clients discuss sensitive, traumatic, and even hidden psychological problems.

And fourth, we'll look at a study demonstrating the effectiveness of what many believe to be the single most important breakthrough ever in treating people with anxiety: Valium.

CHOOSING YOUR PSYCHOTHERAPIST
Smith, Mary Lee, and Glass, Gene V. (1977) Meta-analysis of psychotherapy outcome studies. *American Psychologist*, 32, 752–60.

Imagine for a moment that you are experiencing a difficult emotional time in your life. You consult with your usual support network of friends and family members, but you just cannot seem to work things out. Finally, when you have endured the pain long enough, you decide to seek some professional help: psychotherapy. Psychotherapy simply means therapy for psychological problems; you don't have to be crazy to need it. In fact, the vast majority of people treated by psychotherapists are *not* mentally ill, but are simply having problems in their life. Since you are an informed, intelligent person, you do some reading on psychotherapy and discover that there are many different approaches available. You read about various types of behavior therapies, such as "systematic desensitization" (see the reading on the work by Wolpe) and "behavior modification." Behavioral therapies such as those focus on the specific behaviors that are making you unhappy, and help you change them using techniques borrowed from classical and operant conditioning. You also find that there are several kinds of non-behavioral therapies, such as the Freudian-based "psychodynamic therapy," "transactional analysis," "rational emotive" therapy, and "client-centered" therapy. These therapies, while they use different techniques, all try to put you in touch with the underlying psychological reasons for your unhappiness and help you change through experiencing greater insight into your inner self (see Hock and Mackler, 1991, for a more complete discussion of the various forms of psychotherapy).

Now you are really confused. Which one should you choose? What you would really like to know now is (1) Does psychotherapy really work, and (2) which method works the best? Well, it may (or may not) help you to know that over the past 40 years, psychologists have been asking the same questions. While many comparison studies have been done, most of them have tended to support the method used by the psychologists conducting the study. In addition, most of the studies were rather small in terms of both the number of subjects and the research techniques used. And to make matters worse, the studies are spread over a wide range of books and journals, making a fully informed judgment extremely difficult to arrive at.

To fill this gap in the research literature on psychotherapy techniques, Mary Lee Smith and Gene Glass, at the University of Colorado, undertook in 1977 the task of compiling virtually all of the studies on psychotherapy effectiveness that had been done up to that time and analyzing them together. By searching through 1,000 various magazines, journals, and books, they selected approximately 500 studies that had tested the effects of counseling and psychotherapy. The researchers then applied a technique developed by Glass called "meta-analysis" to the data from all the studies to determine overall and relative effectiveness. A meta-analysis takes the results of many individual studies and integrates them into a larger statistical analysis so that the evidence is combined into a meaningful whole.

THEORETICAL PROPOSITIONS

The goals of Smith and Glass' study were the following (p. 752):

1. to identify and collect all studies that tested the effects of counseling and psychotherapy,
2. to determine the magnitude of the effect of therapy in each study, and
3. to compare the effects of different types of therapy.

The theoretical propositions implicit in these goals was that when this meta-analysis was done, psychotherapy would be shown to be effective, and differences in effectiveness, if any, could be demonstrated.

METHOD

As mentioned in the introduction, Smith and Glass selected 500 studies. Of these, 375 were fully analyzed. Although the studies varied greatly in terms of the research method used and the type of therapy assessed, all the studies examined at least one group that received psychotherapy compared with another group that received a different form of therapy or no therapy at all (a control group). The most important finding in all the studies for Smith and Glass to include in their meta-analysis was the *magnitude of the effect of therapy*. This effect size was obtained for any outcome measure of the therapy that the original researcher chose to use. Often, studies provided more than one measurement of effectiveness, or the same measurement may have been taken more than once. Examples of outcomes used to assess effectiveness were increases in self-esteem, reductions in anxiety, improvements in school work, and improvements in general adjustment. Wherever possible, all of the measures used in a particular study were included in the meta-analysis.

A total of 833 effect sizes were computed from the 375 studies. These included approximately 25,000 subjects in each of the combined experimental and control groups. The authors reported that the average age of the subjects in the studies was 22 years. They had received an average of 17 hours of therapy from therapists with an average of three-and-a-half years of experience.

You can imagine what a tedious and time-consuming task this kind of analysis was. When dealing with such large amounts of data it is important that researchers take great care to ensure that the information is recorded and calculated consistently and correctly. Therefore each study analyzed was coded in exact ways to obtain the desired data regarding experience of therapist, type of therapy, type of outcome measure used, characteristics of subjects, and so on. The coding of the two authors and their four assistants was analyzed for 20 of the studies and the agreement was above 90 percent for all the data categories.

RESULTS

First, Smith and Glass compared all the treated subjects with all the untreated subjects for all types of therapy and all measures of outcome. They found that "the average client receiving therapy was better off than 75 percent of the untreated controls. . . . The therapies represented by the available outcome calculations moved the average client from the 50th percentile to the 75th percentile" (pp. 754–55). Percentiles indicate the percentage of individuals whose scores on any measurement fall beneath the specific score of interest. For example, if you score in the 90th percentile on an aptitude test, it means that 90 percent of those who took the same test scored lower than you. Furthermore, only 99 (or 12 percent) of the 833 effect sizes were negative (meaning the client was worse off than before therapy). The authors pointed out that if psychotherapy were ineffective, the number of negative effect sizes should equal 50 percent, or 417.

Second, various measures of psychotherapy effectiveness were compared across all of the studies. These findings are represented in Figure 1. As is clear from the chart, all of the outcomes demonstrated that therapy, in general, was more effective than no treatment.

FIGURE 1   Combined effectiveness of all studies analyzed for four outcome measures.

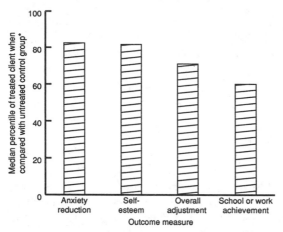

*If there had been no improvement, the clients would have scores of 50. If their condition had become worse, their scores would have been below 50.
(adapted from p. 756)

Third, Smith and Glass compared the various psychotherapy methods found in the studies analyzed using similar statistical procedures. A summary of the more familiar psychotherapies may be found in Figure 2.

Finally, Smith and Glass combined all the various methods into two "superclasses" of therapy: a behavioral superclass consisting of systematic desensitization, behavior modification, and implosion, and a non-behavioral superclass made up of the remaining types of therapy. When they analyzed all the studies in which behavioral and non-behavioral therapies were compared with no-treatment controls, all differences between the two superclasses disappeared (73rd vs. 75th percentile, relative to controls).

DISCUSSION

As is clear from all of the results, psychotherapy appeared to be successful in treating various kinds of problems (Figure 1).
In addition, no matter how the different types of therapy were divided or combined, the differences among them were found to be insignificant (Figure 2 and other percentile findings).

Smith and Glass drew three conclusions from their findings. One is that psychotherapy works. The results of the meta-analysis clearly support the assertion that people who seek therapy are better off with

FIGURE 2   Comparison of the effectiveness of seven methods of psychotherapy.

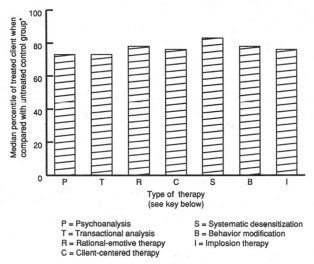

P = Psychoanalysis   S = Systematic desensitization
T = Transactional analysis   B = Behavior modification
R = Rational-emotive therapy   I = Implosion therapy
C = Client-centered therapy

*As in Figure 1, any score above 50 indicates improvement.
(adapted from p. 756)

the treatment than they were without it. Second, "despite volumes devoted to the theoretical differences among different schools of psychotherapy, the results of research demonstrate negligible differences in the effects produced by different therapy types. Unconditional judgments of superiority of one type or another of psychotherapy . . . are unjustified" (p. 760). And third, the authors point out that the knowledge and information researchers and therapists have about psychotherapy's effectiveness is lacking because the information has been spread too thinly across multitudes of publications. Therefore, they suggested that this study was a step in the right direction toward solving the problem, and that research using similar techniques deserves further attention.

IMPLICATIONS AND SUBSEQUENT RESEARCH

The findings in Smith and Glass' study made the issue of psychotherapy effectiveness less confusing for consumers, but more confusing for therapists. Those who choose psychotherapy as a career often have an investment in believing that one particular method (theirs) is more effective than others. However, the conclusions from Smith and Glass' study have been supported by subsequent research (see Smith, Glass, and Miller, 1980, and Landman and Dawes, 1982). One of the outcomes of this line of research is an increase in therapists who take an eclectic approach to helping their clients, meaning that they draw from several methods. In fact, 40 percent of all therapists in practice consider themselves to be eclectic. This percentage is by far the largest of all of the other specific approaches. By being eclectic, these therapists do not confine themselves to any one method, but choose among the various techniques and combine them to develop a treatment plan that best fits the client and the problem he or she is facing.

It would be a mistake to conclude from this and similar studies that all psychotherapy is equally effective for all problems and all people. These studies take a very broad and general overview of the effectiveness of therapy. However, depending on your personality and the circumstances of your specific problem, some therapies might be more effective *for you* than others. For example, it has been demonstrated that behavior therapies are significantly more effective than non-behavioral approaches in the treatment of phobias.

The most important thing to consider when choosing a therapist may not be the type of therapy at all, but rather what your expectations of psychotherapy are, and the characteristics of the therapist. If you believe that psychotherapy can help you, and you enter the therapeutic relationship with optimistic expectations, the chances of successful therapy are greatly increased. The connection you feel with the therapist can also make an important difference. If you see your therapist as genuine, caring, warm, and able to achieve empathy with you, you are much more likely to experience effective and rewarding therapy (Hock and Mackler, 1991).

The importance of the interpersonal aspects of psychotherapy was demonstrated in a study by Strupp and Hadley (1979). University students who were having difficulties with anxiety were assigned to either professionally trained or untrained therapists. The trained therapists were experienced, licensed psychotherapists. The untrained therapists were professors at the university who were known to be interested in and helpful to students, but none had ever been trained in psychotherapy or worked in any related profession. There was also a control group of student subjects who had the same problems and went through the same assessment procedures as the other subjects, but their therapy sessions were delayed until the results of the study were obtained. The findings indicated that the students assigned to both the trained and the untrained therapists improved significantly more than the controls, did but that no differences existed between the two groups. The most favorable outcomes were reported by students whose therapists, trained or not, helped them to discuss their problems, focused on the present rather than the past, and encouraged them to become involved in new social activities.

Smith and Glass' study was a milestone in the history of psychotherapy in that it removed much of the temptation for researchers to try to prove the superiority of a specific method and instead, focused on how best to help those in psychological pain. Future research may now concentrate on clarifying those factors that serve to produce the fastest and most satisfying therapeutic experience.

HOCK, R., and MACKLER, M. (1991) *Do you need psychotherapy?* Manuscript, New England College.
LANDMAN, J., and DAWES, R. (1982) Psychotherapy outcome: Smith and Glass' conclusions stand up under scrutiny. *American Psychologist*, 37, 504–16.
SMITH, M., GLASS, G., and MILLER, T. (1980) *The benefits of psychotherapy*. Baltimore: John Hopkins University Press.
STRUPP, H., and HADLEY, S. (1979) Specific vs. non-specific factors in psychotherapy: A controlled study of outcome. *Archives of General Psychology*, 36, 1125–36.

RELAXING YOUR FEARS AWAY
Wolpe, Joseph (1961) The systematic desensitization treatment of neuroses. *The Journal of Nervous and Mental Diseases*, 132, 180–203.

Before discussing this very important technique in psychotherapy called *systematic desensitization* (which simply means decreasing in an organized way your level of anxiety over something), the concept of neurosis should be clarified. *Neurosis* is now a somewhat outdated term that was used to refer to a group of psychological problems of which extreme anxiety was the central characteristic. Today such problems are called "anxiety disorders." We are all familiar with anxiety, and sometimes experience a high degree of it in situations that make us nervous, such as public speaking, job interviews, exams, and so on. However, when someone suffers from an anxiety disorder, the reactions are much more extreme, pervasive, frequent, and debilitating. Often such disorders interfere with a person's life so that normal and desired functioning is impossible.

The most common anxiety-related difficulties are phobias, panic disorder, and obsessive-compulsive disorder. If you have ever suffered from one of them you know that it is not your ordinary garden-variety anxiety, but a kind of anxiety that takes control of your life. This chapter's discussion of Joseph Wolpe's work in treating those disorders will focus primarily on phobias.

The word *phobia* comes from Phobos, the name of the Greek god of fear. The ancient Greeks painted images of Phobos on their masks and shields to frighten their enemies. A phobia is a fear; but more than that, it is an *irrational* fear. In other words, it is a fear reaction that is out of proportion with the reality of the event. For example, if you are strolling down a path in the forest and suddenly happen upon a rattlesnake, coiled and ready to strike, you will feel fear (unless you're Crocodile Dundee or something). This is *not* a phobia, but a normal, rational fear response to a real danger. On the other hand, if you are unable to go to the zoo because you might see a snake in a glass cage, that would probably be considered a phobia. This may sound humorous to you, but to those who suffer from phobias, it's not funny at all. Phobic reactions are extremely uncomfortable events that involve symptoms such as dizziness, heart palpitations, feeling faint, hyperventilation, sweating, trembling, and nausea. A person with a phobia will carefully avoid situations in which the feared stimulus might be encountered. Often, this avoidance can interfere drastically with a person's desired functioning in life.

Phobias are divided into three main types. *Simple* phobias involve irrational fears of animals (such as rats, dogs, spiders, or snakes) or specific situations such as small spaces (claustrophobia) or heights (acrophobia). *Social* phobias are characterized by irrational fears about interactions with others, such as public speaking, or fear of embarrassment. Finally, *agoraphobia* is the irrational fear of being in unfamiliar, open, or crowded spaces. While the various types of phobias are quite different, they share at least two common features: They are all irrational, and they all are treated in similar ways.

Early treatment of phobias centered around the Freudian concepts of psychoanalysis. This view maintains that a phobia is the result of unconscious psychological conflicts stemming from childhood traumas. It further contends that the phobia may be substituting for some other, deeper fear or anger that the person is unwilling to face. For example, a man with an irrational fear of heights (acrophobia) may have been cruelly teased as a small boy by his father who pretended to try to push him off a high cliff. Acknowledging this experience as an adult might force the man to deal with his father's general abusiveness (something he doesn't want to face), so he represses it, and it is expressed instead in the form of a phobia. In accordance with this view of the source of the problem, psychoanalysts historically attempted to treat phobias by helping the person to gain insight into unconscious feelings and release the hidden emotion, thereby freeing themselves of the phobia in the process. However, such techniques, while useful for most other types of psychological problems, have proven relatively ineffective in treating phobias. It appears that even when someone uncovers the underlying unconscious conflicts that may be related to the phobia, the phobia itself persists.

Joseph Wolpe was not the first to suggest the use of a behavioral technique called systematic desensitization, but he is generally credited with perfecting it and applying it to the treatment of anxiety disorders. The behavioral approach differs dramatically from psychoanalytic thinking in that it is not concerned with the unconscious sources of the problem or with repressed conflicts. The fundamental idea of behavioral therapy is that you have *learned* an ineffective behavior (the phobia), and now you must *unlearn* it. This formed the basis for Wolpe's method for the treatment of phobias.

THEORETICAL PROPOSITIONS

Earlier research by Wolpe and others had discovered that fear reactions in *animals* could be reduced by a simple conditioning procedure. For example, suppose a rat behaves fearfully when it sees a realistic photograph of a cat. If the rat is given food every time the cat is presented, the rat will become less and less fearful, until finally the fear response disappears entirely. The rat had originally been conditioned to associate the cat photo with fear. However, the rat's response to being fed was *incompatible* with the fear response. Since the fear response and the feeding response cannot both exist at the same time, the fear was *inhibited* by the feeding response. This incompatibility of two responses is called "reciprocal inhibition" (when two responses inhibit each other, only one may exist at a given moment). Wolpe proposed the more general proposition that "if a response inhibitory to anxiety can be made to occur in the presence of anxiety-provoking stimuli . . . the bond between these stimuli and the anxiety will be weakened" (p. 180). He also argued that human anxiety reactions are quite similar to those found in the animal lab and that the concept of reciprocal inhibition could be used to treat various human psychological disorders.

In his work with people, the anxiety-inhibiting response was deep relaxation rather than "feeding." The idea was based on the theory that you *cannot* experience deep physical relaxation and fear at the same time. As a behaviorist, Wolpe believed that the reason you have a phobia is that you learned it sometime in your life through the process of classical conditioning, by which some object became associated in your brain with intense fear (see the reading on Pavlov's research). We know from the work of Watson (see the reading on Watson's study with Little Albert) and others that such learning is possible even at very young ages. So, in order to treat your phobia, you must experience a response that is inhibitory to fear or anxiety (relaxation) while in the presence of the feared situation. Will this treatment technique work? Wolpe's article reports on 39 cases randomly selected out of 150, where the subjects' phobias were treated by the author using his systematic desensitization technique.

METHOD

Imagine that you suffer from an irrational fear of heights called acrophobia. This problem has become so extreme that you have trouble climbing onto a ladder to trim the trees in your yard or going above the second floor in an office building. Your phobia is interfering so much with your life that you decide to seek out psychotherapy from a behavior therapist such as Joseph Wolpe. Your therapy will consist of several stages.

Relaxation Training

The first several sessions will deal very little with your phobia. Instead, the therapist will focus on teaching you how to relax your body. Wolpe recommended a form of progressive muscle relaxation introduced by Edmund Jacobson in 1938 that is still in common therapeutic use today. The process involves tensing and relaxing various groups of muscles (such as the arms and hands, the face, the back, the stomach, the legs, etc.) throughout the body until a deep state of relaxation is achieved. This relaxation training may take most of your first five or six sessions with the therapist. After the training, you are able to place yourself in this state of relaxation whenever you want. It should be noted that for most of the cases reported in this article, Wolpe also incorporated hypnosis to ensure full relaxation, but this has been shown to be usually unnecessary for effective therapy.

Construction of an Anxiety Hierarchy

The next stage of the process is for you and your therapist to develop a list of anxiety-producing situations or scenes involving your phobia. The list would begin with a situation that is only slightly uncomfortable and proceed through increasingly more frightening scenes until finishing with the most anxiety-producing event. The number of steps in a patient's hierarchy varies from five or six to 20 or more. Table 1 shows what might appear on your list for your phobia of heights, as well as a hierarchy directly from Wolpe's article by a patient suffering from claustrophobia.

Desensitization

Now comes the actual unlearning. According to Wolpe, no *direct* contact with the feared situations is necessary to reduce a person's sensitivity to them. The same effect could be accomplished through

TABLE 1   Anxiety Hierarchies

ACROPHOBIA*

1. Walking over a grating in the sidewalk.
2. Sitting in a third-floor office near the window (not a floor-to-ceiling window).
3. Riding an elevator to the 45th floor.
4. Watching window washers 10 floors up on a platform
5. Standing on a chair to change a lightbulb.
6. Sitting on the balcony with a railing of a fifth-floor apartment.
7. Sitting in the front row of the second balcony at the theater.
8. Standing on the third step of a ladder to trim bushes in the yard.
9. Standing at the edge of the roof of a three-story building with no railing.
10. Driving around curves on a mountain road.
11. Riding as a passenger around curves on a mountain road.
12. Standing at the edge of the roof of a 20-story building.

*(adapted from Goldstein, Jamison, and Baker, 1980, p. 371)

CLAUSTROPHOBIA*

1. Reading of miners trapped.
2. Having polish on fingernails without access to remover.
3. Being told of someone in jail.
4. Visiting and unable to leave.
5. Having a tight ring on finger.
6. On a journey by train (the longer the journey, the more the anxiety).
7. Traveling in an elevator with an operator (the longer the ride, the more the anxiety).
8. Traveling alone in an elevator.
9. Passing through a tunnel on a train (the longer the tunnel, the greater the anxiety).
10. Being locked in a room (the smaller the room and the longer the duration, the greater the anxiety).
11. Being stuck in an elevator (the greater the time, the greater the anxiety).

*(adapted from Wolpe, p. 197)

description and imagination. Remember, you developed your phobia through the process of association, so you will eliminate the phobia the same way. First, you are instructed to place yourself in a state of deep relaxation as you have been taught. Then the therapist begins with the first step in your hierarchy and describes the scene to you: "You are walking down the sidewalk and you come to a large grating. As you continue walking you can see through the grating to the bottom 10 feet below." Your job is to imagine the scene while remaining completely relaxed. If this is successful, the therapist will proceed to the next step: "You are sitting in an office on the third floor . . . ," and so on. If at any moment during this process you feel the slightest anxiety, you are instructed to raise your index finger. When this happens, the presentation of your hierarchy will stop until you have returned to full relaxation. Then the descriptions will begin again from a point farther down the list so that you can maintain your relaxed state. This process continues until you are able to remain relaxed through the entire hierarchy. Once you accomplish this, you might repeat the process several times in subsequent therapy sessions. In Wolpe's work with his clients the number of sessions for successful treatment varied greatly. Some people claimed to be recovered in as few as six sessions, while one took nearly 100 (this was a patient with a severe phobia of death, plus two additional phobias). The average number of sessions was around 12. This, by the way, was considerably fewer than the number of sessions generally required for formal psychoanalysis, which usually lasted years.

The most important question relating to this treatment method is this: Does it work?

RESULTS

The 39 cases reported in Wolpe's article suffered from many different phobias. The themes of their hierarchies included, among others, claustrophobia, storms, being watched, crowds, bright light, wounds, agoraphobia, falling, rejection, and snakelike shapes. The success of their therapy was judged by the patients' own reports and by occasional direct observation. Generally, patients who report improvement and gradual recovery describe the process in ways that lead Wolpe to accept their reports as credible. The desensitization process was rated as either completely successful (freedom from phobic reactions), partially successful (phobic reactions of 20 percent or less of original strength), or unsuccessful.

For the 39 cases there were a total of 68 phobias treated. Sixty-two of these (in a total of 35 patients) were judged to be completely or partially successful. This was a success rate of 91 percent. The remaining six hierarchies (9 percent) were unsuccessful. The average number of sessions needed for successful treatment was 12.3. Wolpe explained that most of the unsuccessful cases displayed special problems that did not allow for proper desensitization to take place, such as an inability to imagine the situations presented in the hierarchy.

Critics of Wolpe, mainly from the psychoanalytic camp, claimed that his methods were only treating the symptoms and not the underlying cause of the anxiety. They maintained that other symptoms would appear to replace the ones treated in this way. They likened it to a leaking dike; when one hole is plugged, another appears. Related to this was the question of how lasting this treatment would be. Any form of therapy would be of little value if the symptoms returned soon after the sessions ended. Wolpe responded to criticisms and questions by obtaining follow-up reports from 25 of the 35 patients who had received successful desensitization at various times from six months to four years after treatment. Upon examining the reports he wrote, "There was no reported instance of relapse or new phobias or other neurotic symptoms. I have never observed resurgence of neurotic anxiety when desensitization has been complete or virtually so" (p. 200).

DISCUSSION

The discussion in Wolpe's article focuses on responding to the skepticism of the psychoanalysts at the time his research was done. During the 1950s, psychoanalysis was a very common and popular form of psychotherapy. As behavior therapies began to make their way into the mainstream of clinical psychology, a great deal of controversy was created, much of which continues in various forms today. Wolpe pointed out that the desensitization method offered several advantages over traditional psychoanalysis (see p. 202 of the original study):

1. The goals of psychotherapy can be clearly stated in every case.
2. Sources of anxiety can be clearly defined.
3. Changes in the patient's reactions during descriptions of scenes from the hierarchy can be measured during the sessions.
4. Therapy can be performed with others present (Wolpe found that having others present, such as therapists in training, during the sessions did not interfere with the effectiveness).
5. Therapists can be interchanged if desired or necessary.

SUBSEQUENT RESEARCH

Since Wolpe published this article, and a book on the use of reciprocal inhibition in psychotherapy (Wolpe, 1958), the use of systematic desensitization has grown to the point that now it is considered the treatment of choice for anxiety disorders, especially for phobias. This growth has been due in large part to more recent and more scientific research on the effectiveness of the method.

A well-known study by Gordon Paul (see Paul, 1969) treated college students who suffered from extreme phobic anxiety in public speaking situations. First, all the subjects were asked to give a short, ad-libbed speech to an unfamiliar audience. Their degree of anxiety was measured by observer's ratings of visible anxiety, physiological measures such as pulse rate and perspiration of the palms, and a self-report questionnaire. The students were then randomly assigned to three different treatment groups: (1) systematic desensitization, (2) insight therapy (similar to psychoanalysis), or (3) no treatment (control). Experienced therapists carried out the treatment in five sessions. All the subjects were then placed in the same public speaking situation, and all the measures of anxiety were taken. Figure 1 summarizes the results. On the physiological measures, only systematic desensitization differed significantly from the group that received no treatment and was significantly more effective in reducing anxiety as measured by observers and self-report. Even more convincing was that in a two-year follow-up, 85 percent of the desensitization group still showed significant improvement, compared with 50 percent of the insight group.

CONCLUSION

Wolpe was quick to point out that the idea of overcoming fear and anxiety was not new. "It has long been known that increasing measures of exposure to a feared object may lead to the gradual disappearance of the fear" (p. 200). In fact, you already knew this yourself, even if you had never heard of systematic desensitization prior to reading this chapter. Imagine a child who is about 13 years old and has a terrible phobia of dogs. This fear is probably the result of a frightening experience with a dog when the child was much younger, such as being jumped on by a big dog, being bitten, or even having a parent who was afraid of dogs (learning through modeling; see the reading on the work of Albert Bandura). Because of this experience, the child developed an association between dogs and fear. If you wanted to cure this child of

FIGURE 1   Results of treatment for anxiety*

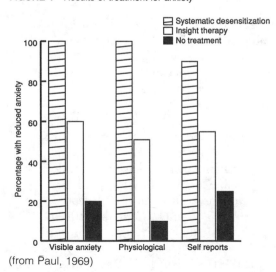

(from Paul, 1969)

the fear of dogs, you would have to somehow break that association. How might you do it? Most people's first response to this question is, "Buy the child a puppy!" If that's what you thought of, you have just recommended a form of systematic desensitization.

GOLDSTEIN, M., BAKER, B., and JAMISON, K. (1980) *Abnormal psychology*. Boston: Little, Brown.
PAUL, G.L. (1969) Outcome of systematic desensitization: Controlled investigation of individual technique variations and current status. In C. FRANKS (ed.), *Behavior therapy: Appraisal and status*. New York: McGraw-Hill.
WOLPE, J. (1959) *Psychotherapy through reciprocal inhibition*. Palo Alto, Calif.: Stanford University Press.

PICTURE THIS!
Murray, Henry A. (1938) *Explorations in personality*. New York: Oxford University Press, pp. 531–45.

In the previous section, a method used by clinical psychologists for exposing underlying aspects of personality called the "projective test" was discussed in relation to Rorschach's inkblot technique. The idea behind Rorschach's test, you'll recall, was to allow individuals to place or *project* their own interpretations onto objectively meaningless and unstructured forms. You'll also recall that Rorschach examined a subject's focus on the location in the inkblot, the various specific features of that location, and statements regarding movement of the figure to draw conclusions about the subject's personality characteristics. The content of the subject's interpretation was also taken into account, but was of secondary importance.

Several years after Rorschach developed his test, Henry A. Murray, at the Harvard Psychological Clinic, and his assistant, Christiana D. Morgan, developed a very different form of a projective test called the *thematic apperception test*, or "TAT," which focused *entirely* on the content of the subjects' interpretations. Rather than formless shapes like Rorschach's inkblots, the TAT consists of black-and-white drawings depicting people in various ambiguous situations. The client or subject is asked to make up a story about the drawing. The stories are then analyzed by the therapist or researcher to reveal hidden unconscious conflicts (*apperception* means conscious perception).

The theory behind the TAT was that when you observe human behavior, either in a picture or in real life, you will interpret that behavior according to the clues that are available in the situation. When the causes for the behavior are clear from available clues, your interpretation will not only be correct, but it will be in substantial agreement with other observers. However, if the situation is vague and it is difficult to find reasons for the behavior, your interpretation will be more likely to reflect something about yourself—about your own fears, desires, conflicts, motives, etc. For example, imagine you see the faces of a man and a woman looking up into the sky with different expressions on their faces: He looks terrified, but she is laughing. As you observe the situation further, you see that they are waiting in line for a ride on "Colossus," the mega-rollercoaster at the Magic Mountain amusement park in California. It is not difficult to interpret the couple's behavior in this situation and your analysis would probably be more or less the same as that of other observers. Now imagine seeing the same expressions in isolation, without any situational clues to explain the behavior. If you were asked, "What are these people experiencing?," your answer would depend on your *internal* interpretation and, therefore, might reveal more about *you* than about the people you are observing. Furthermore, because of the ambiguity of the isolated behavior, different observers' answers would vary greatly. This is the idea behind Morgan and Murray's Thematic Apperception Test, which to this day is a very popular tool among psychotherapists for helping their clients.

THEORETICAL PROPOSITIONS

At the most basic level, the theory underlying the TAT, like that of the Rorschach test, is that people's behavior is driven by unconscious forces. Implicit in this notion is an acceptance of the principles of psychodynamic psychology developed originally by Freud (see the discussion of Freud's theories). In this view, unconscious conflicts must be exposed for accurate diagnosis and successful treatment of psychological problems to take place. This was the purpose of Rorschach's inkblot test, discussed in the previous section, and it was also the goal of Murray's TAT.

Morgan and Murray wrote, "The purpose of this procedure is to stimulate literary creativity and thereby evoke fantasies that reveal covert and unconscious complexes" (p. 530). The way they conceived of this process was that a person would be shown ambiguous drawings of human behavior. In trying to explain the situation, the subject would become less self-conscious and less concerned about being observed by the therapist. This would, in turn, cause the person to become less defensive and reveal inner wishes, fears, and past experiences that might have been repressed. Murray also pointed out that part of the theoretical foundation for this test was that "a great deal of written fiction is the conscious or unconscious expression of the author's experiences or fantasies" (p. 531).

METHOD

In the test's original conceptualization, subjects were asked to guess the events leading up to the scene depicted in the drawing and what they thought the outcome of the scene would be. After testing the method, it was determined that a great deal more about the psychology of subjects could be obtained if they were simply asked to make up a story about the picture, rather than asked to guess the facts surrounding it.

The pictures themselves were developed to stimulate fantasies in the subjects about conflicts and important events in their own experiences. Therefore, it was decided that each picture should involve at least one person with whom the subject could easily identify. Through trial and error with several hundred pictures, a final set of 20 was chosen. Since the TAT is in common usage today, many believe that widespread publication of the pictures used might compromise its validity. However, it is difficult to understand the test without being able to see the type of drawings chosen. Therefore, Figure 1 is one of the original drawings that was under consideration but was not ultimately chosen as one of the final 20. Figure 2 is a single sample selected from the 20 drawings that constituted Murray's original TAT.

An early study of the TAT was conducted by Morgan and Murray and reported in Murray's 1938 book cited at the beginning of this chapter. The subjects for that study were men between the ages of 20 and 30. Each subject was seated in a comfortable chair facing away from the experimenter (as has been commonly practiced by psychotherapists when administering the TAT). These are the exact instructions given to each subject:

> This is a test of your creative imagination. I shall show you a picture and I want you to make up a plot or a story for which it might be used as an illustration. What is the relation of the individuals in the picture? What has happened to them? What are their present thoughts and feelings? What will be the outcome? Do your very best. Since I am asking you to indulge your literary imagination, you may make your story as long and as detailed as you wish (p. 532).

The experimenter handed the subject each picture in succession and took notes on what the subject said for each one. Each subject was given one hour. Due to the time limitations, most subjects only completed stories for about 15 of the 20 drawings.

A few days later the subjects returned and were interviewed about their stories. In order to disguise the true purpose of the study, subjects

FIGURE 1   From Henry A. Murray, Thematic Apperception Test. Cambridge, MA. Harvard University Press. Copyright © 1943 by the President and Fellows of Harvard College. © 1971 by Henry A. Murray. Reprinted by permission of the publishers.

were told that the purpose of the research was to compare their creative experiences with those of famous writers. Subjects were reminded of their responses to the pictures and were asked to explain what their sources for the stories were. They were also given a free-association test, in which they were to say the first thing that came to mind in response to words spoken by the experimenter. These exercises were designed to determine to what extent the stories the subjects made up about the drawings reflected their own personal experiences, conflicts, desires, and so on.

RESULTS AND DISCUSSION

Murray and Morgan reported two main findings from this early study of the TAT. The first was the discovery that the stories the subjects made up for the pictures came from four sources: (1) books and movies, (2) real-life events involving a friend or a relative, (3) experiences in the subject's own life, and (4) the subject's conscious or unconscious fantasies (see p. 533 of the original study).

The second and more important finding was that the subjects clearly projected their own personal, emotional, and psychological existence into their stories. One such example reported by the authors was that most of the subjects who were students identified the person in one of the drawings as a student, but none of the non-student subjects did so. In another example, the subject's father was a ship's carpenter, and the subject had strong desires to travel and see the world. This fantasy appeared in his interpretations of several of the drawings. For instance, when shown a drawing of two workers in conversation, the subject's story was, "These two fellows are a pair of adventurers. They always manage to meet in out-of-the-way places. They are now in India. They have heard of a new revolution in South America and they are planning how they can get there. . . . In the end they work their way there on a freighter" (p. 534). Murray reports that, without exception, every person who participated in the study injected aspects of their personalities into their stories.

To further illustrate how the TAT reflects personal characteristics, the authors report one subject in detail. 'Virt' was a Russian Jew who had emigrated to the United States after terrible childhood experiences during World War I, including persecution, hunger, and separation from his mother. Picture No. 13 of the TAT, was given the following written description by Murray and Morgan: "On the floor against the couch is the huddled form of a boy with his head bowed on his right arm. Beside him on the floor is an object which resembles a revolver" (p. 536). Virt's story about this drawing was as follows:

> Some great trouble has occurred. Someone he loved has shot herself. Probably it is his mother. She may have done it out of poverty. He being fairly grown up sees the misery of it all and would like to shoot himself. But he is young and braces up after a while. For some time he lives in misery, the first few months thinking of death (p. 536).

It is interesting to compare this story with other, more recent stories made up about the same drawing:

> 1. A 35-year-old junior high school teacher: "I think that this is someone who has been put in prison for something he did not do. He has denied that he committed any crime and has been fighting and fighting his case in the courts. But he has given up. Now he is completely exhausted, depressed, and hopeless. He made a fake gun to try to escape, but he knows this won't work either" (author's files).

2. A 16-year-old high school student: "This girl is playing hide-and-seek, probably with her brothers. She is counting from one to a hundred. She is sad and tired because she is never able to win and always has to be 'it.' It looks like the boys were playing some other game before because there's a toy gun here" (author's files).

You don't have to be a psychotherapist to make some predictions about the inner conflicts, motives, or desires that these three people might be projecting onto that one drawing. These examples also demonstrate the remarkably diverse responses that are possible on the TAT.

Murray and Morgan reported that, in addition to insights into unconscious conflicts, the TAT was useful in revealing specific hidden characteristics such as aggressive tendencies, creativity, and achievement motivation. Finally, the researchers measured each subject's level of optimism by rating the outcomes of their stories on a scale from -2 (very negative) to $+2$ (very positive). To find a subject's "optimism score," the ratings were totaled and divided by the number of stories. It was reported that the overall optimism or pessimism score for each subject coincided with other information obtained in the interviews.

CRITICISMS AND RELATED RESEARCH

Although the TAT uses stimuli that are very different from Rorschach's inkblot test, it has been criticized on the same grounds of poor reliability and validity (see the reading on Rorschach's test for additional discussion of these issues). The most serious reliability problem for the TAT is that different clinicians offer differing interpretations of the same set of TAT responses. Some have suggested that therapists may unknowingly inject their own unconscious characteristics onto the subject's descriptions of the drawings. In other words, the interpretation of the TAT might be a projective test for the clinician who is administering it!

In terms of validity (that is, the extent to which the TAT truly measures what it is designed to measure), several types of criticisms have been cited frequently. If the test measures underlying psychological processes, then it should be able to distinguish between, say, normal people and people who are mentally ill, or between different types of psychological conditions. However, research has shown that it fails to make such distinctions. In a study by Eron (1950), the TAT was administered to two groups of male veterans. Some were students in college and others were patients in a psychiatric hospital. When the results of the TAT were analyzed, there were no significant differences found between the two groups or among psychiatric patients with different illnesses.

Other research has questioned the ability of the TAT to predict behavior. For example, if a person includes a great deal of violence in the stories and plots used to describe the drawings, this does not differentiate between aggression that merely exists in the subject's fantasies and the potential for real violent behavior. For some people, it is possible to fantasize about aggression without ever expressing violent behavior, while for others, aggressive fantasy will predict actual violence. Since TAT responses do not indicate into which category a particular person falls, the test is of little value in predicting aggressive tendencies (see Anastasi, 1982, pp. 587–88).

Another basic and very important criticism of the TAT (which could be made of the Rorschach inkblot technique as well) relates to whether the projective hypothesis itself is valid. The assumption underlying the TAT is that subjects' stories about the drawings reveal something about their stable, unconscious processes; about *who they are*. There is scientific evidence to suggest, however, that responses to projective tests such as the Rorschach and TAT may depend upon temporary and situational factors. What this means is that if you are given the TAT on Monday, just after work, when you've had a big fight with your boss, and then again on Saturday, just after you've returned from a relaxing day at the beach, the stories you make up for the drawings might be completely different on the two occasions. Critics argue that, to the extent that the stories are different, the TAT has only tapped into your temporary state and not your "real" underlying self.

As a demonstration of this criticism, numerous studies have found variations in TAT performance relating to the following list of influences: hunger, lack of sleep, drug use, anxiety level, frustration, verbal ability, characteristics of the person administering the test, the attitude of the subject about the testing situation, and the subject's cognitive abilities. In light of these findings, Anne Anastasi, one of the leading authorities on psychological testing, has written, "Many types of research have tended to cast doubt on the projective hypothesis. There is ample evidence that alternative explanations may account as well or better for the individual's responses to unstructured test stimuli" (Anastasi, 1982, p. 589).

CONCLUSION

One of the most remarkable aspects of projective tests such as the TAT and the Rorschach inkblot test is that in spite of a massive body of evidence condemning them as invalid, unreliable, and possibly based on faulty assumptions, they are to this day among the most frequently used psychological tests. The fact that clinicians continue to be enthusiastic about these tools while experimental psychologists grow increasingly wary is a key point of contention between those two groups. How can this contradiction be reconciled? The most commonly argued answer to this question is that the way the TAT and the Rorschach test are actually used in psychotherapy is not as tests at all, but rather as extensions of the usual interviews that occur between clinicians and their patients. It follows, then, that these tests are applied by therapists in very individual ways to open channels of communication with clients and enter psychological domains that might have been hidden without the stories provided by the TAT. As one practicing psychotherapist explains, "I don't score my clients' responses on the TAT or use them for diagnosis, but the drawings are a wonderful and valuable vehicle for bringing to light troubled areas in a client's life. The identification and mutual awareness of these issues that flows from the TAT allows for more focused and effective therapy" (author's files).

ANASTASI, A. (1982) *Psychological testing*, 5th ed. New York: Macmillan.
ERON, L. (1950) A normative study of the thematic apperception test. *Psychological Monographs*, 64, (whole number 315).

A CHEMICAL CALM
Whitehead, William E., Blackwell, Barry, and Robinson, Ann (1978) Effects of diazepam on phobic avoidance behavior and phobic anxiety. *Biological Psychiatry*, 13, 59–64.

When you first read the title of the article at the top of this page, you may not have immediately recognized the topic. But this study by William Whitehead and his colleagues was an early scientific examination of the effects of something everyone recognizes: *Valium*. This is not to say that everyone has used Valium. It is estimated, however, that over half of all adults in the United States will take Valium or a similar drug during their lifetime. The reason for this amazing statistic is that Valium treats the most common ailment in contemporary society: *anxiety*. There is a memorable scene in the film *Starting Over* in which Burt Reynolds' character is having a panic attack in the middle of Bloomingdales' furniture section in New York. His brother, a psychiatrist (played by Charles Durning), rushes in, speaks softly to him for a minute, then turns to the crowd of New Yorkers that has gathered to watch and asks, "Does anyone have a Valium?" As the camera cuts to the crowd, every person is reaching simultaneously into his or her pockets and purses to provide the requested medication.

"Valium" is actually a brand name for a drug called *diazepam*. Diazepam is a member of a category of drugs called the *benzodiazepines*, or "anti-anxiety" drugs, also referred to as "minor tranquilizers." Other familiar medications falling into this category, though not identical to Valium, are Librium and Xanax. Diazepam was developed and marketed under the name Valium in the mid-1960s. By 1973 it had become the most often prescribed drug in the United States, surpassing birth control pills and painkillers. In 1973, there were 80 million prescriptions written for Valium and Librium combined. Looking back, there is little question that those drugs revolutionized how the behavioral sciences viewed and treated the psychological problem of anxiety. Since Valium is now available in its generic form, the term diazepam will be used throughout the remainder of this discussion.

When doctors prescribed diazepam for anxiety, the patient was usually instructed to take the medication on a regular schedule, such as twice or three times per day, to prevent the occurrence of anxiety symptoms in general. However, many patients chose instead to take it only when they felt they needed it: when facing a particularly anxiety-producing event, such as a public speaking engagement or air travel.

It is interesting to note that more than 10 years after its introduction, and after literally tons of the drug had been prescribed, there were few scientific studies demonstrating the effectiveness of diazepam when used on this as-needed basis. This study by Whitehead and his associates was one of the earliest to test diazepam in a specific fear situation called "phobic anxiety."

A phobia is an *irrational* fear of an object or a situation. The key difference between a phobia and a normal fear is that a phobia involves fearful reactions that are exaggerated out of proportion with the reality of the actual danger (see the discussion of phobias related to the work of Joseph Wolpe). It has been said that a phobia is a fear that is so intense, a person would jump out of a moving car to get away from the feared object!

Whitehead, Blackwell, and Robinson had two goals in their study. One goal was to test the effectiveness of diazepam in reducing anxiety in situations where individuals are exposed to the objects of their phobias. In addition to this, they wanted to evaluate the "behavioral approach method" of measuring a fear response. This method simply measures how closely you are willing to approach a feared object; theoretically, the closer the approach, the lower the anxiety.

THEORETICAL PROPOSITIONS

The researchers hypothesized that diazepam would reduce phobic anxiety. If this prediction proved to be correct, it would support the use of the medication on a situational, as-needed basis. The assumption underlying this idea was that phobic anxiety is fundamentally the same as other types of anxiety. Thus, if the researchers could prove diazepam's effectiveness for phobias, its use would be validated for other non-phobic situations involving high levels of anxiety.

In addition, the authors believed that the closeness of approach by a phobic individual to the feared object would be a sensitive and objective measurement of anxiety as well as an index of the effectiveness of the tranquilizer drug. They pointed out that such a measure had been used previously in evaluating various forms of psychotherapy and should transfer well to this context. The most common method of determining how much anxiety is being experienced at a particular moment is to ask the person to rate or describe it. This self-report method, while providing useful information about a person's subjective state, is often more prone to errors in interpretation than more objective measures. Therefore, Whitehead, et al., decided to incorporate both self-report and behavioral approach measures in their study of diazepam.

METHOD

Subjects for this experiment were recruited through an advertisement in the classified section of the newspaper which invited people with phobias of cats or cockroaches to participate in a drug study. In exchange for their participation, they were promised free behavioral therapy for their phobias. Eleven roach phobics, two cat phobics, and one snake phobic answered the ad and were chosen to participate in the study. The snake phobic was male, and all the others were female. (Careful, don't start getting Freudian over this!)

A double-blind experimental procedure was used in this study. This means that neither the subjects or the experimenter administering the medication knew whether the real diazepam or a placebo was taken by each subject. This procedure is extremely important in studies such as this to ensure that the beliefs and expectations of the participants do not interfere with the real effects of the drug.

All subjects were tested twice on their level of anxiety: once before, and again two hours after taking a pill that either consisted of 10 milligrams of diazepam or was a placebo pill. Two measures were obtained from each subject. First, subjects were instructed to approach as closely as they could to the phobic object (real cats, roaches, and snakes were present in the lab). The distance between a subject and the feared object was measured. Also, the subjects were asked to verbally rate the amount of anxiety they felt on a scale from 0 (no anxiety) to 10 (maximum anxiety). The results of the experiment were obtained by comparing the anxiety before and after the drug to the anxiety before and after the placebo.

RESULTS

Figure 1 illustrates the actual distances to which the subjects were able to approach the feared objects before and after diazepam or the placebo. The change in the drug group was significantly greater than that for the placebo group. In addition, the closest distance at which the subjects were able to approach the objects was reduced by 55 percent following the drug, but by only 23 percent for the placebo group.

Since phobic anxiety increases as the distance to the feared object decreases, the subjective ratings by the subjects were multiplied by an arbitrary fraction of the distance to arrive at the data summarized in Figure 2. Clearly the reduction in subjective anxiety was far greater for the diazepam group. In terms of percentages, subjective anxiety dropped by 37 percent following diazepam, but by only 10 percent following the placebo.

DISCUSSION

Whitehead and his collaborators stated the significance of their findings as follows:

> These data show that a single 10-mg oral dose of diazepam is effective at reducing both the subjective anxiety and the behavioral avoidance of feared objects by phobic patients. It is reasonable to infer that a similar dose of diazepam would ameliorate situational fears, such as examination anxiety, which are not usually classified as phobias (p. 63).

This was an important finding because, as mentioned previously, many people use diazepam on an occasional, as-needed basis, and this study supported the effectiveness of that strategy.

FIGURE 1 Comparison of approach distances, Diazepam vs. placebo.

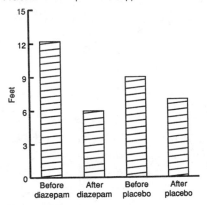

(from p. 62)

The authors also pointed out that the behavioral approach measurement of anxiety appeared to be a very useful method of determining the effectiveness of an anti-anxiety drug in a single session. Prior to this study, since patients were assumed to be taking the medication on a regular basis, outcomes had to be evaluated over long periods of time, which presented numerous methodological problems. Based on this research, the evaluation process for new tranquilizer drugs could be simplified and expedited.

In closing, Whitehead, et al., mentioned one limitation to their method. Although it has been estimated that as many as 11 people in every 1,000 suffer from animal phobias, only 14 people in a city of over 1 million residents (Cincinnati) were willing to participate in the study. While the authors did not speculate as to the reason for the small response to the ad, it probably is this: If you are so fearful of something that it has become a phobia, you tend to avoid it at all costs, and you would not be eager to participate in research with it! The researchers suggested that similar methods could be adapted to fears that are common among university undergraduates, such as test anxiety, fear of public speaking, or anxiety over asking members of the opposite sex for a date. This, they propose, "would ensure an endless supply of subjects" (p. 64).

SUBSEQUENT RESEARCH

Today, the medical and behavioral science communities know a great deal more about diazepam and the related anti-anxiety drugs than they did in 1978 when this study was conducted. Through the first 15 years or so that diazepam was available, it enjoyed the reputation of a "benign little anxiety-reducer." All responsible professionals now acknowledge that it was overprescribed by doctors and often abused by patients. More

FIGURE 2 Comparison of subjective anxiety ratings, Diazepam vs. placebo.

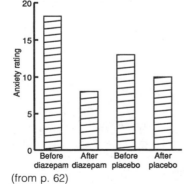

(from p. 62)

recent research has determined that diazepam and the other benzodiazepines are not so benign and can, in fact, produce serious negative side effects.

The most dangerous of these side effects is physical addiction. Continued use of diazepam over long periods of time produces tolerance, so that larger and larger doses of the drug are needed to create the same tranquilizing effect. The body can become dependent on the drug, and if it is suddenly stopped, serious withdrawal symptoms will result, such as insomnia, extreme agitation, loss of appetite, convulsions, and even psychotic reactions (hallucinations and delusions).

There are several other side effects associated with frequent use of diazepam. It has been shown that the effects of the drug can interfere with intellectual functioning, especially related to complex learning tasks. Furthermore, this side effect may continue longer than the actual anti-anxiety effect of the drug (Gray, 1984).

Another recently discovered problem with diazepam has been termed *rebound anxiety*. This phenomenon occurs when someone has been taking the drug to control anxiety over an extended period of time. When the drug is discontinued, even for a short time, the anxiety the person was experiencing before taking the medication returns with an even greater degree of severity. To combat this new level of anxiety, larger doses of the drug are used, which only leads to greater tolerance, greater potential rebound anxiety, greater abuse, and eventually dangerous side effects (see Chouinard, et al., 1983, for a complete discussion of this issue). The extent of such problems is of even greater concern when you consider the huge numbers of people who use the drug.

In addition to reducing anxiety, diazepam and related medications are commonly used to treat insomnia. These drugs are very effective in assisting a person to fall asleep and stay asleep. However, the negative effect is that the drug suppresses REM, or dreaming, sleep. When REM sleep is interrupted, the brain tries to catch up on dreaming by spending more time in REM on subsequent nights (see the reading on the work by Dement for a discussion of this "REM-rebound" effect). So the more the drug is used, the greater the REM deprivation and, consequently, the greater the decrease in the quality of the person's sleep.

Finally, one of the most widely expressed concerns of mental health professionals concerning anti-anxiety medications such as diazepam is that they constitute a simplistic method of coping with problems in life. If such drugs are too easy to obtain and use, they can mask serious psychological difficulties that may require professional attention. This, in turn may prevent people from developing internal coping strategies or obtaining the psychotherapy they need (see Gray, 1984). In the same way that pain alerts us that something is physically wrong, anxiety is a signal that warns us of potential psychological problems that need to be "fixed." If use of anti-anxiety drugs blocks that signal, people may feel as if everything is fine, while the problems become worse because of lack of proper treatment. In other words, the use of diazepam may be the psychological equivalent of disconnecting the smoke alarm in your house because you can't stand the noise it makes!

CONCLUSION

The medical profession has become increasingly aware of the dangers of diazepam and, consequently, the number of prescriptions has dropped about 20 percent. In addition, there is now an increased emphasis on non-drug stress-reduction techniques such as bio-feedback, self-hypnosis, meditation, and progressive relaxation. Such treatments have reduced the demand for anti-anxiety medications. Diazepam has dropped from first to fifth place on the list of most-prescribed drugs in the United States.

There is no doubt that diazepam and the other anti-anxiety drugs are here to stay. Although their dangers are now widely recognized, they continue to serve an extremely useful purpose in helping people cope with periods of stress and anxiety. Individuals with severe, life-limiting, and even debilitating anxiety disorders (such as panic disorder, agoraphobia, fear of air travel, and so on) are often able to live relatively normal lives with the help of these drugs. Also, minor tranquilizers are often useful in life events involving acute anxiety, such as intense grief over the death of a loved one, loss of employment, or withdrawal from alcohol addition.

Diazepam and all of the minor tranquilizers should be judiciously prescribed with respect for the drug and not dispensed freely as "psychological bandaids." When appropriate, psychotherapy should be recommended along with the medication so that the underlying causes of the anxiety might be addressed. If simple guidelines such as these are followed, anti-anxiety drugs can safely help those who, at times, find coping in today's society a seemingly insurmountable task.

CHOUINARD, G., LABONTE, A., FONTAINE, R., and ANNABLE, L. (1983) New concepts in benzodiazepine therapy: Rebound anxiety and new indications for the more potent benzodiazepines. *Progress in Neuro-psychopharmacology and Biological Psychiatry*, 7, 669–73.

GRAY, J. (1984) *The neuropsychology of anxiety*. New York: Oxford University Press.

TEN

SOCIAL PSYCHOLOGY

Social psychology is the branch of psychology that looks at how your behavior is influenced by that of others and how their behavior is influenced by you. It is the study of human interaction. This psychological subfield is vast and covers a wide array of topics, from romantic relationships to group behavior to prejudice, discrimination, and aggression. This is probably the area in psychology that most non-psychologists find the most relevant. We all constantly interact with others, and it is meaningful to us to learn more about the psychological processes involved. Social psychology may also be the research domain that contains the greatest number of landmark studies.

While it is certainly difficult to select a few studies as the most famous and influential in social psychology, the four chosen for this section clearly changed psychology by (1) providing new insights into human social behavior, (2) sparking new waves of research to either confirm, refine, or contest the original findings, and (3) creating heated controversy that ultimately enriched the field in general.

First is an early study that surprised behavioral scientists by suggesting that people's attitudes about a person or object do not always predict how they will behave toward that person or object. Second is a recounting of a crucial study that demonstrated scientifically the power of conformity in determining behavior. The third study presented revealed a surprising phenomenon called the "bystander effect," which says that the more people who witness an emergency, the less likely anyone is to help. And finally we arrive at what may be the most famous (and in some ways, infamous) study in the history of psychology: Stanley Milgram's study of blind obedience to authority.

NOT PRACTICING WHAT YOU PREACH
LaPiere, Richard T. (1934) Attitudes and actions. *Social Forces*, 13, 230–37.

Stanford psychologist Richard LaPiere's study 1934 may have generated more subsequent research projects in the history of psychology than any other presented in this book. It was a study about "social attitudes": the attitudes you hold about other people or groups of people. It is logical to think that a person's attitude about an "attitude object" (either a person or a thing) will influence that person's behavior toward the object. If you tell me your attitude toward brussels sprouts is one of hate and disgust, I would predict that when faced with those little green vegetables, you will very likely refuse to eat them. And I would probably be correct.

In the early years of psychological science, there was an untested assumption that this correspondence between attitude and behavior was generally true, whether the subject of the attitude was vegetable preferences or opinions regarding other people (social attitudes). Consequently, it was quite common for psychologists and sociologists to measure attitudes through the use of questionnaires, and then assume that the measured attitude would be reflected in future behavior when the attitude object is actually encountered.

LaPiere questioned this assumption, particularly as it pertained to social attitudes. To illustrate his criticism, he used the example of a researcher asking American men the question, "Would you get up to give an Armenian woman your seat in a streetcar?" (Remember, this article was published in 1934!) Whatever the answer, LaPiere explained, the response would only be a symbolic (or hypothetical) response to a symbolic situation, and would not necessarily predict what a man would actually do if faced with a real Armenian woman on a real crowded streetcar. Even so, most researchers would, according to LaPiere, be quite willing to suggest that they could predict the respondents' actual behavior from the symbolic attitude as measured by the answer to the hypothetical question. Not only that, but the same researchers might even draw conclusions about the overall relationship between Americans and Armenians based on the same data. LaPiere argued that the assumption researchers were making of a direct correspondence between symbolic behavior (responses on questionnaires) and real behavior was far too simple, unwarranted, and probably wrong

Throughout the following discussion of LaPiere's famous study, it is important to keep in mind that in the 1930s, there was a great deal of racial and ethnic prejudice and discrimination in American society. This is not to say that such attitudes do not exist today, but 60 years ago discriminatory practices were generally more widespread, blatant, and accepted. For example, it was a common practice for hotels and restaurants to have policies refusing service to members of certain racial or ethnic groups. LaPiere decided to capitalize on such discriminatory policies to test his idea that spoken attitudes are often poor predictors of actual behavior.

THEORETICAL PROPOSITIONS

During 1930 and 1931, LaPiere traveled extensively with a young Chinese student and his wife. "Both were personable, charming, quick to win the admiration and respect of those with whom they had the opportunity to become intimate" (p. 231). There was in the United States then a great deal of prejudice and discrimination toward anyone of Asian descent. Because of this, LaPiere reported feeling quite apprehensive when, early in their trip, the three of them approached the clerk in the best hotel "in a small town noted for its narrow and bigoted attitude toward Orientals" (p. 231). So he was surprised when they all were immediately and politely accommodated. LaPiere went on to explain, "Two months later I passed that way again, phoned the hotel, and asked if they would accommodate 'an important Chinese gentleman.' The reply was an unequivocal 'No.' That aroused my curiosity and led to this study" (p. 232).

The theory implied in LaPiere's study was that, contrary to prevailing beliefs, people's "social actions" track very poorly with their spoken social attitudes. In other words, what people say is often not what they do.

METHOD

This study was conducted in two distinctly separate parts. The first part focused on actual behavior, while the second assessed related symbolic attitudes.

Real Behavior Phase

LaPiere and his Chinese friends traveled by car twice across the United States as well as up and down the full length of the Pacific Coast. Their journey totaled approximately 10,000 miles. From a careful examination of LaPiere's article, it appears that his research on attitudes was not the purpose of the trip, but rather was coincidental. For one thing, LaPiere did not inform the Chinese couple that he was making careful observations of the treatment they received wherever they went. His justification for this was that had they known, they might have become self-conscious and altered their behavior in some way that would have made the study less valid.

Between 1930 and 1933, the travelers approached 67 hotels, auto camps, and "tourist homes" (whatever those were) for accommodations. They ate at 184 restaurants and cafés. LaPiere kept "accurate and detailed records" of the responses of hotel clerks, bell boys, elevator operators, and waitresses to the presence of the Chinese couple. So that reactions would not be unduly altered because of his presence, LaPiere often let the Chinese couple secure the room or other accommodations while he took care of the luggage, and whenever possible he allowed them to enter restaurants before him. The treatment the Chinese couple received will be discussed in detail shortly.

Symbolic Behavior Phase

In the second part of the study LaPiere mailed questionnaires to all of the establishments they had visited. He allowed six months to pass between the actual visit and the mailing of the questionnaire. His reason for this delay was to allow the effect of the Chinese couple's visit to fade.

The question of primary interest on the questionnaire was, "Will you accept members of the Chinese race as guests in your establishment?" These questionnaires were returned by 81 of the restaurants and cafés and 47 of the lodging establishments. This was a response rate of 51 percent.

To further ensure that the questionnaire responses were not directly influenced by the Chinese couple's visit, LaPiere also obtained responses to the same questionnaire from 32 hotels and 96 restaurants located in the same regions of the country, but not visited by the travelers.

So now, after nearly three years, LaPiere had the data necessary to make a comparison of social attitudes with social behavior.

RESULTS

LaPiere reported that of the 251 hotels and restaurants they patronized on their travels, there was only *one* instance in which they were denied service because of the ethnicity of his companions. This single rejection, in a small California town, was described by LaPiere as occurring at a "rather inferior auto camp." The proprietor came toward the car and upon seeing the occupants said, "No. I don't take Japs!" This ugly experience aside, most of their other experiences involved average or even above-average treatment, although at times the treatment was altered due to "curiosity" about the Chinese couple. LaPiere explained that in 1930, outside the Pacific Coast region, Chicago, and New York, most people in the United States had little experience with, and perhaps had never even seen, people of Asian heritage. Table 1 summarizes LaPiere's ratings of the service they received. As you can see, in all but a very few establishments, the services they received was rated by LaPiere to be the same as or better than he would have expected if he had been traveling alone.

The responses to the questionnaires mailed to the establishments six months later and those mailed to the places not visited are summarized in Table 2. Nearly all (over 90 percent) of the hotels, campgrounds, tourist homes, restaurants, and cafés visited by LaPiere and the Chinese couple replied that they would *not* serve Chinese individuals! In addition, the distribution of responses from the establishments not visited are virtually the same, indicating that the findings were not somehow caused by the travelers' recent visit. On the contrary, the one "yes" response to the questionnaire came from the manager of a small auto camp who enclosed a "chatty letter describing the nice visit she had had with a Chinese gentleman and his sweet wife during the previous summer" (p. 234).

DISCUSSION

LaPiere's discussion of his findings focused on the lack of validity of questionnaires in determining a person's true attitude. He contended that "it is impossible to make direct comparisons between the reactions secured through questionnaires and from actual experience" (p. 234). He pointed out that if a Chinese person were to consult the findings of the questionnaire prior to setting out on a tour of the United States (in 1930), he would undoubtedly decide to stay home! However, LaPiere's friends enjoyed an almost discrimination-free trip and became increasingly confident about approaching new social situations without fear of rejection or embarrassment.

So was LaPiere suggesting that we eliminate the use of questionnaires altogether? No. He suggested that such data might be useful in determining people's symbolic attitudes about issues that would remain symbolic. For example, he allowed that questionnaires could measure political attitudes and even predict for whom someone will vote (later research found that these predictions are often poor as well), but

TABLE 1   LaPiere's Ratings of Services Received

QUALITY OF RECEPTION	LODGINGS	RESTAURANTS AND CAFÉS
Very much better than expected if investigator had been alone	25	72
Good, but different because of increased curiosity	25	82
Equal to normal expectations	11	24
Perceptibly hesitant for racial reasons	4	5
Definitely, but temporarily, embarrassing	1	1
Not accepted	1	0
Total	67	184

(adapted from p. 235)

this information would provide little information about how that person will behave if he meets the candidate on the street or at a party. Another example of an acceptable use of questionnaire data was the measurement of religious attitudes. LaPiere pointed out that "an honest answer to the question 'Do you believe in God?' reveals all there is to be measured. 'God' is a symbol; 'belief,' a verbal expression" (p. 235).

His conclusion was that if you want to predict how someone will *behave* when actually faced with a certain situation or another person, a verbal reaction to a symbolic situation (that is, an attitude questionnaire) is wholly inadequate. He contended that social attitudes can only be reliably measured by studying human behavior in actual social situations. His article ended with what might be interpreted as a warning to other researchers:

> The questionnaire is cheap, easy, and mechanical. The study of human behavior is time-consuming, intellectually fatiguing, and depends for its success on the ability of the investigator. The former method gives

TABLE 2   Number of Questionnaire Responses to Question: Will You Accept Members of the Chinese Race as Guests in Your Establishment?

ANSWER	LODGINGS VISITED	RESTAURANTS VISITED	LODGINGS NOT VISITED	RESTAURANTS NOT VISITED
No	43	75	30	76
Undecided, depends on circumstances	3	6	2	7
Yes	1	0	0	1

(adapted from p. 234)

quantitative results, the latter mainly qualitative. . . . Yet it would seem far more worthwhile to make a shrewd guess regarding that which is essential than to accurately measure that which is likely to prove quite irrelevant (p. 237).

CRITICISMS AND SUBSEQUENT RESEARCH

It seems that psychologists reacted to LaPiere's findings almost as an athlete would react to being challenged to a competition. A great deal of research was generated, and this response took three directions. First, there have been several strong criticisms leveled at LaPiere's findings. Second, researchers set about trying to determine why attitude assessments fail to predict actual behavior. And third, behavioral scientists have attempted to determine the conditions under which attitude measurements will reliably predict behavior.

LaPiere's methods were criticized on the basis that a simple yes-no answer to a question in a letter is not a valid measurement of a person's attitude regarding a specific group of people. For example, the image of "members of the Chinese race" in the minds of the respondents may have been very different from the Chinese couple they actually encountered. Another criticism has been that only half of the places the three travelers visited responded to the questionnaire. It is possible that those who took the time to respond may have been the ones with the strongest prejudiced attitudes against Asians. Finally, after six months, there was the possibility that the person responding to the letter was not the same person who met the travelers face to face.

However, nearly 40 years after LaPiere's findings were published, another researcher reviewed the research that had accumulated over the years and concluded that the correlation between measured attitudes and actual behavior was indeed weak and perhaps non-existent (Wicker, 1969). Many researchers have focused their attention on trying to determine why this inconsistency exists. Many reasons have been proposed (see Fishbein and Ajzen, 1975, for a complete discussion), but only a few of them will be discussed here.

First, you have many attitudes that may compete with each other. Which attitude will exert the most influence on your behavior depends on the specifics of the situation. Second, there are times when you might behave in ways that are contrary to your attitudes because you have no alternative, such as situations in which your job or a friendship depends on a certain action. Third, social pressures and the human desire to avoid embarrassment can exert strong influences that may produce behaviors that are inconsistent with attitudes. Fourth, "force of habit" may weaken the connection between attitude and behavior. An example of this is the smoker who has become convinced that smoking is bad, but continues to smoke because the habit is stronger than the attitude.

So this question remained: When, if ever, will attitude measurements be successful in predicting behavior? Recently, there has been a major research effort to identify the factors that produce greater consistency between attitudes and behavior. These factors can be summarized into the following four categories (see Sears, Peplau, and Taylor, 1991):

1. *Strength of the attitude.* The stronger you feel toward certain people or situations, the more likely you are to behave accordingly when you encounter them in person. On the other hand, weak or ambivalent attitudes may exert little or no influence on your behavior.

2. *Stability of the attitude.* This factor deals with how your attitudes change over time. Attitudes that are stable predict behavior better than those that change with time. Measuring voters' attitudes about a candidate three weeks prior to an election may tell you very little about voting behavior three weeks later. Ideally, for an accurate attitude-behavior connection they should be measured at nearly the same time.

3. *Relevance of attitude to the behavior.* If you measure someone's attitude about sports, it is likely to be a poor predictor of how often they attend athletic events. Some early studies asked people if they believed in God, and then tried to use their answers to predict their attendance in church. It didn't work. The conclusion here is that attitudes will predict behavior much better if the attitude measured relates as exactly as possible to the behavior of interest. To demonstrate this, one study asked a group of college women about their attitudes toward birth control and asked another similar group about their attitudes toward using birth control pills during the next two years. The correlation between the measured attitude and actual use of birth control pills during the following two years was 0.08 (non-significant) for the first group, but 0.57 (highly significant) for the specific-attitude group (Davidson and Jaccard, 1979).

4. *Salience of the attitude.* If an attitude you hold toward something or someone is salient, it is conspicuous, important, and readily accessed from your memory. The more salient the attitude, the more likely it will predict your behavior. Suppose you have a positive attitude about the act of donating blood. If a friend or family member has recently had surgery that required a lot of blood, your attitude about giving blood is probably much more salient than usual. Under these circumstances, you are more likely to give blood than at other times, even though the attitude itself did not change.

CONCLUSION

The research on attitudes and behavior constitutes a huge body of literature, of which only a minuscule sample has been included here. Behavioral scientists may never unravel all the complexities of this relationship, but the research continues. As theories and methods have been refined and perfected over the years, evidence has increased to suggest that our attitudes do play an important role in determining our behavior. It is no longer a question of whether attitudes predict behavior, but exactly *how* and *when* they do so. What is most important in the present context is that the beginning of all this interest in the attitude-behavior connection began with a single study by LaPiere over a half-century ago.

DAVIDSON, A., and JACCARD, J. (1979) Variables that modulate the attitude-behavior relation: Results of a longitudinal survey. *Journal of personality and social psychology*, 37, 1364–76.

FISHBEIN, M., and AJZEN, I. (1975) *Belief, attitude, intention, and behavior: An introduction to the theory and research*. Reading, Mass.: Addison-Wesley.

SEARS, D.O., PEPLAU, L.A., and TAYLOR, S.E. (1991) *Social psychology*. Englewood Cliffs, N.J.: Prentice Hall, 150–53.

WICKER, A. (1971) Attitudes vs. action: The relationship between verbal and overt behavior responses to attitude objects. *Journal of Social Issues*, 25, 41–78.

THE POWER OF CONFORMITY
Asch, Solomon E. (1951) Opinions and social pressure. *Scientific American*, 193, 31–35.

Do you consider yourself to be a conformist, or are you more of a non-conformist? Most of us probably like to think that we are conformist enough to not be considered terribly strange or frightening, and non-conformist enough to demonstrate that we are individuals and capable of independent thinking. Psychologists have been interested in the concept of conformity for decades. It is easy to see why, when you remember that psychology tries to study the influences on human behavior. The differences in the amount to which people conform can help us a great deal in predicting the behavior for various individuals.

When psychologists talk about conformity, they refer to an individual's behavior that adheres to the behavior patterns of a particular group of which that individual is a member. The usually unspoken rules or guidelines for behavior in a group are called "social norms." If you think about it, you can probably remember a time in your life when you behaved in ways that were out of sync or in disagreement with your attitudes, beliefs, or morals. Chances are you were in a group in which everyone was behaving that way, so you went along with them. This indicates that sometimes conformity is a powerful force on our behavior and can even at times make us do things that conflict with our attitudes, ethics, and morals. Therefore, conformity is clearly very worthy of interest and study by behavioral scientists. It was not until the early 1950s that someone decided to make a systematic study. That someone was Solomon Asch. His experiments offered us a great deal of new information about conforming behavior and opened many doors for future research.

THEORETICAL PROPOSITIONS

Suppose you are with a group of people that you see often, such as friends or co-workers. The group is discussing some controversial issue or political candidate. It quickly becomes clear to you that everyone in the group shares one view, which is the opposite of your own. At one point the others turn to you and ask for your opinion. What are you going to do? The choices you are faced with are to state your true views and risk the consequences; to agree with the group consensus even though it differs from your opinion; or, if possible, to sidestep the issue entirely.

Asch wanted to find out just how powerful the need to conform is in influencing our behavior. Although conformity often involves general and vague concepts such as attitudes, ethics, morals, and belief systems, Asch chose to focus on a much more obvious form: perceptual conformity. By examining conforming behavior on a simple visual comparison task, he was able to study this phenomenon in a controlled laboratory environment.

If conformity is as powerful a force as Asch and many others believed, then researchers should be able to manipulate a person's behavior by applying group pressure to conform. This is what Asch set about testing in a very elegantly designed series of experiments, all incorporating a similar method.

METHOD

The visual materials consisted simply of pairs of cards with three different lengths of vertical lines (called comparison lines) on one and a single standard line the same length as one of three comparison lines on the other (see Figure 1). Here is how the experimental process worked. Imagine you are a subject who has volunteered to participate in a "visual perception study." You arrive at the experiment room on time and find seven other subjects already seated in a row. You sit in the empty chair at the end of the row. The experimenter reveals a pair of cards and asks you to determine which of the three comparison lines is the same length as the standard line. You look at the lines and immediately decide on

FIGURE 1 An example similar to Asch's line judging task cards.

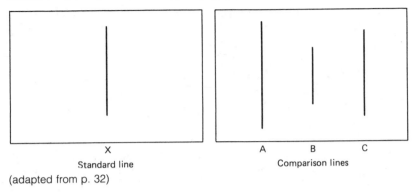

X
Standard line

A   B   C
Comparison lines

(adapted from p. 32)

the correct response. Starting at the far end of the row away from you, each subject is asked individually for his or her answer. Everyone gives the correct answer, and when your turn comes you give the same obviously correct answer. The card is changed, the same process happens, and—once again, no problem—you give the correct answer along with the rest of the group. On the next trial, however, something odd happens. The card is revealed and you immediately choose in your mind the correct response. (After all, this is not difficult.) But when the other subjects give their answers, they all choose the wrong line! And they all choose the *same* wrong line. Now, when it is your turn to respond again, you pause. You can't believe what is happening. Are all these other people blind? The correct answer is obvious. Isn't it? Have *you* gone blind? Or crazy? You now must make a decision like the one described above with your friends or co-workers. Do you maintain your opinion (after all, the lines are right in front of your nose), or do you conform and agree with the rest of the group?

As you have probably figured out by now, the other seven "subjects" in the room were not subjects at all, but confederates of the experimenter. They were in on the experiment from the beginning and the answers they gave were, of course, the key to this study of conformity. So, how did the real subjects in the study answer?

RESULTS

Each subject participated in the experimental situation several times. Approximately 75 percent of them went along with the group's consensus at least once. Considering all trials combined, subjects agreed with the group on the incorrect responses about one-third of the time. Just to be sure that the line lengths could be accurately judged, a control group of subjects were asked to individually write down their answer to the line comparison questions. Subjects in this group were correct 98 percent of the time.

DISCUSSION AND RELATED RESEARCH

The powerful effects of group pressures to conform were clearly demonstrated in Asch's study. If individuals are willing to conform to a group of people they hardly know about a clearly incorrect judgment, how strong must this influence be in real life, where groups exert even stronger forces and issues are more ambiguous? Conformity as a major factor in human behavior, the subject of widespread speculation for years, had now been scientifically established.

Asch's results were extremely important to the field of psychology in two crucial ways. First, as discussed above, the real power of the social pressure to conform was demonstrated clearly and scientifically for the first time. Second, and perhaps even more important, this early research sparked a huge wave of additional studies that continue right up to the present. The body of research that has accumulated since Asch's early studies has greatly elaborated our knowledge of the specific factors that determine the effects conformity has on our behavior. Some of these findings follow:

1. *Social support.* Asch conducted his same experiment with a slight variation. He altered the answers of the confederates so that in the test condition one of the seven gave the correct answer. When this occurred, only 5 percent of the subjects agreed with the group consensus. Apparently, a single ally is all you need to "stick to your guns" and resist the pressure to conform. This finding has been supported by several later studies (see, for example, Morris and Miller, 1975).

2. *Attraction and commitment to the group.* Later research has demonstrated that the more attracted and committed you are to a particular group, the more likely you are to conform to the behavior and attitudes of that group (see Forsyth, 1983). If you like the group and feel that you belong with them (they are your "reference group") your tendency to conform to that group will be very strong. This becomes even clearer if you imagine a situation in which you are in the company of a group that you do not identify with and, if the truth be known, you really do not like. Obviously your desire to conform to the norms, standards, and beliefs of this group will be minimal.

3. *Size of the group.* At first, research by Asch and others demonstrated that the tendency to conform increases as the size of the group increases. However, upon further examination, it was found that this connection is not so simple. While it is true that conformity increases as the size of the group increases, this only holds for groups up to six or seven members. As the group size increases beyond this number, conformity levels off, and even decreases some-what. This is shown graphically in Figure 2. Why is this? Well, Asch has

FIGURE 2 The relationship between group size and conformity.

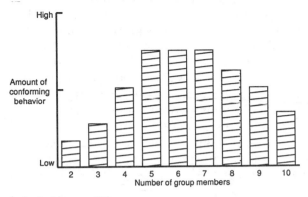

(adapted from p. 35)

suggested that as the group becomes large, people may begin to suspect the other members of working together purposefully to affect their behavior and they become resistant to this obvious pressure.

4. *Sex.* Do you think there is a difference between men and women in their tendency or willingness to conform? Early studies that followed Asch's work indicated that women seemed to be much more willing to conform than men. This was such a strong and frequently repeated finding that it entered the psychological literature as an accepted difference between the sexes. However, more recent research is drawing this notion into question. It now appears that many of the early studies (conducted by men) inadvertently created testing conditions that were more familiar and comfortable for men in those days than for women. Psychologists know that people will tend to conform more when placed in a situation where the appropriate behavior is unclear. Therefore, the finding of greater conformity among women may have simply been a systematic error caused by subtle (and unintentional) biases in the methods used. More recent research under better controlled conditions has failed to find this sex difference in conformity behavior (see Sistrunk and McDavid, 1971, for a discussion of these gender-related issues).

There are other areas related to the issue of conformity that have been studied as well. These include, but are not limited to, cultural differences, the amount of information available when making decisions about conforming, the role of norms, the amount of privacy, and so on. Nearly all general textbooks on social psychology include a more complete discussion of those factors.

CRITICISMS

Asch's work on conformity has received widespread support and acceptance. In addition, it has been replicated in many studies under a wide variety of conditions. A line of criticism commonly heard concerns whether Asch's findings can be generalized to situations in the real world. In other words, does a subject's answer in a laboratory about the length of some lines really have very much to do with conforming behavior in life? This is a valid criticism to make for all research about human behavior that is carried out in a controlled laboratory setting. What this criticism says is, "Well, maybe the subjects were willing to go along with the group on something so trivial and unimportant as the length of a line, but in real life, and on important matters, they would not conform so readily." It must be pointed out, however, that while real-life matters of conformity can certainly be more meaningful, it is equally likely that the pressures for conformity from groups in the real world are also proportionately stronger.

FORSYTH, D. (1983) *An introduction to group dynamics*. Monterey, Calif.: Brooks/Cole.
MORRIS, W., and MILLER, R. (1975) The effects of consensus-breaking and consensus-preempting partners on reduction in conformity. *Journal of Experimental Social Psychology*, 11, 215–23.
SISTRUNK, F., and MCDAVID, J. (1971) Sex variable in conforming behavior. *Journal of Personality and Social Psychology*, 17, 200–07.

TO HELP OR NOT TO HELP
Darley, J.M., and Latané, B. (1968) Bystander intervention in emergencies: Diffusion of responsibility. *Journal of Personality and Social Psychology*, 8, 377–83.

One of the most influential events in the history of psychology and psychological research was not an experiment or a discovery made by a behavioral scientist, but a news item about a violent and tragic event in New York City that was picked up by most media news services across the United States. (This story continues to be well known due to its frequent re-telling in psychology texts.) In 1964, Kitty Genovese was returning to her apartment in a quiet, middle-class neighborhood in Queens after closing the Manhattan bar that she managed. As she left her car and walked toward her building, she was viciously attacked by a man with a knife. As the man stabbed her several times, she screamed for help. One neighbor yelled out his window for the man to "leave that girl alone," at which the attacker began to walk away. But then he turned, knocked Genovese to the ground and began stabbing her again. She continued to scream until finally someone telephoned the police. The police arrived two minutes after they were called, but Genovese was already dead and her attacker had disappeared. The attack had lasted 35 minutes. During police investigations it was found that 38 people in the surrounding apartments had witnessed the attack, but only one had eventually called the police. One couple (who said they assumed the police had been called by someone) had moved two chairs next to their window in order to watch the violence. The murderer was never found.

It was clear that if someone had acted sooner to help Genovese, she probably would have survived. New York City and the nation was appalled by the seeming lack of caring on the part of so many neighbors who had failed to try to stop this violent act. People attempted to find a reason for the inaction. The alienation caused by living in a large city was blamed; the neighborhood of Queens was blamed; basic human nature was blamed.

The Genovese tragedy sparked the interest of psychologists, who set out to try to better understand what psychological forces might have been at work to prevent all those people from helping. There is an area of psychology that studies what behavioral scientists call "pro-social behavior," or behavior that produces positive social consequences. Topics falling into this research area include altruism, cooperation, resisting temptation, and helping behavior. If you witness an emergency situation in which someone may be in need of help, there are many factors that may affect your decision to step in and offer assistance. John Darley at New York University and Bibb Latané at Columbia, both social psychologists, were among those who wanted to examine these factors. They termed this behavior of helping in emergencies "bystander intervention" (or in this case, non-intervention).

Have you ever been faced with a true emergency? Contrary to what you may think from watching T.V. and reading newspapers, emergencies are not very common. Darley and Latané estimated that the average person will encounter fewer than six emergencies in a lifetime. This is good and bad: good for obvious reasons, bad because when you do find yourself facing an emergency, you will have to decide what to do without the benefit of very much experience. Society dictates that we take action to help in emergencies, but often, as in the famous Genovese case, we do not. Why is this? Could it be because we have so little experience that we do not know what to do? Is it because of urban living or human nature, according to popular belief?

Following the Genovese murder, Darley and Latané met to analyze the bystanders' reactions. They proposed that the large number of people who witnessed the event *decreased* the willingness of individuals to step in and help. So they set out to test this theory experimentally.

THEORETICAL PROPOSITIONS

Your common sense might tell you that the more bystanders there are in an emergency, the more likely someone will intervene. But Darley and Latané hypothesized just the opposite. They believed that the reason no one took steps to help Kitty Genovese was a phenomenon they called "diffusion of responsibility." That is, as the number of bystanders in an emergency increases, the greater is the belief that "someone else will help, so I don't need to." Have you ever witnessed an accident on a busy street or arrived at the scene of one soon after it has happened? Chances are that as you drove by you made the assumption that someone surely has called the police or ambulance by now, and therefore you did not feel the personal responsibility to do so. But imagine discovering the same accident on a deserted country road with no one else around. Would your response be different? So would mine!

The concept of diffusion of responsibility formed the theoretical basis for this chapter's study. The trick was to re-create a Genovese-like situation in the laboratory so that it could be manipulated and examined systematically. Darley and Latané were very ingenious in designing an experiment to do this.

METHOD

For obvious reasons it would not be practical or even possible to reproduce the events of the Kitty Genovese murder for experimental purposes. Therefore, a situation needed to be devised that would approximate or simulate a true emergency so that the intervention of bystanders could be observed. In this experiment, Darley and Latané told students in an introductory psychology class at New York University that they were interested in studying how students adjust to university life in a highly competitive, urban environment and what kinds of personal problems they were experiencing. The students were asked to discuss their problems honestly with other students, but to avoid any discomfort or embarrassment, they would be in separate rooms and would speak with each other over an intercom system. This intercom, they were told, would only allow one student to speak at a time. Each student would be given two minutes, after which the microphone for the next student would be activated for two minutes, and so on.

Of course, all of this was a cover story designed to obtain natural behavior from the subjects and to hide the true purpose of the experiment. The most important part of this cover story was the way the students were divided into three different experimental conditions. The subjects in group 1 believed that they would be talking with only one other person; those in group 2 believed there would be two other people on the intercom; and the group 3 subjects were told that there were five other people on the line. In reality, each subject was alone and all the other voices were on tape.

Now that the size of the groups was varied, some sort of emergency had to be created. The researchers decided that a very realistically acted epileptic seizure would be widely interpreted as an emergency. As the discussions over the intercom system between the subjects and the other "students" began, subjects heard the first student, a male, tell about his difficulties concentrating on his studies and problems adjusting to life in New York City. He then added, with some embarrassment, that he sometimes had severe seizures, especially when under a lot of stress. Then the conversation switched to the next student. In group 1, the actual subject's turn came next, whereas in the other two conditions, the subject heard one or more other students speak before his or her turn. After the subject spoke it was the first student's turn again. This is when the emergency occurred. The first student spoke normally as before, but then began to have a seizure (remember, this was all on tape). Latané and Darley quote the seizure in detail in a later report:

> I-er-um-I think I-I need-er-if-if could-er-er somebody er-er-er-er-er-er give me a little-er-give me a little help here because-er-I-er-I'm-er-h-h-having a-a-a real problem-er right now and I-er-if somebody could help me out it would-it would-er-er s-s-sure be good . . . because-er-there-er-ag cause I er-I-uh-I've got one of the-er-sei—er-er-things coming on and-and-and I could really use some help so if somebody would-er give me a little h-help-uh-er-er-er-er c-ould somebody-er er-help-er-uh-uh-uh [choking sounds] . . . I'm gonna die-er-er . . . help-er-er-seizure [chokes, then quiet]. (Latané and Darley, 1970, pp. 95–96)

To the subjects this was clearly an emergency. There was no question that the "student" was in trouble and needed help immediately. In order to analyze the responses of the subjects, Darley and Latané measured the percentage of subjects in each condition who helped the student in trouble (helping was defined as leaving the cubicle and notifying the experimenter of the problem). They also measured the amount of time it took subjects to respond to the emergency and try to help. Subjects were given four minutes to respond, after which the experiment was terminated.

RESULTS

The findings from this study offered strong support for the researchers' hypothesis. As subjects believed there were a greater number of others present, the percentage who reported the seizure quickly (during the attack itself) decreased dramatically (see Figure 1). Even among those who eventually did help, the amount of delay in helping was greater when more "bystanders" were present. For group 1, the average delay in

FIGURE 1   Number of subjects in each condition who helped during seizure.

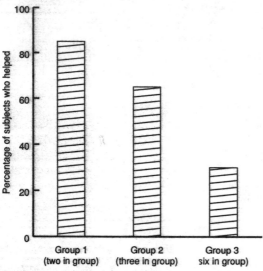

(adapted from data on p. 380)

responding was less than one minute, whereas for group 3 it was over three minutes. Finally, the total number of subjects who reported the seizure at all varied among the groups in a similar way. All of the subjects in group 1 reported the emergency, but only 85 percent of group 2 and 60 percent of group 3 did so at any time during the four-minute period.

DISCUSSION

As in the real-life case of Kitty Genovese, you might think that the subjects in this study were simply apathetic and uncaring toward the victim having the seizure. However, Darley and Latané are quick to point out that this was not the reason for the inaction of subjects in groups 2 and 3 (or of Genovese's neighbors). All the subjects reported experiencing a great deal of anxiety and discomfort during the attack and showed physical signs of nervousness (trembling hands, sweaty palms). The researchers concluded, therefore, that the reason for their results must lie in the difference in the number of other people the subjects believed were present. Whenever your behavior is changed because of the presence of others, this is called "social influence." Obviously, social influence played a significant role in this study. But we are still left wondering why. What was it about the presence of others that was so influential?

Well, Darley and Latané claimed to have demonstrated and supported their theory of diffusion of responsibility. As the number of people in the group increased, the subject felt less personal or individual responsibility to take action to help in the emergency. It was easier in groups 2 and 3 for the subjects to assume that someone else would handle the problem. In a related point, it is not only the responsibility for helping that is shared when others are present, but also the potential guilt or blame for not helping. Since helping others is considered to be a positive action in our culture, refusing or failing to help carries shameful connotations. If you are the only person present in an emergency, the negative consequences of not helping will be much greater than if others are there to bear some of the burden for non-intervention.

Another possible explanation for this type of social influence is something that psychologists have termed "evaluation apprehension." Darley and Latané contended that part of the reason we fail to help when others are present is that we are afraid of being embarrassed or ridiculed. Imagine how foolish you would feel if you were to spring into action to help someone who did not need or want your help. I remember a time when, as a teenager, I was swimming with a large group of friends at a neighbor's pool. As I was about to dive from the board I saw the neighbor's 13-year-old daughter lying face down on the bottom of the pool. I looked around and no one else seemed to be aware of or concerned about this apparent emergency. Was she drowning? Was she joking? I wasn't sure. Just as I was about to yell for help and dive in for the rescue, she swam lazily to the surface. I had hesitated a full 30 seconds out of the fear of being wrong. Many of us have had experiences such as this. The problem is they teach us the wrong thing: that helping behavior carries with it the possibility of looking foolish.

SIGNIFICANCE OF THE FINDINGS

From this and other studies, Darley and Latané became the leading researchers in the field of helping behavior and bystander intervention. Much of their early work is included in their book *The Unresponsive Bystander: Why Doesn't He Help?* (Latané and Darley, 1970). In this work they outline a model for helping behavior that has become widely accepted in the psychological literature on helping. They proposed that there are five steps you would go through before intervening in an emergency.

Step 1. You, the potential helper, must first *notice* that an event is occurring. In the study this chapter examines, there was no question that such notice would occur, but in the real world, you may be in a hurry or your attention may be focused elsewhere, and you might completely fail to notice the event.

Step 2. Next, you must *interpret* the situation as one in which help is truly needed. This is a point at which fear of embarrassment exerts its influence. Again, in the present study, the situation was not ambiguous and the need for help was quite clear. In reality, however, most potential emergencies contain some degree of doubt or ambiguity, such as in my swimming pool example. Or, imagine you see a man stagger and pass out on a busy city sidewalk. Is he sick or just drunk? How you interpret the situation will influence your decision to intervene. Many of those who failed to help in the Genovese case claimed that they thought it was a lover's quarrel and did not want to get involved.

Step 3. You have to assume personal *responsibility*. This will usually happen immediately if you are the only bystander in the emergency. If others are also present, however, you may instead place the responsibility on them. This step was the focus of this chapter's experiment. The more people present in an emergency, the more diffused the responsibility, and the less likely help will occur.

Step 4. If you assume responsibility, you then must *decide* what action to take. Here, if you do not know what to do or you do not feel capable of taking the appropriate action, you will be less likely to help. In our present study, this issue of competence did not play a part, since all that the subject had to do was report the seizure to the experimenter. But if a crowd were to witness a pedestrian run over by a car, a member of the group who was a doctor, a nurse, or a paramedic would be more likely to intervene because he or she would know what to do.

Step 5. Finally, after you've decided what action to take, you have to take it. Just because you know what to do doesn't guarantee that you will do it. Now you will weigh the costs and benefits of helping. Are you willing to personally intervene in a fight in which one or both of the participants has a knife? What about victims of accidents—can you help them, or will you make things worse by trying to help (the competence issue again)? If you get involved, can you be sued? What if you try to help and end up looking like a fool? Many such questions, depending on the situation, may run through your mind before you actually take action.

Figure 2 illustrates how helping behavior may be short-circuited or prevented at any one of these stages.

SUBSEQUENT FINDINGS AND CRITICISMS

Both the Kitty Genovese murder and the experiment we have been discussing here involved groups of onlookers who were out of contact with each other. What do you suppose would happen if the bystanders could see and talk to each other? Perhaps they could analyze the emergency, decide on ways of dividing up the helping action, and encourage each other to help. Also, since helping others is expected in our culture, we might expect that when other people could watch and

FIGURE 2 Latané and Darley's model of helping.

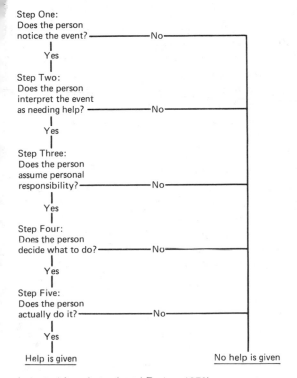

Step One:
Does the person
notice the event? ——————No——

Yes

Step Two:
Does the person
interpret the event
as needing help? ——————No——

Yes

Step Three:
Does the person
assume personal
responsibility? ——————No——

Yes

Step Four:
Does the person
decide what to do? ——————No——

Yes

Step Five:
Does the person
actually do it? ——————No——

Yes

Help is given

No help is given

(adapted from Latané and Darley, 1970)

judge each other, they would be more likely to "do the right thing" and intervene. However, Darley and Latané believed that in some cases even groups in close contact would be less likely than individuals to help. This would be especially true, they theorized, when the emergency is somewhat ambiguous.

Imagine you are sitting in a waiting room and smoke begins to stream in through a vent. You become concerned and look around at the others in the room. Everyone else appears quite calm and unconcerned. Through a process known as "social comparison" you decide your reaction to the smoke must be exaggerated, and you decide against taking any action. Why? Because if you take action and are wrong (maybe it wasn't smoke, just vapor from the air conditioner), you fear ridicule and embarrassment, as discussed earlier. What you don't realize is that everyone in the room is feeling the same as you and hiding it, just as you are, to avoid embarrassment! So everyone is comparing their reaction with everyone else's, and no one is doing anything about the smoke. Sound unbelievable? Well, it's not.

Latané and Darley (1968) tested this idea in a slightly later study by creating the situation just described. Psychology students volunteered to participate in interviews to "discuss some of the problems involved in life at an urban university." When they arrived for the interview, they were seated in a room and asked to fill out a preliminary questionnaire. After a few minutes, smoke began to pour into the room through a vent. The smoke was a special mixture of titanium dioxide and water vapor so as not to be dangerous to the subjects. After several minutes the smoke became so thick that vision in the room was obscured. Subjects were timed to see how long they would wait to intervene and report the smoke to the experimenter. Some of the subjects were in the room alone; others were with two confederates, believed by the subject to be other participants, who behaved very passively when the smoke appeared; and still other subjects were in the room in groups of three. Once again, Latané and Darley's results supported their theory. Fifty-five percent of the subjects in the alone condition reported the smoke within the first two minutes, while only 12 percent of the subjects in the other two groups did so. Moreover, after four minutes 75 percent of the alone group had acted, but no additional subjects in the other groups ever reported the smoke.

There have been over a hundred studies by Darley and Latané and others on this issue of bystander intervention. The findings are extremely consistent. There are certain conditions in which the bystander effect does not occur, such as when the members of the group are friends or acquaintances, but when groups of strangers are faced with an emergency, the usual result is inaction.

CONCLUSION

The results of this research may seem rather pessimistic, but it should be stressed that this research deals with an extremely specific situation in which people fail to help. There are frequent examples of people helping other people every day, of altruistic and even heroic acts. This research is important, however, not only to explain a perplexing human behavior, but to help change it. Hopefully as more people become aware of the bystander effect, they will make the extra effort to intervene in an emergency, even if others are present. In fact, research has actually demonstrated that when people have learned about the bystander effect, they are more likely to help in emergencies (Beaman, et al., 1978). The bottom line is, never assume that others have intervened or will intervene in an emergency. Always act as if you are the only person there.

BEAMAN, A., BARNES, P., KLENTZ, B., and MCQUIRK, B. (1978) Increasing helping rates through information dissemination: Teaching pays. *Personality and Social Psychology Bulletin*, 4, 406–11.

LATANÉ, B., and DARLEY, J.M. (1968) Group inhibition of bystander intervention in emergencies. *Journal of Personality and Social Psychology*, 10, 215–21.

LATANÉ, B., and DARLEY, J.M. (1970) *The unresponsive bystander: Why doesn't he help?* New York: Appleton-Century-Crofts.

OBEY AT ANY COST
Milgram, S. (1963) Behavioral study of obedience. *Journal of Abnormal and Social Psychology*, 67, 371–78.

If someone in a position of authority ordered you to deliver an electrical shock of 350 volts to another person because the other person answered a question incorrectly, would you obey? Neither would I. If you met someone who was willing to do such a thing, you would probably think of him or her as cruel and sadistic. This study by Stanley Milgram of Yale University set out to examine the idea of obedience and produced some shocking and disturbing findings.

Milgram's research on obedience may be the most famous and widely recognized in all of psychology's history. It is included in every general psychology text and every social psychology text. If you talk to students of psychology, more of them are familiar with this study than with any other. Out of this study came a book by Milgram (1974) on the psychology of obedience and a film about the research itself that is widely shown in college and university classes. Not only is this experiment referred to in discussions of obedience, but it has also been highly influential in issues of research methodology and the ethics of using human subjects in psychological research.

Milgram's idea for this project grew out of his desire to investigate scientifically how people could be capable of carrying out great harm to others simply because they were ordered to do so. Milgram was referring specifically to the millions of hideous atrocities committed on command during World War II, but also, more generally, to the inhumanity that has been perpetrated throughout history by people following the orders of others. It appeared to Milgram that in some situations, the tendency to obey is so deeply ingrained and powerful that it cancels out a person's ability to behave morally, ethically, or even sympathetically.

When behavioral scientists decide to study some complex aspect of human behavior, their first step is to gain control over the behavioral situation so that they can approach it scientifically. This can often be the greatest challenge to a researcher, since many events in the real world are difficult to re-create in a laboratory setting. So Milgram's problem was how to cause one person to order another person to physically injure a third person without anyone actually getting injured.

THEORETICAL PROPOSITIONS

Milgram's primary theoretical basis for this study was that humans have a tendency to obey other people who are in a position of authority over them, even if, in obeying, they violate their own codes of moral and ethical behavior. He believed that, for example, individuals who would never intentionally inflict pain on another would, when placed in a subordinate position to a powerful authority figure, inflict pain on a third person because they are ordered to do so.

METHOD

Probably the most ingenious portion of this study is the technique that was developed to test the power of obedience in the laboratory. Milgram designed a rather scary-looking shock generator: a large electronic device with 30 toggle switches labeled with voltage levels starting at 15 volts and increasing by 15-volt intervals up to 450 volts. These switches were labeled in groups such as "slight shock," "moderate shock," and "danger: severe shock." The idea behind this was that a subject could be ordered to administer electric shocks at increasing levels to another person. Please note, before you conclude that Milgram was truly sadistic himself, that this was a very realistic-looking *simulated* shock generator, and no one ever actually received any painful shocks.

The subjects for this study were 40 males between the ages of 20 and 50. There were 15 skilled or unskilled workers, 16 white-collar sales-or businessmen, and nine professional men. They were recruited through newspaper ads and direct-mail solicitation asking for subjects to be paid participants in a study about memory and learning at Yale University. Each subject participated in the study individually. In order to obtain an adequate number of subjects, each was paid $4.50 (remember, these are 1963 dollars). All subjects were clearly told that this payment was simply for coming to the laboratory, and it was theirs to keep no matter what happened after they arrived. This was to ensure that subjects did not behave in certain ways because they were fearful of not being paid.

In addition to the subjects, there were two other key participants: a confederate in the experiment (a 47-year-old accountant) posing as another subject, and an "actor" (dressed in a gray lab coat, looking very official) playing the part of the experimenter.

As a participant arrived at the social interaction laboratory at Yale, he was seated next to another "subject" (the confederate). Obviously, the true purpose of the experiment could not be revealed to subjects, since this would completely alter their behavior. Therefore, a "cover story" was given by the experimenter, who explained to the subjects that this was a study on the effect of punishment on learning. The subjects then drew pieces of paper out of a hat to determine who would be the teacher and who would be the learner. This drawing was rigged so that the true subject always became the teacher and the accomplice was always the learner. Keep in mind that the "learner" was a confederate in the experiment, as was the person playing the part of the "experimenter."

The "learner" was then taken into the next room and was, with the subject watching, strapped to a chair and wired up with electrodes (complete with electrode paste to "avoid any blisters or burns") connected to the shock generator in the adjoining room. The learner, although his arms were strapped down, was able to reach four buttons marked a, b, c, and d, in order to answer questions posed by the teacher from the next room.

The learning task was thoroughly explained to the teacher and the learner. Briefly, it involved the learner memorizing connections between various pairs of words. It was a rather lengthy list and not an easy memory task. The teacher-subject would read the list of word pairs and then test the learner's memory of them. The teacher was instructed by the experimenter to administer an electric shock each time the learner responded incorrectly. Most important, *for each incorrect response, the teacher was to move up one level of shock on the generator*. All of this was simulated so realistically that no subject suspected that the shocks were not really being delivered.

The learner-confederate's responses were preprogrammed to be correct or incorrect in the same sequence for all the subjects. Furthermore, as the amount of voltage increased with incorrect responses, the learner began to shout his discomfort from the other room (in prearranged, prerecorded phrases, including the fact that his heart was bothering him), and at the 300-volt level he pounded on the wall and demanded to be let out. After 300 volts he became completely silent and refused to answer any more questions. The teacher was instructed to treat this lack of a response as an incorrect response and to continue the procedure.

Most of the subjects would turn to the experimenter at some point for guidance on whether to continue the shocks. When this happened, the experimenter ordered the subject to continue, in a series of commands increasing in severity as more prodding was necessary:

Command 1:   Please continue.
Command 2:   The experiment requires that you continue.
Command 3:   It is absolutely essential that you continue.
Command 4:   You have no other choice, you must go on.

A measure of obedience was obtained simply by recording the level of shock at which each subject refused to continue. Since there were 30 switches on the generator, each subject could receive a score of 0 to 30. Subjects who went all the way to the top of the scale were referred to as "obedient subjects" and those who broke off at any lower point were termed "defiant subjects."

RESULTS

Would the subjects obey the commands of this experimenter? How high on the voltage scale did they go? What would you predict? Think of yourself, your friends, people in general. What percentage do you think would deliver shocks all the way through the 30 levels; all the way up to 450 volts—"danger: severe shock"? Well, before discussing the actual results of the study, Milgram asked a group of Yale University seniors, all psychology majors, as well as various colleagues to make such a prediction. The estimates ranged from 0 percent to 3 percent, with an average estimate of 1.2 percent. That is, no more than three people out of a hundred were predicted to deliver the maximum shock.

Table 1 summarizes the shocking results. Upon command of the experimenter, every subject continued at least to the 300-volt level, which was when the confederate banged on the wall to be let out and stopped answering. But most surprising is the number of subjects who obeyed orders to continue all the way to the top of the scale.

Although 14 subjects defied orders and broke off before reaching the maximum voltage, 26 of the 40 subjects, or 65 percent, followed the experimenter's orders and proceeded to the top of the shock scale. This is not to say that the subjects were calm or happy about what they were doing. Many exhibited signs of extreme stress and concern for the man receiving the shocks, and even became angry at the experimenter. Yet they obeyed.

TABLE 1   Level of Shock Delivered by Subjects

NUMBER OF VOLTS TO BE DELIVERED	NUMBER WHO REFUSED TO CONTINUE AT THIS LEVEL
Slight shock	
15	0
30	0
45	0
60	0
Moderate shock	
75	0
90	0
105	0
120	0
Strong shock	
135	0
150	0
165	0
180	0
Very strong shock	
195	0
210	0
225	0
240	0
Intense shock	
255	0
270	0
285	0
300	5
Extreme intensity shock	
315	4
330	2
345	1
360	1
Danger: severe shock	
375	1
390	0
405	0
420	0
XXX————	
435	0
450	26

(from Milgram, 1963, p. 376)

There was concern that some of the subjects might suffer psychological distress from having gone through the ordeal of shocking another person, especially when the learner had ceased to respond for the last third of the experiment. To help alleviate this anxiety, after the subjects finished the experiment, they received a full explanation (called a debriefing) of the true purpose of the study and of all the procedures, including the deception that had been employed. In addition, the subjects were interviewed as to their feelings and thoughts during the procedure and the confederate "learner" was brought in for a friendly reconciliation with each subject.

DISCUSSION

Milgram's discussion of his findings focused on two main points. The first was the surprising strength of the subjects' tendency to obey. These were average, normal people who agreed to participate in an experiment about learning, not sadistic, cruel individuals in any way. Milgram points out that from childhood these subjects had learned that it is immoral to hurt others against their will. So, why did they do so? The experimenter was a person in a position of authority, but if you think about it, how much authority did he really have? He had no power to enforce his orders, and subjects would lose nothing by refusing to follow orders. Clearly the situation carried a force of its own that somehow made obedience significantly greater than was expected.

The second key observation made during the course of this study was extreme tension and anxiety manifested by the subjects as they obeyed the experimenter's commands. Again, it might be expected that such discomfort could be relieved simply by refusing to go on, and yet this is not what happened. Milgram quotes one observer (who watched a subject through a one-way mirror):

> I observe a mature and initially poised businessman enter the laboratory smiling and confident. Within 20 minutes he was reduced to a twitching, stuttering wreck who was rapidly approaching a point of nervous collapse . . . . At one point he pushed his fist into his forehead and muttered, 'Oh, God! Let's stop it.' And yet he continued to respond to every word of the experimenter and obeyed to the end (p. 377).

Milgram listed several points at the end of the article to attempt to explain why this particular situation produced such a high degree of obedience. In summary, from the point of view of the subject, his main points were that (1) if it's being sponsored by Yale, it must be in good hands, and who am I to question such a great institution; (2) the goals of the experiment appear to be important, and therefore, since I volunteered, I'll do my part to assist in the realization of those goals; (3) the learner, after all, also voluntarily came here and he has an obligation to the project too; (4) hey, it was just by chance that I'm the teacher and he's the learner—we drew lots and it could have just as easily been the other way around; (5) they're paying me for this, I'd better do my job; (6) I don't know all that much about the rights of a psychologist and his subjects, so I will yield to his discretion on this; and (7) they told us both that the shocks are painful, but not dangerous.

SIGNIFICANCE OF THE FINDINGS

Milgram's findings have held up quite well in the nearly 30 years since this article was published. Milgram himself repeated the procedure on similar subjects outside of the Yale setting, on unpaid college student volunteers, and on women subjects, and he found similar results each time.

In addition, he expanded further on his findings in this study by conducting a series of related experiments designed to reveal the conditions that promote or limit obedience (see Milgram, 1974). He found that the physical, and therefore emotional, distance of the victim from the teacher altered the amount of obedience. The highest level of obedience (93 percent going to the top of the voltage scale) occurred when the learner was in another room and could not be seen or heard. When the learner was in the same room with the subject and the subject was required to force the learner's hand onto a shock plate the rate of obedience dropped to 30 percent.

Milgram also discovered that the physical distance of the authority figure to the subject also influenced obedience. The closer the experimenter, the greater the obedience. In one condition, the experimenter was out of the room and telephoned his commands to the subject. In this case obedience fell to only 21 percent.

Finally, on a more positive note, when subjects were allowed to punish the learner by using any level of shock they wished, no one ever pressed any switch higher than No. 2, or 45 volts.

CRITICISMS

While Milgram's research has been extremely influential in our understanding of obedience, it has also had far-reaching effects in the area of the ethical treatment of human subjects. Even though no one ever received any shocks, how do you suppose you would feel, knowing you had been willing to shock someone (possibly to death) simply because a person in a lab coat told you to? Critics of Milgram's methods (see Baumrind, 1964, and Miller, 1986) claim that unacceptable levels of stress were created in the subjects during the experimental sessions. Furthermore, it has been argued that the potential for lasting effects existed. When the deception is revealed to subjects at the end of their ordeal, they may feel used, embarrassed, and possibly distrustful of psychologists or legitimate authority figures in their future lives.

Another line of criticism focused on the validity of Milgram's findings. The basis for this criticism was that since the subjects had a trusting and rather dependent relationship with the experimenter, and the laboratory was an unfamiliar setting, obedience found there did not represent obedience in real life. Therefore, critics claim, the results of

Milgram's studies were not only invalid, but because of this poor validity the treatment his subjects were exposed to could not be justified.

Milgram responded to criticisms by surveying subjects after they had participated. He found that 84 percent of his participants were glad to have participated, and only about 1 percent regretted the experience. In addition, a psychiatrist interviewed 40 of the subjects who were judged to have been the most uncomfortable in the laboratory and concluded that none had suffered any long-term effects. As to the criticism that his laboratory findings did not reflect real life, Milgram said, "A person who comes to the laboratory is an active, choosing adult, capable of accepting or rejecting the prescriptions for action addressed to him" (Milgram, 1964, p. 852).

The Milgram studies reported here have been a focal point in the ongoing debate over experimental ethics involving human subjects. It is, in fact, arguable whether this research has been more influential in the area of social psychology and obedience or in policy formation on the ethical treatment of human subjects in psychological research.

BAUMRIND, D. (1964) Some thoughts on the ethics of research: After reading Milgram's "Behavioral Study of Obedience." *American Psychologist*, 19, 421–23.

MILGRAM. S. (1964) Issues in the study of obedience: A reply to Baumrind. *American Psychologist*, 19, 448–52.

MILGRAM, S. (1974) *Obedience to authority*. New York: Harper & Row.

MILLER, A.G. (1986) *The obedience studies: A case study of controversy in social science*. New York: Praeger.